# TEACHING MUSIC HISTORY

*For Teachers and Students*

*May we learn well from each other the skills necessary
to experience music's magic and mystery*

# Teaching Music History

*Edited by*
MARY NATVIG
*Bowling Green State University, USA*

**Ashgate**

© Mary Natvig 2002

Published by
Ashgate Publishing Limited
Gower House
Croft Road
Aldershot
Hants GU11 3HR
England

Ashgate Publishing Company
131 Main Street
Burlington, VT 05401-5600 USA

Ashgate website: http://www.ashgate.com

**British Library Cataloguing in Publication Data**
Teaching music history
   1.Music - History and criticism - Instruction and study
   I.Natvig, Mary
   780.7'11

**Library of Congress Cataloging-in-Publication Data**
Teaching music history / edited by Mary Natvig.
   p. cm.
   Includes bibliographical references and index.
   ISBN 0-7546-0129-3
   1.Music in universities and colleges. 2.Music--Instruction and study. I.Natvig, Mary, 1957-

MT18 .T38 2002
780'.71'1--dc21
                                    2001053479

ISBN 0 7546 0129 3

Printed and bound in Great Britain by MPG Books Ltd, Bodmin, Cornwall

# Contents

*List of Contributors*                                                          *vii*
*Introduction*                                                                    *ix*


**Approaches to the Music History Survey**

1        Providing Context: Teaching Medieval and Renaissance Music    3
         *Patrick Macey*

2        Teaching Baroque Music to the Bright and Interested          13
         and Ignorant
         *Kenneth Nott*

3        What Chopin (and Mozart and Others) Heard: Folk, Popular,    25
         "Functional," and Non-Western Music in the
         Classic/Romantic Survey Course
         *Ralph P. Locke*

4        Teaching Music History (After the End of History):           43
         "History Games" for the Twentieth-Century Survey
         *Robert Fink*


**Teaching Non-Majors: The Introductory Course**

5        Interdisciplinary Approaches to the Introduction to          69
         Music Course
         *Maria Archetto*

6        The "Why" of Music: Variations on a Cosmic Theme             77
         *Marjorie Roth*

7        *First Nights*: Awakening Students' Critical Skills in a        95
         Large Lecture Course
         *Noël Bisson*

**Topics Courses**

8        Teaching "Women in Music"                                      111
         *Mary Natvig*

9        Teaching Film Music in the Liberal Arts Curriculum             121
         *Michael Pisani*

10       Don't Fence Me In: The Pleasures of Teaching                   145
         American Music
         *Susan C. Cook*

**General Issues**

11       Teaching at a Liberal Arts College                             157
         *Mary Hunter*

12       Teaching in the Centrifugal Classroom                          169
         *Pamela Starr*

13       The Myths of Music History                                     181
         *Vincent Corrigan*

14       Score and Word: Writing about Music                            193
         *Carol A. Hess*

15       Peer Learning in Music History Courses                         205
         *J. Peter Burkholder*

16       Creating Anthologies for the Middle Ages and Renaissance       225
         *Russell E. Murray, Jr.*

Bibliography                                                            239

Index                                                                  259

# List of Contributors

*Maria Archetto*
Oxford College of Emory University

*Noël Bisson*
Cabot Postdoctoral Fellow at the
Bok Center for Teaching and Learning,
Harvard University

*J. Peter Burkholder*
Indiana University

*Susan C. Cook*
University of Wisconsin

*Vincent Corrigan*
Bowling Green State University

*Robert Fink*
University of California, Los Angeles

*Carol A. Hess*
Bowling Green State University

*Mary Hunter*
Bowdoin College

*Ralph P. Locke*
The Eastman School of Music of the University of Rochester

*Patrick Macey*
The Eastman School of Music of the University of Rochester

*Russell E. Murray, Jr.*
University of Delaware

*Mary Natvig*
Bowling Green State University

*Kenneth Nott*
The Crane School of Music

*Michael Pisani*
Vassar College

*Marjorie Roth*
Nazareth College (Rochester, NY)

*Pamela Starr*
University of Nebraska

# Introduction

*Mary Natvig*

This collection of essays is intended for those who teach a college-level music history or music appreciation course: from the graduate student who finds him or herself in front of a class for the first time to the seasoned professor having to teach outside of his/her specialty; from musicologists seeking to enrich their teaching expertise to performers looking for a life raft after learning they must teach a university music history course.

The idea for the book grew out of my personal needs as a faltering college teacher, a career that began only one year after receiving my own undergraduate degree. As the violin/viola teacher in a small liberal arts college, I was also required to teach a medium-sized (about 45 students) music appreciation course to music majors and non-majors. I had a master's degree in musicology but had never taught in a classroom. I spent hours each night on detailed lectures, poring over a variety of sources, compulsively over-preparing as I was sure I would get questions I could not answer. My youth, however, worked in my favor. My "cool" factor brought me marvelous teaching evaluations. I *thought* I was a fantastic, natural teacher and I coasted in that happy oblivion for several years. Then one fall I unknowingly stepped through a door marked "middle age," which wiped off my youthful patina and left me an unvarnished teacher of a difficult and unpopular course. For the first time in my life my teaching evaluations were less than glowing—some were downright nasty. By this time I had full academic qualifications: a Ph.D. in musicology, and at least ten years of teaching experience at two different institutions. I was one year from tenure. I thought I was getting better as a teacher, but something in those evaluations told me that whatever I had done right before was no longer working. The problem was, I did not know exactly what it was that had worked or why. And I really did not know what was so different about my teaching that particular semester that warranted poor evaluations. Of course my colleagues told me not to worry about it—some semesters are better than others. In actuality it was not the evaluations that bothered me, but the internal voice that said I needed to become more conscious about my teaching—not necessarily more conscientious (I was that), but more aware, knowledgeable, and purposeful in how and what I taught.

Musicologists rarely discuss in a public forum our roles as teachers in spite of the fact that, for many of us, teaching is what occupies us most of the time. Although there have been a few worthwhile panels on teaching at sessions of the American Musicological Society, they are usually tucked away over a noon hour or opposite an evening concert. Surely many of us confer privately about our choice of texts, syllabi, types of assignments, etc., and I imagine that most of us commiserate regularly about issues such as lack of time, large class sizes, and inadequate student preparation. Recently, email has facilitated such discussions, both privately and on professional lists. Although many of us have absorbed a kind of collective wisdom about how to teach music history, we, unlike our colleagues in music theory and music education, have rarely committed our pedagogical ideas to print.

Since very few of us have engaged in writing about our teaching, I found that conversing with colleagues about what worked for them in the classroom was the most effective way for me to re-evaluate my own teaching. I borrowed and stole ideas, tried them out and molded them to my own and my students' personalities, needs, and abilities. I read and continue to read what is available on teaching at the college level,[1] in particular the few essays devoted to teaching music history.[2] But I still find that informal conversations with others in my field provide the best way to learn about the art of teaching. This book is the result of many of those informal interactions.

There are sixteen essays included, written from numerous perspectives on a variety of topics. The first section concerns courses that comprise the basic music history survey, usually intended for music majors. The second deals with "music appreciation" courses, or one-semester introductions to music for the non-major. Section three includes three "special topics" courses: women in music, film music, and American music. (Other topics, such as world music or ethnomusicology, opera, symphonic literature, etc., are not included simply because of the need to limit the scope and length of the book; consider those served here as the appetizers rather than the whole meal.) The fourth and final section explores general issues such as writing, using anthologies, musical mythologies, and approaches to teaching in various situations.

Other topics, not defined by the four broad sectional divisions, permeate all or many of the essays. Integrating social history or cultural context into the music history classroom is an idea discussed by Patrick Macey in his essay on the Medieval/Renaissance survey, by Ralph Locke in his discussion of the Classic/Romantic periods, and Mary Hunter, Noël Bisson, Marjorie Roth, and Susan Cook among others. Robert Fink explicitly frames his course on contemporary music as "the deliberate foregrounding of music as intellectual history." Fink writes, "my insights about musical structure seemed less redundant when linked to contemporaneous beliefs about aesthetics, politics, religion, and sexuality." And Maria Archetto's essay on teaching to non-music majors further places the study of music within the context of other cultural fields. Her course is founded on the premise that "students without much previous knowledge of [music as a discipline] respond well when their music course material is combined with the study of topics [art history, philosophy, psychology] that relate music to other fields of study."

Most of the writers also acknowledge the current shift in our discipline, and hence in pedagogical thinking, regarding the choice of repertory that we teach. In 1950 Elizabeth E. Kaho surveyed the music literature taught at 168 four-year colleges and universities that offered a degree in music. She found what would be considered today a remarkably similar body of works presented to music students at each of those institutions.[3] Forty five years later, Bruno Nettl would label this our "central repertory." He sees "the music school as an institution for both study and advocacy—advocacy of the Western art music tradition, particularly the common-practice period, 1720–1920."[4] In spite of Nettl's observation, however, and in spite of the continued emphasis of music schools on "classical music," this repertory, or "canon," as many of us knew it, is currently under fire (pun intended). Most of us have had to confront the ramifications of its instability, often by restructuring our own "canons" in the courses we teach. Susan Cook, Ralph Locke, Mary Natvig, and Michael Pisani directly challenge the traditional canon by including music in their classes that was never remotely connected to the traditional music school repertory: American music, ethnic music, women's music, and film music. At the same time, they struggle with the canonical implications of the music that they do include. Also, Russell Murray writes about canons as part of his essay on constructing anthologies (constructing canons?) and suggests the implications of the content of anthologies on student learning. Though his essay focuses on early music, the concepts that he discusses can be applied to any period. Other contributors, though not directly addressing the specific repertory they teach, acknowledge the changing canon by placing it in quotations—a nod to the current ambiguity of the term.

Numerous authors ponder the question of how to organize a course, with time constraints and the problem of varied student backgrounds foremost in their concerns. Noël Bisson, Susan Cook, Mary Natvig, Michael Pisani, and Marjorie Roth all address the issue of teaching non-majors and the discrepancies in musical literacy that result. Marjorie Roth uses "roadmaps" directing students via text and instrumentation through musical forms. Noël Bisson writes of TA-run workshops for students needing extra help with musical concepts in Harvard's *First Nights*, as well as placement of students into small group sections based on musical background. Mary Hunter's essay focuses on the special considerations of teaching both music majors and non-majors in the same courses, particularly when those courses are not electives for the music majors but a part of their core curriculum.

The contributors to this volume are all traditionally trained musicologists with successful teaching records. They are in various stages of their careers, from those just beginning to those on the verge of retirement. In the minds of our students some of us may be perceived as contemporary and "hip," some as traditional and stodgy; and some, I suppose, are looked upon as just plain odd. (What normal person would spend years of her life on the Latin-texted works of Antoine Busnoys, for instance—as Kerman says, "Love is a many-clangored thing.")[5] We teach in a variety of institutions, from eastern liberal arts colleges and prestigious coastal universities, to huge midwestern state-supported institutions and professional conservatories. We teach music majors, non-music majors, the talented and not so talented, some motivated and some bored. What binds us together is our love of music and our commitment to teaching others about its beauty, passion, and power. The external rewards in our field are few. However, the ability to change a life, to move a soul, soothe a spirit, and spark an intellect, though not measurable by worldly standards, are the benefits of our profession. As we ourselves have been formed by a life in music, so we seek to impart the joys of a musical life to our students.

*Many people have contributed greatly to this volume, and while I wish I could name them all, they will, for practical reasons, have to remain anonymous. Their anonymity in no way diminishes my gratitude for their assistance and encouragement. There are a few, however, whose names I must reveal. To Ralph P. Locke, Carol A. Hess, Rob Haskins, Marilyn Shrude, and my husband, William Engelke, I say thank you from the bottom of my heart.*

**Notes**

1    Here are a few that I have found helpful and inspiring: 1) Robert Blackey, ed., *History Anew: Innovations in the Teaching of History Today* (Long Beach, CA: The University Press, 1993), in particular the essay by Russell H. Hvolbek entitled "History and Humanities: Teaching as Destructive of Certainty"; 2) Walter Kaufmann, *The Future of the Humanities: Teaching Art, Religion, Philosophy, Literature and History* (New Brunswick: Transaction Publishers, 1977/revised with new material, 1995); 3) Alan Brinkley, Betty Dessants, Michael Flamm, et al., *The Chicago Handbook for Teachers: A Practical Guide to the College Classroom* (Chicago: The University of Chicago Press, 1999); and 4) though not specifically a manual on teaching, I have found Peter Sacks's *Generation X Goes to College: an eye-opening account of teaching in postmodern America* (Chicago: Open Court, 1996) to be a thought-provoking and unfortunately accurate glimpse of many of my general university students.

2    See 1) L. Michael Griffel, "Teaching Music," in *Scholars Who Teach: the Art of College Teaching*, Steven M. Cahn, ed. (Chicago: Nelson-Hall, 1978), 193–216; 2) Anne V. Hallmark, "Teaching Music History in Different Environments," in *Musicology in the 1980s: Methods, Goals, Opportunities*, D. Kern Holoman and Claude V. Palisca, eds. (New York: Da Capo Press, 1982), 131–143; 3) *Musicology and Undergraduate Teaching*. The College Music Society Report No. 6 (Boulder, CO: College Music Society, 1989) with forward, introduction and four essays by Elliott S. Schwartz, Anne Dhu Shapiro, James A. Hepokoski, Kenneth Levy, Margaret Murata, and Katherine T. Rohrer; 4) James Parakilas, "Teaching Introductory Music Courses with a 'More Comprehensive Perspective,'" *College Music Symposium* 30 (1990): 112–16; 5) Roger Rideout, "The German Model in Music Curricula," *College Music Symposium* 30 (1990): 106–11; 6) Mary DuPree, "Beyond Music in Western Civilization: Issues in Undergraduate Music History Literacy," *College Music Symposium* 30 (1990): 100–5; 8) *Papers from the Dearborn Conference on Music in General Studies*, College Music Society, 1984; and 9) Mark Mazullo, "Music Appreciation Revisited," *College Music Society Newsletter* (electronic version) (September, 2000).

3    Elizabeth E. Kaho, *Analysis of the Study of Music Literature in Selected American Colleges* (New York: Teachers College, Columbia University, 1950).

4    Bruno Nettl, *Heartland Excursions: Ethnomusicological Reflections on Schools of Music* (Urbana and Chicago: University of Illinois Press, 1995), 101.

5    Joseph Kerman, *Contemplating Music: Challenges to Musicology* (Cambridge, MA: Harvard University Press, 1985), 32.

# Approaches to the Music History Survey

Chapter One

# Providing Context: Teaching Medieval and Renaissance Music

*Patrick Macey*

Because the music of the Middle Ages and Renaissance seems impossibly remote from the experience of most college students, it can be effective to begin with a brief discussion of the term culture. By asking the students to take an imaginary trip to some European country (assuming the repertory in the course is European music), they can identify several of the ways that one experiences a foreign culture. Take Italy, for example: that would include the language, food (from aioli to zabaglione), clothing, architecture, sculpture, painting, religious observances, politics, and of course music, from pop to opera to chant. The point is that culture is learned and passed on from generation to generation, and a music history course is one means of passing on musical culture (the students could easily suggest some other means of learning musical culture as well).

A survey of the music of the Middle Ages and Renaissance will maintain a clear focus for the students if one keeps the social context for music making to the fore. One can emphasize that real, living individuals performed and cared strongly, even passionately, about this music. Far from a cobwebbed artifact, it is rather a vehicle for living human expression, and it needs performers to bring it to life. Contexts could include: monastic life, especially that of Benedictines from the sixth to tenth centuries, in monasteries built in remote wilderness far from secular influence (including nuns in monasteries who performed for the Mass and Office); Charlemagne's politically inspired move to standardize the practice of chant in his realm; the rise in the twelfth and thirteenth centuries of urban cathedrals and polyphony; the crusades and songs of courtly love; the political corruption and social upheavals of fourteenth-century France (vividly satirized in the songs of the *Roman de Fauvel*); the dissonant yet sensual polyphonic songs of Machaut, whose progressions based on doubled leading tones seem to express the professions of love and desire in Machaut's courtly love texts; the Black Death and Boccaccio's response to it in the *Decameron*, where at the end of each day the ten young people dance and sing an Italian ballata. The possibilities for relating the arts and cultural context to musical production are rich and varied.

One further note: if this music is to make more than a passing impression on students, they will need to perform it themselves. Of course it is not difficult to sing much of the repertory in class; as well, small groups of students in the class who have good singing voices could prepare individual pieces for more polished performances. Students who experience this music first-hand will appreciate that it is not a desiccated art, but rather an engaging and lively one.

Some specific comments on particular repertory may prove useful for supplementing standard textbooks such as Grout and Palisca's *History of Western Music*. When discussing chant, one could provide a brief but long-range overview of the variety of musical genres that served to prepare the high-point of the first half of the Mass, the Gospel, and this survey could range from the earliest chants all the way to Mozart in the late eighteenth century. The interlude between the reading of the Epistle and the Gospel provided a moment of special musical eloquence in the Mass and prepared the congregation for the reading of the Gospel. Some of the earliest Gregorian chants are melismatic Graduals, whose elaborate melodies provided the opportunity for solo singers to unleash rhapsodic roulades of melody. Eventually an equally melismatic Alleluia was added, and by Frankish times in the eighth century a new type of chant, the syllabic sequence, in turn found a place after the Alleluia. Thus the interval between the Epistle and Gospel provided an outlet for various styles of musical elaboration and creativity. By the twelfth and thirteenth centuries, precisely these chants—the Gradual and Alleluia—were chosen by composers at Notre Dame in Paris for elaborate polyphonic settings performed by solo singers in organum style. Christopher Page constructs a vivid and imaginative account of the unstable working conditions at Notre Dame for the young clerks of Matins who performed organum, clerks who were approximately the same age as the college students in our classes.[1] By the 1500s, with the onset of the Lutheran Reformation, the congregation now participated actively in the liturgy and worshipers sang a chorale or "Graduallied" between the Epistle and Gospel in the Lutheran Mass. In the Catholic Mass of the later sixteenth and seventeenth centuries, one could hear instrumental pieces—canzonas—during this portion of the service; repertory includes canzonas for instrumental ensemble by Giovanni Gabrieli for St. Mark's in Venice, and canzonas for organ by Girolamo Frescobaldi, who was organist at St. Peter's in Rome in the first half of the seventeenth century (see the series of pieces titled "canzon dopo l'espistola" in Frescobaldi's *Fiori musicali*, 1635). By the late seventeenth century Arcangelo Corelli was composing trio sonatas called church sonatas ("sonata da chiesa") that could be performed after the Epistle at Mass.[2] Finally, Mozart's seventeen Epistle sonatas were composed for performance in the 1770s during the Gradual at Mass in the cathedral of Salzburg.

The sequence is of course another musical insertion before the reading of the Gospel, and most textbook discussions focus on late examples such as twelfth-century works by Hildegard of Bingen, or the *Dies irae* from the thirteenth century. Here again one could provide a broader view of the sequence, one that extends back to the earliest examples from the ninth century all the way to the nineteenth century. The most engaging and informed comments on the earliest sequences are by Richard Crocker, who emphasizes how clear melodic shapes and repetition of phrases in conjunction with the arrangement of the text in couplets vividly distinguish this genre from the less predictable style of Gregorian chant, such as melismatic Graduals.[3] The Ensemble Gilles Binchois has produced a superb recording that brings the sequences of Notker to life, especially the opening selection in honor of St. Gall, *Dilecte Deo Galle*.[4] The use of sequences extends far beyond the Middle Ages, and in particular nineteenth-century composers quoted the *Dies irae* in a number of instrumental works, from the finale of the *Symphonie fantastique* by Berlioz, to Liszt's *Totentanz*, to the works of Rachmaninoff. One could spend a few minutes discussing why medieval chant—and this chant especially—appealed to nineteenth-century composers; historical context could include the rise of gothic themes in literature, as in Mary Shelley's *Frankenstein* (1818), and in architecture, for example, the Houses of Parliament in London, including Big Ben (begun 1836). The appeal of the Middle Ages—the "age of faith," for many in the nineteenth century—can be seen partly as a reaction to the rationalism of the Enlightenment, which produced the upheavals of the French revolution and the subsequent Napoleonic wars, and witnessed the abolishment of traditional religion in France. After the Congress of Vienna in 1815, France saw the reinstatement of Catholicism and a renewed interest in preserving the architectural heritage of gothic cathedrals, many of which had been pulled down during the Revolution. The revival of Gregorian chant occurred in conjunction with the same movement of restoration.[5]

Moving to the fourteenth century, the allegorical figure of Fortune and her wheel can serve to illuminate the unstable and uncertain character of social life in this century, as it does in works such as the *Roman de Fauvel* and Machaut's *Remède de Fortune*. The *Roman de Fauvel* offers a rich opportunity to contextualize music in the early part of the century, with its combination of poetic satire and musical interpolations, and its focus on contemporary political corruption in France. The story of the rise to power of Fauvel, in the allegorical guise of a horse who represents various vices, can be summarized briefly for the students. It includes the goddess Fortune, who plays the central role in Fauvel's ascent to prominence. Seeing her favor, and in order to prevent his inevitable fall as Fortune's wheel continues to turn, he schemes to win her fickle hand in marriage and thereby wrest control of her wheel.

Fauvel reflects to himself (lines 1715ff):

| | |
|---|---|
| *Trestout me vient a volenté* | Everything happens according to my will; |
| *Moult sui riches et bien renté* | I am rich and very influential |
| *Par mon sens et par ma fallace.* | thanks to my wits and shrewdness. |
| *J'ay bien de Fortune la grace:* | I am in the good graces of Lady Fortune, |
| *Du tout a mon vouloir tournie,* | who is wholly receptive to my wishes. |
| *Moult m'a donné grant seigneurie:* | She has given me a grand domain: |
| *Du monde, qui est sa maison,* | contrary to Reason she has made me |
| *M'a fait seigneur maugré Raison ...* | lord of the world, which is her home ... |
| *Or ay je pensé d'autre part* | Now, I have come to the conclusion that |
| *Que Fortune, qui tout depart,* | Dame Fortune, who rules over everyone, |
| *Il ne puet estre qu'el ne m'aime* | cannot do otherwise than love me, |
| *Quant si grans honneurs en moy* | since she has given me such great honors. |
| *seime.* | |
| *Puis qu'elle m'a fait si grant mestre,* | Because she has made me such a grand |
| | master, |
| *Il ne pourroit nulement estre* | it is not possible that she has given me |
| *Que elle ne m'ait sans fallace* | her love and her grace |
| *Donnee s'amour et sa grace;* | without some deeper motive. |
| *Et elle n'est pas mariee* | And she is not married, |
| *Ne moy aussi, qui a lié bee,* | nor am I, and I am bound to her; |
| *Et croy, qui li en parleroit,* | and I believe that if I spoke to her, |
| *Que moult tost s'y acorderoit.* | she would receive me cordially. |
| *Et se j'espousee l'avoie,* | And if I were to marry her, |
| *De sa roe mestre seroie.*[6] | I would then be master of her wheel! |

In the monophonic ballade that follows this exchange, *Douce dame debonaire*, Fauvel crouches at the feet of Lady Fortune and asks for her hand in marriage.[7] Fortune scorns his advances in no uncertain terms: "Fie on you, tool of the wicked ... never will I give you my love." The song is a dialogue between the two characters, and not only does its text spoof the conventions of courtly love, but it also adopts the high style of the *grand chant* found in trouvère songs from the thirteenth century. The dramatic gesture of the falling scale at the opening occurs in other trouvère songs, as do the simple rhythms of longs and breves (dotted or undotted half notes, and quarter notes).[8] The *Roman de*

*Fauvel* of course contains pieces in a wealth of musical styles, including many isorhythmic motets, and the reversals of Fortune's wheel are symbolized in the music and text of one of them, *Tribum/Quoniam/Merito*, attributed to Philippe de Vitry.[9]

Fortune again comes to the fore in the most notable and accomplished French narrative love poem of the fourteenth century, Machaut's *Remède de Fortune* (1340s).[10] The remedy for the reversals of fortune is not despair, but rather hope, and this allegorical figure guides the lover during his trials. The poem features seven musical interpolations in the form of chansons sung by the lover or by Hope, including examples of the lai, ballade, rondeau and virelai (four are monophonic and three polyphonic). The monophonic virelai, *Dame a vous sans retollir*, occurs as the lover comes across his lady dancing with her friends in a meadow outside her castle, and she asks him to join in and sing a virelai as they dance. He responds with *Dame a vous*. The song can be easily contextualized by reading the narrative passage in the poem that leads up to its performance.[11] The illumination in the original manuscript that depicts the scene, as well as the music for the virelai, is available in a modern color reproduction.[12]

Turning to the fifteenth century, one should take just a moment to play a remarkable recording of Dufay's isorhythmic motet *Apostolo glorioso*.[13] I have never encountered such mastery of sonority and verve of phrasing in any other performances of Dufay's music. Later in the century, study of music in Italy can profitably focus on distinctive styles of patronage at four courts: Milan, Ferrara, Florence, and Mantua. In the 1470s Italy witnessed a remarkable rise in imported Franco-Flemish singers and composers, nowhere more than in Milan, where Duke Galeazzo Maria Sforza employed more than thirty singers in his choir. Diplomatic correspondence from his court provides a lively account of Galeazzo's zeal in recruiting the best singers; he was an ardent lover of music and wished to create a chapel that would outshine any other in Europe, including those of the Duke of Burgundy and the King of Naples.[14] Indeed, Galeazzo's brazen campaign to lure singers away from the court of Naples created a diplomatic scandal and nearly caused a complete break in relations between the two courts. The letters that passed between Galeazzo and his ambassadors in Naples provide an entertaining account of Galeazzo's scheming, as well as his flustered attempts to extricate himself when his schemes were exposed.[15] Recent research reveals that Josquin des Prez did not serve in Galeazzo's chapel in the 1470s, as previously believed, but he was in fact active in Milan somewhat later, in the 1480s; in 1484–85 he was in the service of Cardinal Ascanio Sforza and in early 1489 (perhaps earlier) he was a singer for the cardinal's brother, Ludovico il Moro, the ruler of Milan.[16] Leonardo da Vinci moved from Florence to Milan at the same time as Josquin, so the two may have encountered one another there. It now appears that Josquin's famous *Ave Maria ... virgo serena* was copied in the early 1480s, and chances are good that he composed it after his arrival in Milan,[17] in emulation of the so-called Milanese style of the 1470s, in which motets by Gaspar van Weerbeke and Loyset Compère emphasize clear presentation of the words through paired imitative duets that lead up to full four-voice sections, often in homophony.

For Ferrara, Josquin composed distinctive music for Duke Ercole I d'Este, including his *Missa Hercules dux Ferrariae* and the psalm motet *Miserere mei, Deus*; in both works he expands traditional techniques of musical construction over a cantus firmus to create new levels of rhetorical intensity in music. For contemporary documents, students can read the letters in which Ercole's agents offer opposing recommendations regarding the best man to head the duke's chapel: Josquin or Heinrich Isaac.[18]

While the emphasis in Milan and Ferrara during the closing decades of the fifteenth century seems to have been on sacred music, Florence and Mantua each produced distinctive types of secular music. Lorenzo de' Medici brought Isaac to Florence in the mid-1480s, and Lorenzo commissioned musical settings of his own texts, including love songs and carnival songs.[19] The prevailing homophony of the three-voice settings—of carnival songs in particular—is well suited to outdoor performance, and this is illustrated in a contemporary wood-cut that shows Lorenzo listening to a performance of one of his own carnival songs by two boys and three men, all wearing masks.[20] Florentines adopted the music of obscene carnival songs for singing sacred laudas during the post-carnival season of Lent, and a vivid example is the Song of the Chimney Sweeps, *Visin, visin visin*, whose music served for the lauda *Gesù, Gesù, Gesù*.[21] When the fanatical Dominican friar Girolamo Savonarola rose to a position of power after Lorenzo's death in 1492, he quashed the performance of carnival songs altogether, but encouraged the singing of laudas, including those on texts that he wrote himself.[22] He recognized the unparalleled importance of music as a means of uniting the youth of Florence behind his cause of social and spiritual reform.

In Mantua, Isabella d'Este married into the ruling Gonzaga family and promoted a different kind of secular music, the frottola.[23] In contrast to Florentine carnival songs, frottolas were intimate chamber music for a solo singer with various possibilities for instrumental accompaniment: lute or harpsichord, or even viols, or a combination thereof. Isabella had her own private chamber, her *studiolo*, in which she sang and accompanied herself in the performance of frotttolas.[24] She even commissioned paintings for the walls of her *studiolo* that showed mythological and allegorical scenes, several of which emphasized music. The most notable is Andrea Mantegna's *Parnassus*

(1497). One can easily show students a reproduction of this painting (now in the Louvre), which depicts Apollo singing to his lyre on the left, while the muses sing and dance in the center, and Mercury holds a panpipe on the right. At the top of an earthen arch stand Venus and Mars symbolizing Isabella and her consort, who oversee the harmonious realm of Parnassus, a metaphor for Isabella's ideal of her own court. She speaks in her own words about the importance of music in her letters to Ferrara; here she asks her father, Ercole d'Este, for the loan of his *maestro di cappella*, Giovanni Martini, so that she can continue to study music in Mantua.[25]

Finally, one can trace musical developments from Ferrara, Florence, and Mantua to the end of the sixteenth century, particularly in the genres of the madrigal, from Arcadelt in Florence to Cipriano de Rore, Luzzasco Luzzaschi, and Gesualdo in Ferrara, and Monteverdi in Mantua, and even to monody and early opera in Florence and Mantua.[26] The roots of the new musical developments can be found in the intense cultivation of music at north Italian courts in the preceding century.

These few thoughts can help create a cogent narrative for the teaching of music from the Middle Ages and Renaissance; many readers will no doubt already have come up with them on their own, and other approaches will occur to the imaginative teacher. Whatever approach one takes, one should always attempt to give full value to the expressive possibilities—preferably in live performances—of music that wholly engaged patrons and performers in the Middle Ages and Renaissance.

### Notes

1    Christopher Page, *The Owl and the Nightingale: Musical Life and Ideas in France 1100–1300* (Berkeley: University of California Press, 1989), 144–54.

2    See Stephen Bonta, "The Uses of the *Sonata da Chiesa*," *Journal of the American Musicological Society* 22 (1969): 54–84, especially 78–79, 82.

3    Richard L. Crocker, *The Early Medieval Sequence* (Berkeley: University of California Press, 1977), 1–4 (on Notker), 370–71, 374–76, and 385.

4    Ensemble Gilles Binchois, *Musique et Poesie a Saint-Gall: Sequences et tropes du IX$^e$*, Harmonia Mundi France, HMC 905239 (1997); transcription and discussion in Crocker, *Early Medieval Sequence*, 264–65.

5    Katherine Bergeron, *Decadent Enchantments: The Revival of Gregorian Chant at Solesmes* (Berkeley: University of California Press, 1998).

6    French text edited in *Le Roman de Fauvel par Gervais du Bus publié d'apres tous les manuscrits connus*, ed. Arthur Långfors (Paris, 1914–19), 65–67.

7    For the music and first stanza, see Archibald T. Davison and Willi Apel, eds., *Historical Anthology of Music* (Cambridge, MA: Harvard University Press, 1946 and 1949), I: 16; all three stanzas are translated along with the music in

Samuel N. Rosenberg and Hans Tischler, eds., *The Monophonic Songs in the Roman de Fauvel* (Lincoln: University of Nebraska Press, 1991), 58. A hilarious performance can be found on Studio der Frühen Musik, dir. Thomas Binkley, *Roman de Fauvel,* Reflexe LP C 063–30 103 (1972).

8    See Wulf Arlt, "Jehannot de Lescurel and the Function of Musical Language in the *Roman de Fauvel* as Presented in BN fr. 146," in *Fauvel Studies,* ed. Margaret Bent and Andrew Wathey (Oxford: Clarendon Press, 1998), 27 and 30.

9    See Margaret Bent, "Fauvel and Marigny: Which Came First?" in *Fauvel Studies,* 43–46.

10   Guillaume de Machaut, *Le Jugement du roy de Behaigne and Remède de Fortune,* ed. James I. Wimsatt and William W. Kibler, music ed. Rebecca A. Baltzer (Athens: University of Georgia Press, 1988). The complete French poem is provided with a translation on facing pages, and Machaut's seven chansons are included in an appendix.

11   Machaut, *Remède,* 355–61; the song is edited on p. 430. A good recording is by Ensemble Project Ars Nova, *Remède de Fortune,* New Albion Records, Inc., NA068CD (1994). Here the tenor soloist is accompanied by an added vielle, and tutti voices join in for the refrain. Another recording for just one soloist, Emma Kirkby, is on Gothic Voices, *The Mirror of Narcissus: Songs by Guillaume de Machaut,* Hyperion Records, CDA66087 (1987).

12   François Avril, *Manuscript Painting at the Court of France: The Fourteenth Century (1310–1380)* (New York: George Braziller, 1978), 87 (in color). The original music for *Dame a vous* is shown under the illuminated scene. All the illuminations are reproduced in black and white in Wimsatt, ed., *Remède de Fortune,* except for the color frontispiece, which shows blindfolded Fortune turning her wheels.

13   The Binchois Consort, *Dufay: Music for St. James the Greater,* Hyperion Records, CDA66997 (1998).

14   For Galeazzo's grand plan to finance his chapel with benefices from churches in his realm, see the letter in William F. Prizer, "Music at the Court of the Sforza: The Birth and Death of a Musical Center," *Musica disciplina* 43 (1989): 157.

15   See the translations in Paul A. and Lora M. Merkley, *Music and Patronage at the Sforza Court* (Turnhout: Brepols, 1999), 41–53.

16   See Lora Matthews and Paul Merkley, "Iudochus de Picardia and Jossequin Lebloitte dit Desprez: The Names of the Singer(s)," *Journal of Musicology* 16 (1998): 200–26.

17   Joshua Rifkin, unpublished paper.

18   For the original letters of 14 August and 2 September 1502, with English translations, see Lewis Lockwood, "Josquin at Ferrara: New Documents and Letters," in *Josquin des Prez: Proceedings of the International Josquin Festival Conference,* ed. Edward E. Lowinsky and Bonnie J. Blackburn (London: Oxford University Press, 1976), 130–33. The letter of 2 September is also translated

in Piero Weiss and Richard Taruskin, eds., *Music in the Western World: A History in Documents* (New York: Schirmer Books, 1984), 99.

19    Lorenzo's ballata, *Un di lieto giamai,* with music by Isaac is edited in Heinrich Isaac, *Five Italian Songs for Three Voices or Instruments*, ed. Bernard Thomas, Thesaurus musicus 28 (London: London Pro Musica, 1981); also in DTO 28, p. 44. For a recording, see The Medieval Ensemble of London, *Heinrich Isaac: Chansons, Frottole and Lieder*, L'Oiseau-lyre, Decca Recording Co., LP 410 107–1 (1984). For carnival, Lorenzo's *Sian galanti di Valenza* (Song of the Perfumers), has a three-voice setting, perhaps also by Isaac; for an edition and recording, see Patrick Macey, *Bonfire Songs: Savonarola's Musical Legacy* (Oxford: Clarendon Press, 1998), 42–43.

20    Reproduced in Macey, *Bonfire Songs*, 36.

21    For an edition of the carnival song and a recording of both the carnival song and laude, see Macey, *Bonfire Songs*, 44–47.

22    For discussions of Savonarolan laude in the 1490s, see Macey, *Bonfire Songs*, chapters three and four (also the recordings on the accompanying CD). For complete editions of the music and translations of the multiple stanzas of text, see *Savonarolan Laude, Motets and Anthems,* ed. Patrick Macey, *Recent Researches in the Music of the Renaissance* 116 (Madison: A-R Editions, 1999).

23    For a brief and insightful biographical account of the lives of Isabella and her sister Beatrice, see Maria Bellonci, "Beatrice and Isabella d'Este," in J. H. Plumb, *The Italian Renaissance* (New York: Houghton Mifflin Co., second ed. 1985), 285–301.

24    For a floor plan of the Gonzaga palace in Mantua that shows Isabella's *studiolo* and her "giardino secreto" (private garden), see *Splendours of the Gonzaga*, ed. David Chambers and Jane Martineau, Catalogue of Exhibition in the Victoria & Albert Museum, London, 1981–82 (Milan: Cinisello, 1981), xxiii.

25    The letters are published and translated in William F. Prizer, "Una 'Virtu Molto Conveniente A Madonne': Isabella D'Este as a Musician," *Journal of Musicology* 17 (1999): 10–49, esp. 10–15.

26    A fascinating study of the treatment of erotic texts in madrigals by Arcadelt, Giaches de Wert, Marenzio, and Monteverdi is Laura Macy, "Speaking of Sex: Metaphor and Performance in the Italian Madrigal," *Journal of Musicology* 14 (1996): 1–34. For discussion of erotic themes and music in the late sixteenth-century French chanson, see Kate van Orden, "Sexual Discourse in the Parisian Chanson: A Libidinous Aviary," *Journal of the American Musicological Society* 48 (1995): 1–41; and idem, "An Erotic Metaphysics of Hearing in Early Modern France." *The Musical Quarterly* 82 (1998): 678–91.

# Chapter Two

# Teaching Baroque Music to the Bright and Interested and Ignorant

*Kenneth Nott*

I take my title from a wise passage in Jaroslav Pelikan's *The Idea of the University: A Reexamination*. Lamenting the pervasiveness of scholarly jargon in academic circles, Pelikan comments on how it

> afflicts the writing of many scholars even when they are addressing their work to a nonspecialized audience... . Usually the counterpart to the audience for this kind of writing that a publishing scholar can find is the class at an undergraduate lecture. If the students there are well informed in general but poorly informed in particular, if they are bright and interested and ignorant, they correspond to the readers, or at any rate the potential readers, of a scholar's books. The scholar can have no better practice for the writing of such books than a continued exposure to undergraduate teaching. For when undergraduates are puzzled, their wrinkled brows show it; when readers are puzzled, they decide not to buy the book.[1]

It is easy to lose sight of the benefits that teaching undergraduate music history holds for the teacher. In our zeal to impart to students everything that we know and love about the repertory in question, in our struggles to deal with the "so few teaching hours and so much we'd like our students to learn problem,"[2] we perhaps focus too much on the challenges of teaching undergraduate music history without giving sufficient recognition to the benefits for students and especially teachers. As a colleague of mine in the music theory department recently remarked, "the students are our best teachers."

This is not to say that teaching undergraduate music history is without its challenges, but we need to recognize exactly what those challenges (and opportunities) are. Each semester, the undergraduate music history instructor comes in contact with students who, as Pelikan described them above, are "well informed in general but poorly informed in particular." Having met a rigorous and competitive audition requirement, they come to their undergraduate program prepared to invest a significant amount of time, talent, and money to pursue training in an art that may well become their life's work.

They are ready, some even hungry, to learn the literature of this art. Moreover, there is a chance for them to discover how other musicians lived out their commitment to music and how their art contributed to the life of their community. For the teacher, there is an important opportunity to back away from the intense details of scholarly work and address broader issues, an exercise that can be extremely beneficial to that work. As Pelikan puts it, "one fundamental reason for the contribution that undergraduate teaching makes to scholarly writing and publishing is that both of these activities call for going beyond the data and details of research to hypothesis and generalization." In an undergraduate course

> The professor is obliged to draw connections and contrasts and to locate the work in its broader context. Eventually it is the professor's obligation to carry out that same assignment ... also as a scholarly author. The professor comes to that obligation of the scholar far better prepared after having first taken it on as an undergraduate teacher.[3]

This brings to mind an incident that happened to me a couple of years ago. After reading a paper at a musicological conference in Germany, an American colleague of mine complimented me on the clarity of the presentation. My response: "I teach undergraduates; I have to be clear."

Though the "audience" in a music history class is already "sold" on the importance of music, it is also very much a captive one. In the letter of self-evaluation that accompanied my tenure application, I observed: "no one, or practically no one, comes to Hartt to study music history, but everyone has to take it." Music history (along with music theory and ear training) as a required course of study runs the risk of becoming a necessary evil, or worse, in the eyes of the students. This sample from several years' worth of student evaluations of my undergraduate classes testifies to the reputation that music history enjoys among some students: "[He] even got me interested in music history! (1988)," "Dr. Nott actually makes history enjoyable (1991)," "[he] makes what can be a very dull subject exciting (1996)," "I've never been able to learn anything from a history class before this one (1996)." Of course, student evaluations only tell part of the story, and some students elevate griping about music history to the level of an undergraduate ritual on a par with griping about dorm food, which is to say that some will complain, regardless of what the actual experience is. Nevertheless, the teacher of undergraduate music history would be wise to consider where the subject exists in the educational hierarchy of the students and make every effort to help them perceive the course material as both interesting in itself and relevant to their other studies. For example, how often do students perform in class? How often does the class sing and perhaps learn by heart a chant or chorale? Do the future classroom and studio teachers in the class understand what a great teacher, say, Bach was and the extent to which many of his greatest works were pedagogical in intent? In reflecting on fifteen years of teaching undergraduate music history, I have uncovered two basic principles that have guided my work: (1) start with the familiar and (2) be aware of the obstacles that confront your students. These principles are complementary and have in common the idea that the instructor needs to know where the students are. Most of us have a clear idea of where we want the students to be at the end of the course—that is, we have a clear idea of what facts and pieces of music they should know when the course is over—but many of us, especially those just starting out, are sometimes less attentive to the experiences and expectations that students bring to the class. Perhaps distracted by the newness of the experience, or obsessed with finding out which hoops we need to jump through to earn tenure, many beginning instructors pay little heed to the myriad ways, in addition to verbal comments and written evaluations, that students have of telling us how the course is going. It is not unlike the beginning conductor who, in the auditorium seats, can listen with the ears of a seasoned professional, but, once on the podium, wonders where his or her ears have gone. Failure to "listen" to the students in a classroom setting can open the way for a less than satisfactory educational experience for all concerned. These are some of my thoughts on how these two principles can give direction to the teaching of Baroque music.

Start with the familiar. This basic precept may be realized in a number of ways, but one possibility consists of rearranging the sequence of the undergraduate history survey so that it begins with the late seventeenth century, or around the time when major-minor tonality became the basis for the musical language. A decade and a half of undergraduate music history teaching has taught me that beginning the sequence of courses with the Middle Ages, though logical, has its risks. There is so much material that is new and foreign to the average student that many are overwhelmed and even decide early on that music history is complex, confusing, dull, and has no connection with what they are in school for, which is primarily to learn how to perform, compose, or teach. In addition to having to master some of the basic concepts of music history, such as the development of styles and forms, the connection between music and other arts, and its cultural context, students also have to master many new musical elements, such as chant notation, modality, and the liturgy. While many students are able to clear these hurdles, many are not. Why not start at a place where at least the basic musical language is familiar?

Over the years, I have taught and, therefore, come to know very well, three different undergraduate music history sequences. As a graduate teaching fellow and later as an instructor I taught a rigorous, fairly traditional four-semester sequence: (1) Middle Ages to Early Renaissance (or Grout/Palisca, chapters 1–6), (2) Late Renaissance to Baroque (chapters 7–12), (3) Classic to Early Romantic (chapters 13–17), (4) Late Romantic to Twentieth Century (chapters 18–22). A few years later, the department switched to a two-semester survey (Middle Ages to Baroque, Classic to Present) followed by two semesters of elective literature courses (Keyboard Literature, Vocal Literature, Symphonic Literature, etc.), which students took according to their majors. We currently have a three-semester survey (Late Baroque to Classic, Romantic to Present, Middle Ages to Early Baroque) followed by one semester of elective literature courses.

Each configuration has its advantages. The four-semester survey gave students a solid grounding in what is now called the Western art-music canon and also formed a common educational experience that was shared by all Bachelor of Music students, regardless of major. Yet, the survey ate up all twelve credits of the music history requirement and, therefore, prevented most from delving into more specialized literature studies relating to their majors. The two-semester survey/two-semester elective sequence corrected this imbalance, but at the expense of the survey, which was difficult to accomplish in two semesters—even some of the students complained! What tends to happen in a two-semester survey of Western music is that the two "ends" of the survey—very early and very recent music—become marginalized or get cut altogether.

Our current sequence of a three-semester survey/one-semester elective has turned out to be a workable compromise between the first two arrangements, allowing for a more leisurely survey and yet leaving room for some specialized study. Of course, music history can be "packaged" in any number of ways, none absolutely perfect, but the idea of starting the undergraduate sequence with a later time period is a fruitful idea and, in my experience, very successful. The first semester is essentially "Bach to Beethoven," though we actually begin a little earlier (Grout/Palisca, chapter 10) so that certain concepts (which are necessary background to the study of the music of Bach, Handel and Vivaldi) are properly introduced. These include: da capo aria, ritornello form, sonata, and dance suite. Though it may seem odd to introduce undergraduates to cantus firmus technique through the music of Bach, who essentially represents the end of this tradition, from the students' perspective this idea is more easily assimilated when presented through the work of a composer whose name and style are familiar. The examples by Bach of elaboration of pre-existent music found in the most recent edition of the

*Norton Anthology of Western Music* (Cantata BWV 140, *Wachet auf*; the organ chorale, *Durch Adams Fall*; and the last movements from the Credo of the Mass in B Minor) are excellent choices for this purpose. Furthermore, I have been told by the instructor of the medieval segment of the survey that when students come to study organum and Ars antiqua motet in their third semester, they are better prepared to understand the compositional techniques of this less familiar repertory.

Be aware of the obstacles that confront your students. Even though late-Baroque music offers a familiar musical language to most undergraduate music majors, it also, somewhat paradoxically, presents the students with significant obstacles, especially in the vocal music. Baroque opera, in particular, is (for the average undergraduate music major) a foreign, perhaps even bizarre, art form, and this is understandable. Who would not be puzzled by a genre that featured roles for castrated males who play mighty kings and heroes and yet sing in the treble range? And who can blame students for being resistant to the seemingly endless parade of static and predictable da capo arias, when their sense of dramatic pacing has been shaped by Mozart, Verdi and Broadway? I tell students that my initial reaction to opera seria was similar to theirs, but that I now love it deeply and maintain without hesitation that Handel is the equal of Mozart and Verdi in the field of opera.

It is important that students study and arrive at some understanding of Baroque opera since it was the most important and popular genre of its time. Yet it is difficult to teach because it has so many components that need study: musical, literary, dramatic, social, political. But it is this very density that can make it such a rich learning experience (Bach cantatas are also rich in this regard).

In introducing Baroque opera to an undergraduate survey class, I begin by concentrating on the recitative/aria unit, which forms the foundation for most late-Baroque vocal music, opera, as well as oratorio and cantata. If I feel especially brave, I will even improvise a scene, using piano and falsetto voice, to show how the dramatic rhythm of action/reflection is expressed by these two types of vocal music.[4] In this regard, the *Norton Anthology of Western Music* has two drawbacks. The Scarlatti aria ("Mi rivedi" from *Griselda*) has no preceding recitative, since it opens Act II of the opera (and the aria itself is a bit dull) and the scene from Handel's *Giulio Cesare*, though wonderfully dramatic, is too unorthodox formally for introductory purposes.[5] On the other hand, the excerpt from Handel's *Admeto* (as found in the Sarah Fuller anthology) is an excellent choice, giving the student ample secco recitative, followed by an exciting bravura aria whose form is crystal clear, accompagnato recitative, and two more arias.[6] Once the form of the da capo aria, as studied in an anthology excerpt, is analyzed in some detail by the class,

I am able to point out to them how easily the form is heard by playing a recording of another aria (such as "Scenes of horror" from Handel's *Jephtha*). By mastering this one form, they have a way of understanding oratorio and cantata, as well as opera. They have also been introduced to ritornello form, the use of tonality in structuring a coherent form and the late-Baroque predilection for juxtaposing free and strict styles (e.g., recitative-aria, prelude-fugue).

As already mentioned, the complexity of Baroque vocal music resides in the variety of its constituent elements: music, poetry, the rules of drama (in the case of opera), theology (in the case of sacred music), classical literature, social and political context. Yet this very complexity presents an educational opportunity that should not be missed in the undergraduate survey, for from a few excerpts the students can learn a great deal. A scene from a Handel opera (or oratorio) or a well-chosen Bach cantata presents the undergraduate with a microcosm of much of the late-Baroque musical, indeed, cultural universe. Thus, after dealing with what might be called the primary features of a given excerpt (musical form and style, poetic form, plot), the class is ready to move into broader, contextual issues.[7]

One such issue is that of dramatic pacing. For undergraduate music majors, especially for most voice or opera majors, the pacing of Baroque opera is slow, static, and formulaic. This is understandable, since their expectations in this regard have been shaped by opera from Mozart on. A good example for exploring this aspect of Baroque opera could be Scenes three and four from Act I of Handel's *Giulio Cesare* (available in a number of good recorded performances and a decent video performance). In the beginning of Scene 3, Caesar, having arrived in Egypt, is presented with a gift from Achilla, general and counselor to the ruler of Egypt. When the urn is opened, the severed head of Pompey, whom Caesar recently defeated in battle, rolls onto the stage. There follow three full da capo arias (ca. eighteen minutes of music) sung by Caesar, Cornelia (the widow of the decapitated man), and Sesto (his son). In a later operatic style, such a dramatic moment might well trigger a fiery ensemble number with the main characters reacting differently (Caesar with disgust, Cornelia with shock, Sesto vowing revenge) but simultaneously. The point is that later opera moves more quickly and that the faster pacing of this more familiar repertory shapes the expectations of undergraduate music majors and, indeed, much of the modern operatic audience. I like to compare the pacing of Baroque opera to that of a chess game: each character reacts one at a time, positioning him/herself in relation to the other characters in a rather deliberate, methodical manner. The emotional tension builds in a more cumulative rather than sudden manner.

This matter of pacing also comes into play when a single character undergoes an emotional transformation. A classic example of this in nineteenth-century opera would be Rigoletto's great Act II "Cortigiani" scene. Here, Verdi's hunchback jester moves from anger, to begging for pity, to utter desperation in a three-section unit which is not tonally closed: "Cortigiani"—Andante mosso agitato—C minor; "Ah! Eben, piango"—Meno mosso—F minor; "Miei signori"—D-flat major. Rigoletto's descent into despair (and into the flat keys, the scene actually begins in E minor) is rapid and continuous. A composer of Baroque opera had two possibilities for such an emotional plummet: accompanied recitative or consecutive arias. Near the end of the second act of Handel's *Jephtha* (an oratorio which, however, relies heavily on operatic conventions), the main character, on the brink of emotional and spiritual destruction, sings an extraordinary accompanied recitative ("Deeper and deeper still"). This type of recitative allowed the Baroque composer to step outside the bounds of affective unity and regularity of tempo, form, and tonality to create scenes of intense, almost Romantic, drama, something that Handel definitely achieves in this case. The use of separate arias to chart a single character's emotional journey is a more measured though no less effective way of achieving this. The Prison Scene from Act II of Handel's *Theodora* (another operatic oratorio) is a wonderful example of this approach. Here, the imprisoned Theodora makes an emotional journey that is really the opposite of Rigoletto's: from despair to a kind of spiritual exultation. Handel achieves this through a series of separate, discrete movements:

> Sinfonia (G minor)
> Secco recitative ("Oh thou bright sun!")
> Aria (non da capo—F-sharp minor—"With darkness deep, as is my woe")
> Sinfonia (E minor)
> Secco recitative ("But why are thou disquieted, my soul?")
> Aria (da capo—E minor—"Oh that I on wings could rise")

The pacing is different, but the result is the same: chess vs. baseball.

To return to the scene from *Guilio Cesare*, mention should be made of how various aspects of the scene (and the entire opera) are expressive of the prevailing political and social order of Handel's time. The three arias from Scenes three and four are presented according to a social hierarchy: monarch, mother, son (it could also be pointed out that much of the Baroque stage director's job entailed positioning the singers on stage according to their social position). Caesar reacts as befits a just and noble king: he is properly outraged by this gratuitous murder, a serious breach of the rules of war. Cornelia and Sesto, likewise, react according to social norms: the grieving widow and vengeful son. In many ways, opera seria was one of the last great art forms that subscribed to the classical maxim that art should delight and instruct. The portrayal and oftentimes celebration of the social order, so evident in Baroque opera, might be fruitfully compared with the depiction of royalty found in later operas.[8] Students might better appreciate the topsy-turvy Hugoesque world of *Rigoletto* if they come to it with some understanding of the (relatively) more ordered social structure of opera seria.

Studying the vocal music of Bach and Handel inevitably leads to the question of the reputations of these composers during their own lifetimes as compared with the reputations that they currently have. The place they have earned in textbooks and anthologies can mislead students into a false sense of what their historical positions were in the eighteenth century. In the case of Bach, for example, it can be instructive to show how the memory of a composer with, at best, a regional reputation, was kept alive by a number of devoted pupils, some of whom were leading theorists and then, in the following century, was pressed into service by a fast-growing nationalist movement. Thus, the local Lutheran cantor was transformed into "the greatest musical poet and the greatest musical orator that ever existed."[9] By this, I do not mean to minimize Bach's achievement, but I feel it important in an educational setting to relativize it, lest students come away with the impression that a "great" composer's reputation is automatically absolute and lasting. The central position that Bach occupies in the study of Baroque music is a distortion (many would argue a happy distortion) and came about through the tireless efforts of pupils, theorists, offspring, critics, biographers, composers, performers, publishers, editors, even music history teachers. They need to know that the music history textbook of the next century may treat Bach very differently and that, in any case, this music should not be taken for granted and if it is to remain a vital cultural treasure, it still needs the active advocacy of performers, scholars, and listeners.[10]

The case of Handel is different, but equally instructive. Here we have a composer whose fame was international during his lifetime and continued to grow after his death, though in a distorted way. Undergraduates are always surprised to hear that Handel devoted thirty-five years of his professional life to Italian opera and that *Messiah*, only one of twenty oratorios, is not even typical of the genre. For an assignment, I have asked students to visit one of the local music shops and write down which works by Handel are in the store's CD inventory and how many copies of each work there are. At the next class, I try to undo, or at least flesh out, Handel's longstanding reputation as primarily the composer of *Messiah* and *Water Music*. As in the case of Bach, this can trigger discussion of the roles played by the various components of what is called, regrettably, the "Music Industry."

Discussion of topics such as the dissemination of music and the role of arts management or entrepreneurship in our time and earlier periods is intrinsically interesting, helps students better understand the music they are studying, and touches upon their own very real desire to find a meaningful career for themselves in the complex, bewildering "Music Industry" of the early twenty-first century. It is also especially relevant to the growing number of students whose major field of study is arts management or music technology. While some argue that these majors are more appropriately housed in the business and technology schools of the university, I for one welcome these majors into the Bachelor of Music programs at our school. So much of our musical universe is shaped by record producers and arts managers that the better informed about things musical the future practitioners of these professions are, the more likely it is that their universe, or a least a small part of it, will be shaped according to musical values.

The recent work of a number of scholars has made the details of the professional careers and business dealings of a number of composers readily available. "Handel's London—the theatres" by Judith Milhous and Robert D. Hume makes it clear how much more expensive, and thus risky, undertaking an opera was as compared with spoken theatre.[11] Donald Burrows's biography of Handel spells out the details of the composer's efforts to secure the best and most famous singers for his London opera season, the arrangements with the nobility to start and keep afloat the Royal Academy Opera, and his (at first) reluctant turning to English oratorio as a way of finding a financially viable art form that would appeal to the unpredictable English public.[12] For many students, the once stuffy, distant, even sanctimonious composer of *Messiah* takes on a very real, almost contemporary humanity. A similarly humanizing effect can come about for Bach through use of material from Christoph Wolff's newly-published biography.[13] A few short excerpts would give students some insight into the reasons, or possible reasons, for Bach's career choices, the details of his duties and daily life at Leipzig, and the political ups and downs of his various positions. Even details such as diagrams of the Bach family living quarters in the St. Thomas School and an appendix on monetary values during Bach's time go a long way in bringing to life "the greatest musical orator that ever existed." It then seems to students all the more miraculous that, amidst the mundane challenges of their daily personal and professional lives, these composers managed to create works of such lasting power and beauty.[14]

It is important at this stage to emphasize that getting to all of these topics in one course is not possible and it is equally important to see to it that these contextual details, however interesting in themselves, do not distract students from the music, but rather serve to enhance their understanding of and appreciation for this great literature.

Teaching undergraduate music history is a challenging, even exhausting experience. Still, when the challenges are successfully met, it can be every bit as rewarding as graduate teaching, the supposed brass ring on the academic merry-go-round. The great scientist, J. Robert Oppenheimer, once remarked that "the specialization of science is an inevitable accompaniment of progress—yet it is full of dangers and it is cruelly wasteful since so much that is beautiful and enlightening is cut off from most of the world."[15] For those of us who want to see to it that so much beautiful and enlightening music is not cut off from most of the world, all we need is a passion for communicating what we know and love to nonspecialists and a willingness to let those "bright and interested and ignorant" undergraduates teach us how to do it.

## Notes

1    Jaroslav Pelikan, *The Idea of the University: A Reexamination* (New Haven: Yale University Press, 1992), 94.

2    See Ralph Locke's essay, p. 25.

3    Pelikan, *The Idea of the University*, 95.

4    It is important, however, not to present this action/reflection dichotomy as a rigid convention without exceptions. See Reinhard Strohm, *Dramma per Musica: Italian Opera Seria of the Eighteenth Century* (New Haven: Yale University Press, 1997), 11–13.

5    Claude Palisca, ed., *The Norton Anthology of Western Music*, third ed. (New York: W. W. Norton, 1996), I: 395, 572.

6    Sarah Fuller, ed., *The European Musical Heritage: 800–1750* (New York: McGraw-Hill, 1987), 481.

7    There may not be time to address all of these topics in a single class and some might be more appropriate for an upper-level literature course. Still, these are strategies that have worked for me and sparked some interest in students from my classes.

8    Though care should be taken not to oversimplify here. Baroque opera and oratorio could also be critical of the prevailing social order, or at least parts of it. See Strohm, *Dramma per Musica*, chapter 14 and Ruth Smith, *Handel's Oratorios and Eighteenth-Century Thought* (Cambridge: Cambridge University Press, 1995).

9    From the last paragraph of Forkel's *On Johann Sebastian Bach's Life, Genius, and Works*. See Hans T. David and Arthur Mendel, eds., *The New Bach Reader: A Life of Johann Sebastian Bach in Letters and Documents*, revised and expanded by Christoph Wolff (New York: W. W. Norton, 1998), 479.

10    I am reminded here of an incident that took place in my Baroque Seminar a few years ago. At the first class, I asked the small group of graduate and select upper level undergraduate students what they knew about Bach's *Mass in B Minor*. "One of the monuments of Western civilization," came the immediate reply from one of the undergraduate students. When I asked him to explain, he said, "That's what you told us in the survey course." You never know what they will remember!

11    In Donald Burrows, ed., *The Cambridge Companion to Handel* (Cambridge: Cambridge University Press, 1997), 55–63.

12    Donald Burrows, *Handel* (New York: Schirmer, 1994).

13    Christoph Wolff, *Johann Sebastian Bach: The Learned Musician* (New York: W. W. Norton, 2000).

14    I have offered during the summer term a music history elective on "Handel as Arts Manager" designed specifically for music management majors. In addition to lots of music and the above-mentioned details of Handel's professional life, we study copyright, publishing, concert and theater life, and politics in eighteenth-century England.

15    As cited in Pelikan, *The Idea of the University*, 98.

# Chapter Three

# What Chopin (and Mozart and Others) Heard: Folk, Popular, "Functional," and Non-Western Music in the Classic/Romantic Survey Course

*Ralph P. Locke*

Teaching a survey of Western art music in the so-called Classic and Romantic eras (ca. 1730–1880) is one of the great delights and challenges that an instructor of music history can face. Both the delight and the challenge remain vitally alive for me every year, despite (or because of?) having taught the course for twenty-five years now at the Eastman School of Music.

But the passing years have made me more uneasy with certain prevailing assumptions about how to structure such a course and what repertoire to include and exclude. As a result, I have begun to experiment with bringing a certain amount of non-canonical music into the course. It is on that ongoing experiment that I report here. I also glance back occasionally to music before 1750 or glance ahead to the twentieth century, in order to suggest the possible applications of my experiment to courses that treat Western art music of other eras.

## High and wide multiculturalisms

We have so few teaching hours in our courses and so much we would like our students to learn, or at least become glancingly familiar with: factual information, musical repertoires, stylistic trends, representative pieces, and interpretive concepts that help bind all of these together. The task was hard enough in previous decades, when the music history survey sequence, in most colleges and music schools, restricted itself to exploring (or "covering," as some syllabi ambitiously put it) the art-music traditions of Europe and the United States.

The task is harder now. Many of us have come to feel that students, to be culturally literate, need to know more than the accepted masterpieces of

Western art music, such as Monteverdi's *Vespers,* Beethoven's Ninth, and Stravinsky's *Sacre du printemps.*

This feeling of ours is based on several intertwined beliefs. The first and most basic of these is the belief, held more and more widely these days, that human expression can reach significant aesthetic heights—and has done so, in various times and places and settings, not just in European churches, courts, and chambers, or Western (European *and* American) concert halls, opera houses, and avant-garde institutions (such as the Columbia-Princeton lab or Boulez's IRCAM).

This belief leads us to wish to introduce our students to a wider range of musical achievements: the pathbreaking 1920s improvised solos of trumpeter Louis Armstrong, the Country-and-Western songs of Patsy Cline, the hymns to French low life by Jacques Brel, Styne and Sondheim's Broadway musical *Gypsy* (in its various incarnations on Broadway, film, television/video), the harmonic adventures of jazz pianist Bill Evans, the searingly passionate declarations of lesbian singer/songwriter Melissa Etheridge or, to take two non-Western examples, the delicate *erhu* playing of the blind Chinese folk musician Abing and the sometimes hour-long song performances, recorded live and with audible audience response, of Egypt's now-legendary Umm Kulthum. (Every teacher will have his or her own preferred instances of artful music-making—whatever that word "artful" might mean—that lie off the Western art-music axis that leads from Bach to Debussy and beyond. The eight just named are merely my own recent favorites.)

This belief deserves a name: I propose "high multiculturalism." As the examples that I cite suggest, a high multiculturalism underlies the work not only of historical musicologists and music theorists, with their devotion to canonical masterpieces of Western art music, but also of many ethnomusicologists, with their equally intense devotion to the richly elaborated "classical" art-music traditions of Morocco, Afghanistan, India, or Indonesia, or to certain intricate polyphonic traditions of sub-Saharan Africa (e.g., music of the Congolese pygmies).

A very different belief (though not incompatible with the first) is that the world's various musics are of interest and value primarily because—like high mountains—"they are there": i.e., because they are practiced and valued by this or that population, social class, or ethnic group.

Let us call this belief "wide multiculturalism." Not, I stress, "low multiculturalism," as if it were some kind of opposite to the "high" version. Indeed, this second belief often skirts the whole issue of high and low. But this is not to say that questions of aesthetics and value are necessarily ignored in a "wide multiculturalist" approach; rather, when raised, they tend to be treated sociologically. "What are the values and other meanings," the wide multiculturalist asks, "that the given population or group *assigns* to the music that it makes and uses?" A wide multiculturalism is, of course, most often associated with ethnomusicology, but it is finding an increasing place in the work of many historical musicologists who deal with Western art music and other repertoires long treated as relatively autonomous: witness the proliferating studies of musical institutions and how they function, and also of how various musical genres and individual works have been received in different places and times by audiences and critics.

It remains true, though, that wide multiculturalism tends most often to lead us to repertoires that are widely understood as being intertwined with and shaped by concrete aspects of people's non-musical lives in different societal contexts: repertoires as varied as the yodeling systems of Swiss cowherds, various ritual musics of East Asia, the digeridoo of Australia's native population, jump-rope chants of inner-city African-American girls, or festive Sabbath songs of Chassidic Jews in Brooklyn. These repertoires, in other words, maintain a crucial and undisguised *functional* relationship to some other social activity—dancing, courtship, religion, and so on—instead of being apprehended primarily within an aesthetic frame, such as the contemplative listening that is typical of concert traditions. (Pop and other entertainment music most often falls somewhere between these two extremes: it can take place in concert settings—yet, when listened to on the car radio, say, it is inextricably woven into courtship rituals and other relationships among young people: for instance, non-homosexual male bonding.) German musicologists and music sociologists, such as Carl Dahlhaus and Tibor Kneif, tend to label such repertoires as, precisely, *funktionell*, in contrast to music of both the "art" and the "commercial entertainment" varieties. There are, of course, serious limitations to all such terminological systems.[1] I will nonetheless continue to use the word "functional" below, in regard to certain repertoires—including certain Western ones—that differ in profound ways from much of the Western art music that lies at the center of my teaching.

Most of the repertoires just mentioned, whether Western or non-Western, have (or have had) relatively little to do with the Western art-music tradition. But if we think for a moment, we can quickly come up with a number of analogous, equally "functional" repertoires that *have* been demonstrably important for the development of, or have in some way interacted with, Western music over the past two centuries: the Viennese waltz, national anthems (and other musical pieces associated with particular countries and nations), military and political music, and hymns and other relatively simple church music. And, of course, certain non-Western traditions (such as Indonesian gamelan music) *have* influenced the art music of the West.

In any case, whether or not these repertoires did or did not influence a Mozart or a Stravinsky, I am increasingly convinced that they can have a lot to say to students today, even (or especially) pre-professional music students and others who are particularly devoted to Western art-music traditions.

## Constraints on a fully multicultural approach

But it is one thing to *wish* to incorporate folk, popular, non-Western, and heavily "functional" music into our music history courses, and quite another to attempt to put that wish into practice. Especially given that many of us, including myself, remain committed to exposing our students in some systematic way to the art music of the West, from Gregorian chant and Dufay to Schubert, Debussy, Bartók, and, say, Joan Tower. Time simply does not suffice for all that we would like to do.

The time constraint is particularly apparent to those of us who teach music majors (BMus students, and BA music majors). Many of these students come to our music school or conservatory with the hope and intention of playing, studying, and teaching Western art music for the rest of their lives. And many other music-school students—jazz guitarists, say—understand and accept the premise that Western art music is an important part of their training and perhaps of a multipronged career, such as is becoming increasingly common these days.

Some music-school students, I find, are simply aching to hear more Western art music and learn more about it. In part, this is because they feel that they cannot get enough of it in other parts of their lives. And understandably enough: after all, "classical" music, as it is widely called, scarcely exists on radio and TV, and what *is* found there comprises a very narrow selection from a vast and varied set of repertoires. When, I sometimes fret, was the last time our Rochester NPR station chose, on its own, to play a Schubert lied, a Bach cantata, a Renaissance madrigal, any late Stravinsky? Such works are reportedly still considered problematic or annoying by many listeners: "surveys show that vocal music is a turnoff," one radio-station manager told me, as if that "fact" preempted the need for further discussion. The surveys are equally adamant about any music perceived as "dissonant."

Other music students, admittedly, do *not* ache for this knowledge and increased exposure to repertoire yet arguably need it all the more—need, that is, to be provided with a basis for appreciating the achievement and complexity/coherence, the situated aspects and the transcendent/universal ones, of the specific pieces that they are studying and that many of them will spend decades of their lives imparting to (or sharing with, as I like to think of it) others: concert and radio audiences, or college and music-school students of their own, or schoolchildren (in the case of those who will be teaching in the elementary and secondary schools).

Compounding the limitations of time is the fact that the art music of the West is itself an increasingly intractable organism, one that is at once cumulative and ever-evolving. I say that it is ever-evolving because it keeps extending forward: our standard excuses for not discussing the music of the second half of the twentieth century ("it's too recent") ring ever more hollow as each passing decade brings forth memorable new pieces, such as the Ligeti Horn Trio or Michael Torke's witty and deeply affecting opera, *Strawberry Fields*. But its cumulativeness, these days, is no less striking: the performance of early music now forms a truly vibrant (and economically successful) component of mainstream musical life. Giving it short shrift in our courses denies our students access to a major part of the Western musical heritage and to some extraordinarily imaginative explorations by such specialists as Andrew Manze, Paul O'Dette, Fabio Biondi, Ellen Hargis, Christopher Herrick, David Daniels, Christophe Rousset, Carole Cerasi, Jordi Savall, and William Christie, and also by "general practitioners"—those who perform both early and later repertoires—such as Cecilia Bartoli, Lorraine Hunt Lieberson, Philippe Herreweghe, and John Eliot Gardiner.

Of course, having more time with the students would help. So we try to persuade curricular committees to add more credit-hours of required music history. This, we argue, would enable us to add more early and/or recent music, plus some of those other repertoires discussed earlier (folk, pop, non-Western, and Western-functional). But, even if we do win some extra "credits," the problem remains: how can we do even faint justice to so much material, such varied phenomena and concepts?

The usual solutions involve adding a course requirement—World Music, say—or letting the student elect one from among several options, e.g., World Music, History of Jazz, or Popular Music. But such courses, fine things in themselves, also have built-in drawbacks that risk creating inadvertent misimpressions in a student's mind. For example, a course on "Popular Music in the US" (plus The Beatles, of course) may, quite unintentionally, reinforce the unspoken yet widespread notion in the US that continental Europe has never produced anything but art/classical music (except for whatever recent exceptions the student happens to know already, e.g., ABBA and Rammstein). If that pop-music course begins, as it well may, around 1900, it will almost inevitably reinforce the widespread impression that America had no thriving popular-music practitioners and industry before that date. So much for all those dance-music fiddlers, coast to coast, not to speak of "After the Ball" and other parlor ballads that sold in the hundreds of thousands of copies in the last decades of the nineteenth century. If the decision is made, instead, to begin the course around 1950, the result can be even more pernicious, implying (again, unintentionally) that popular music first found its mass market only with Elvis and Chuck Berry, thus effectively negating all awareness of not only those fiddle tunes and parlor ballads but also the marches of Sousa, the "coon songs" of May Irwin, the "sweet" jazz of the Glenn Miller Orchestra (broadcast "live" to the nation over the radio before and during World War II), the antic magic of "Fats" Waller, and the enormous recorded output of such varied singers as Bessie Smith, Bing Crosby, and Hank Williams, not to mention Continental (and ocean-crossing) stars such as Yvonne Printemps, Noel Coward, Marlene Dietrich, and the American-born Josephine Baker.

Yet another such drawback is that, by separating folk, popular, non-Western, and Western-functional repertoires off from the history of Western art music, one loses the opportunity to explore parallels and disparities, interactions and frictions.

All of these drawbacks are more easily avoided if one, instead, integrates various of those other repertoires into the existing sequence of courses on Western art music. I would like, in the remainder of this essay, to discuss the advantages and concomitant disadvantages of this unusual teaching strategy.

## A new solution (and its risks)

"Teach the conflicts," runs Gerald Graff's famous proposal for how to approach the canonical masterpieces with undergraduates.[2] Similarly, we music history teachers would do well, I feel, to problematize (which means, to some extent, historicize) the musical masterwork by revealing the conflicts of its own day that it embodies—as also the conflicts that it gives occasion to when different audiences and commentators have tried, and try today, to make sense of it. I do not propose that we emphasize the conflicts at every single class meeting. But students would profit from our doing it sometimes. And I propose, more specifically, that we try doing it by confronting the masterwork with other musics that it either resembles (and perhaps influenced or was influenced by) or strikingly differs from.

There are a thousand ways to do this, of course. Some involve juxtaposing a work of Western art music with a piece that is from a very different place and time yet resembles it (and of course differs from it) in various technical respects. A piece by Corelli or Couperin, for example, and a John Coltrane cut can be fruitfully compared and contrasted as examples of highly improvisatory embellishment over a relatively simple, conjunct (and sometimes preexisting) melody and/or standard harmonic pattern. Furthermore, the similarities and dissimilarities need not be stylistic or technical but might, instead, be historical, functional (in the terms set out earlier), aesthetic, or any number of other things. Indeed, the two pieces might be chosen because of fundamental dissimilarities that would help the student grasp the specific quality of each piece (and the tradition or traditions that each represents).

My proposal is not unprecedented. In the late 1980s, a committee of scholars of American music argued that teachers should insert specific American musical repertoires into the undergraduate music history sequence at points where the instructor could show them to be relevant. This relevance could be chronological, such as adding music of an American composer of art music—Edward MacDowell, say—to a class or unit involved primarily with the music that formed his or her stylistic and aesthetic context—in this case, Liszt, Brahms, or Grieg. Or the relevance might leap chronology: the teacher might note certain striking parallels in musical technique or social function between repertoires that occurred centuries apart. For example, the students in an early-music survey class might be asked to sing and discuss Billings's "When Jesus Wept" (1770)—though it is centuries "too late"—at the point where they are encountering an analogous vernacular-style, modally inflected round: "Sumer is icumen in" (ca. 1300).[3]

My proposed solution for bringing different repertoires into the existing survey courses may seem less radical than the Billings case, because it does not commit the great (supposed) sin of anachronism. But it is surely more risky than the MacDowell case, because (as we shall see in a moment) it amounts to putting at least a certain amount of "non-art" music on the same pedagogical and curricular level as the canonic masterpieces. Even so, it may well be lambasted as maintaining an apparent *hegemony* of Western art music: as simply throwing a few pieces of folk (parlor, etc.) music into the usual mix, too few to achieve the kind of "critical mass" that gives a repertoire profile in the student's mind.

In the end, I would insist that my solution *is* radical, even (by intention) blasphemous. This solution, as sketched a bit more fully below, teaches the students various things at various points in the semester, most importantly that the musical repertoires that they (and most concertgoing non-musicians) have been repeatedly taught to value by teachers, conductors, and critics was, at the time of its creation, but a single musical strand in a "multi(musico)cultural" fabric. My solution has the merit of dislodging existing preconceptions, allowing the student to hear a familiar or mainstream masterwork afresh, placed back in its own original musical context (or else placed in an intriguingly parallel or even contrasting one). At the same time, it has the added benefit of exposing the student to unfamiliar varieties of musical expression that may be just as compelling, tightly woven, and fascinating (aesthetically, historically or sociologically, or both) as the Mozart, Brahms, and Ravel with which he or she passionately identifies.

My proposed solution, as I have already hinted, is to incorporate selected examples of non-Western and other musics (e.g., Western folk and popular musics, including music of the dance hall and the bourgeois parlor) into a course, or multi-course sequence, that is structured primarily as a chronological survey of Western art music. Such an approach entails compromises on every front, but these may be outweighed, in the teacher's view, by a resulting richness not previously attainable. The instances to be examined in the remainder of this chapter emphasize both the possibilities and the inherent traps in such an effort (including the importance of making the traps explicit to the class).

## Placing Chopin in many musical contexts

Let us start with a readily comprehensible instance. A fifty-minute class devoted nominally to Chopin can naturally incorporate related music of several different kinds. It rarely does so, in my experience, though teachers and textbooks regularly allude to one or more of them. These other musical selections might include:

1. a Bellini aria, since Chopin specifically admired such vocal writing and arguably was influenced by it (and by its prominent exponents, such as the tenor Rubini) in his more florid passages.

2. some Polish folk music.

3. Polish-style pieces by immediate predecessors of Chopin, or contemporaries of Chopin. Numerous examples are easily found in a recent anthology by Wasowska, and some have even been recorded.[4]

4. a piano nocturne by John Field, the "inventor" of that genre, which, in the context of a Chopin lecture, could be presented as destined more for the parlor than the concert stage—hence a kind of "middlebrow" cultural item for daily use by intermediate-level pianists. The Field pieces are, of course, widely available, though sometimes in performances that are either a bit blunt or, the opposite, too droopy and blurrily pedaled.

For present purposes, let us leave the first of these, the Bellini, out of consideration, in part because it already finds a place in the Western art-music survey course, as a "high-art" item of a relatively melodious sort (though Bellini is hardly granted much attention in another branch of the musical academy, namely music theory).[5] This still leaves at least three distinct and interesting musical streams to be explored. No doubt this is still too many to deal with in one fifty-minute class. For, as I mentioned earlier, an obvious downside to the process of including more and different kinds of music besides the masterpieces is that the teacher inevitably leaves him/herself with less time in which to present pieces by Chopin himself and so must play and discuss fewer of them (or else discuss them more briefly than he or she otherwise would have).

Still, by adding in some folk music, or some music by Chopin's less genius-level predecessors and contemporaries, the teacher will have gained the possibility of unrolling before the students such new perspectives as:

1. How orally transmitted folk traditions differ from composed "works." This includes recognizing how the artistic integrity of folk performances was/is often stripped away by well-meaning transcribers, such as Kolberg and other nineteenth-century compilers of folk-tune collections.[6]

2. How Chopin's mazurkas absorb dance rhythms, drones, Lydian fourths, and other stylistic conventions of the folk repertoire—and/or from the folk-evoking parlor works of his Warsaw predecessors—but then elaborate upon them in astonishing, sophisticated ways, creating relatively stable (and undying) musical "works." (One could pause here also to show the differences between various manuscripts and editions of a single Chopin piece, and between different recorded performances of it, thus emphasizing the word "relatively" in the description just given of "relatively stable 'works.'")

3. How Field's nocturnes (which Chopin admired and taught to his piano students) provided Chopin with a genre that he could enrich with more varied and specific figuration and harmonies, while still producing works that are not too difficult technically for the intermediate-level pianist and that therefore might, like the far simpler Field pieces, sell well to significant numbers of purchasers.

I mentioned the drawback of limited time. Another quite serious one is the risk of making the folk music, or the salon mazurkas, or the Field pieces, seem interesting only as rough ore that a "real" musician then turned into gold. This drawback can be lessened, in part, by the teacher's addressing the issue explicitly (problematizing it, rather than sweeping it under the rug—Graff's main point, after all). It also helps if the teacher selects music (and performances) that he or she loves. I recommend the Field Nocturne no. 5 in B-flat, rather than, say, the somewhat blander no. 8 in A major, included in Palisca's *Norton Anthology*, though that one does have a revealing melodic parallel to Chopin's Nocturne in E-flat, op. 9, no. 2.[7] From the folk-music side, Czekanowska's recent CD of Polish folk music gives some marvelous items to choose from, many of them quickly disproving the notion that folk music is simple, artless, and predictable.[8] For example, a class of young musicians skilled in Western art music may be brought to appreciate the rhythmic complexities of this and other "folk" (and "tribal") musics simply by trying to clap along or to transcribe a few seconds' worth.

An additional risk arises with comparisons to folk music. We have no recorded folk performances, of course, from Chopin's era, since recording technology was unknown until several decades after his death. At most, we have those aforementioned transcriptions from the time, which reduce a complex multistrophic and multilayered performance (e.g., a heterophonic rendering over rhythmicized drones) to a single one-line rendering of "the tune" (sometimes omitting even to transcribe the words; or printing the words separately, thereby veiling from sight the ways in which successive stanzas may alter the performance of a tune). And folk music, like everything else in human life, changes in response to multiple influences, social and musical. For one thing, Western art music, including some pieces (or at least tunes) by Chopin, has been familiar to certain village musicians since the advent of recordings and radio. So any resemblances that we excitedly spot may actually indicate an influence of the "reverse" kind, rather like the famous incident of "*Beowulf* in South Dakota." Around 1936 an eager ethnologist doing field research among Native Americans (Ojibwa, I presume) noted that a certain tale showed significant similarities to *Beowulf*; from this the scholar drew fanciful conclusions when a simpler explanation, and the true one, was that another white ethnologist, only months before, had, upon request, shared with her hosts/informants a story from her own culture.[9]

Nonetheless, listening to folk music in the context of Chopin brings many advantages. It raises the question of *why* a composer would/should want to "sound" Polish (Spanish, Norwegian, etc.) in his or her music. And this leads to issues involving nationalism and the building of a local and international career or reputation. Chopin, after all, distinguished himself from some of his contemporary pianist-composer colleagues in part by being the audible representative of a small or marginalized country, by having something stylistically different and fascinating to offer. Which does not mean that he offered it cynically or casually. The point is worth stressing to students, who, I have noticed, are sometimes quick to assume that economic motivations always work at cross-purposes to aesthetic ones. True, this is often the case, as may be seen in some of the more exploitive and limiting aspects of the mass musical marketplace today (which result in the Back Street Boys or Britney Spears). But there are plenty of exceptions: figures who produced works of high and lasting aesthetic quality within a commercial system, including Chopin but also Duke Ellington or the best products of Broadway musical theater.

**Further windows of pedagogical opportunity**

I would like to note more briefly some other connections (comparisons, contrasts) that I have either found valuable and workable in my teaching or would look forward to employing at some future date.

(1) It is worth pointing out to students that folk-music influences preceded the romantic nationalism of Chopin and Liszt. Telemann, for instance, heard folk bands during several trips to a nobleman's estate in Pless (Upper Silesia). In an autobiographical article, he declared that "an observant person could pick up enough ideas from them in a week to last a lifetime. In short, this music contains much valuable material, if it is properly treated." "In time," he added, "I wrote various grand concertos and trios in this manner which I clothed in Italian dress, with divers[e] adagios and allegros."[10]

(2) Whereas Chopin focused heavily on the music of his own native country, Mozart was fascinated by a tradition of "Turkish" music that supposedly represented the music of the elite Janissary troops of the Ottoman Empire. Unfortunately for us today, the Janissaries were suppressed in the 1830s, and their bands along with them, so it is not easy to compare actual Janissary repertoires to Mozart's vision of them. But several examples of Janissary music have been reconstructed and recorded by Turkish cultural authorities; the new versions are based in part on notated melodies that survive from the eighteenth and early nineteenth centuries. As with the Polish folk music, one can point to the rich variation within an actual Janissary performance (as reconstructed on the recordings) and the comparative poverty and insistent, plain-faced repetition of Mozart's version of this kind of music. But there are some revealing resemblances, too. Turkish music is built upon a rhythmic pattern or *usul*, and Mozart has been accused by certain scholars of utterly ignoring these distinctively Middle Eastern patterns. A glance at the music confirms that Mozart, like Beethoven after him, does favor one particular recurrent rhythm in the accompaniments to his "Turkish" movements:

long, short, short, long. If we play for the students a recording of, say, the "Old [Turkish] Army March" from a currently available CD and then either Mozart's rondo *alla turca* from the keyboard sonata in A Major, K. 331, or the Turkish episode from the finale of his Fifth Violin Concerto (also in A major), they can easily be led to see similarities and differences between a Middle Eastern and a Western way of handling the same basic rhythm.[11]

(3) "Northfield," an early New England fuguing tune (1805) by Jeremiah Ingalls, is available on recordings in both a "straight" performance and a highly inflected one, the latter having been recorded "in the field," namely at an Alabama shape-note convention in the 1960s.[12] We can thus trace the way in which this piece traveled from New England, and from its composer's writing desk, to become a vernacular tradition, learned largely by ear, among highly religious rural folk. When using this piece and the recordings, I pose the possibility that some of the vocal slides and tight-throat singing that we hear in the Alabama recording may be similar (in spirit if not in precise technique) to the "wild shouting" that was typical of New England renderings in the early 1800s and that church-music reformers such as Lowell Mason strove successfully to suppress in the 1830s.

(4) Scholars have uncovered a transcribed version of a Puerto Rican folk song that Gottschalk used as the basis for his *Souvenir de Porto Rico*. It is, intriguingly, less syncopated than his version, though this may simply be a result of the homogenization that transcribers forced upon folk melodies in order to make them more readable (or more acceptable) to eyes and ears trained on Western art music.[13] In order to give students a sense of the syncopated sounds that Gottschalk did encounter in the Caribbean, I have played for them a wonderful field recording of a Puerto Rican singer of African origin.[14] It is a different song from the one Gottschalk used, but I point out how this song, too, would probably be "straightened out" in transcription and lose most of its charm. In addition, bringing in this recording has the benefit of raising an important social-historical point: Puerto Rico has been the scene of greater interaction between populations of (ultimately) different origins than students in North America are accustomed to. Thus, my decision to use a singer of African origin (in the coastal town of Loiza Aldea) to illustrate the syncopated rhythms sung by *jibaros* (peasants of Spanish origin living in the inland hill country) is not as implausible as it may sound.

(5) Highly stereotyped French dance music thrived ca. 1860—both as full-length (and one-act) ballets by Adam and Delibes and as quadrilles for domestic dance parties. The forms and styles of such dances are borrowed and

transformed in Tchaikovsky's far more complex and often dramatically more intriguing ballets. Hearing a bit of *Giselle* before hearing a bit of *Swan Lake* may help students grasp the highly conventional contexts in which great composers often work—how he or she uses the conventions and also resists (transcends?) them. It also helps the students understand why Tchaikovsky, despite the distinctly Russian sound of some of his music, tends to be regarded, within a Russian context, as primarily a "Westernizer."

(6) The Hardanger fiddle (*hardingfele*) is a Norwegian folk instrument that has a flat fingerboard and therefore can produce double and triple stops more easily than a concert violin. The instrument is also fitted with several sympathetic strings under the fingerboard, and, since these are often tuned in open fifths, the result is a ringing drone accompanying the (fingered) melody, not unlike the complex sounds of a bagpipe. Edvard Grieg arranged twelve traditional Hardanger fiddle tunes for solo piano, under the title *Slåtter,* op. 72 (1902–3). Heard side by side with the original folk versions, they demonstrate: a) the limitations of trying to notate, for the trained reading eye, what we might call a non-literate "ear- and hand-music" full of rapid improvised ornaments and b) the limitations of trying to reproduce on the piano (an instrument of fixed pitches) a folk music that is full of slides and bent notes. And yet they also demonstrate c) the imaginativeness with which a talented composer can escape these limitations—most notably in the contrasting middle section of piece no. 4, full of melancholic downward chromatic harmonic progressions that are not at all folklike (though the top voice reiterates devotedly the opening motive of the folk tune with which the piece began).[15] Furthermore, at least one of the tunes that Grieg set has now reentered the "folk revival" repertoire, a process that has submitted it to yet further fascinating alteration.[16]

(7) North African traditional music is echoed in the Bacchanale from Saint-Saëns's *Samson et Dalila.* Indeed, Saint-Saëns states plainly in one of his many informative articles that he was given "the oriental theme of the ballet" (the one starting on the fifth degree of the scale and including a major third degree but a flatted second and sixth) by a famed French general who had distinguished himself during the conquest of Algeria.[17]

(8) Indonesian gamelan music exerted a profound influence on Debussy and Britten, but how often, really, do teachers attempt to have students listen to a gamelan recording, or bring the school's gamelan ensemble into class, in order to establish (as with the Janissary recordings above) similarities and differences?

(9) American patriotic songs, Protestant hymns, college songs, and military marches were used for multiple overlapping purposes by Ives. Students need to be presented with these, since so few of them nowadays can be counted on to know the tunes of "Columbia, the Gem of the Ocean," "Bringing in the Sheaves," or perhaps even "How Dry I Am," much less certain items that are nowadays known mainly to band musicians, such as David Wallis Reeve's *Second Regiment Connecticut National Guard March* (ca. 1877, quoted at length in Ives's *Decoration Day* and two other of his pieces; Ives described this march as "inspiring").

(10) Traditional Russian wedding laments (representing the mixed emotions of the bride, the parents, etc.) are evoked in Stravinsky's *Les noces*. Fortunately, the Pokrovsky Ensemble has recorded a selection of these. Unfortunately, on that same CD they also perform *Les noces*, a work that they are technically unfit to handle, though some vocal phrases do sound indelibly "right" (or at least extremely effective) in their throats.[18]

(11) Hungarian folk songs were adapted by Bartók in numerous works. Here one can sometimes compare the very recording that he made in the field with the composition that he based upon the same tune. [19]

(12) The Shaker hymn "Simple Gifts" was used by Aaron Copland in his ballet *Appalachian Spring*. The Shaker traditions are documented in extensive studies by American ethnomusicologists and cultural historians.[20] All of this can help students to understand both the uses of music within a distinctively American social movement and to ponder what made it attractive to Copland, a "composer from Brooklyn," who of course had no Shaker (nor Appalachian) elements in his background. (The family name was originally Kaplan.)

(13) Ghanaian drumming patterns have, by Steve Reich's own admission, deeply influenced numerous of his works such as *Clapping Music*.[21] Parallel listening may, again, reveal significant similarities and differences, allowing the student to appreciate each type of music for its own distinctive qualities. (Fortunately, Reich has named some of the sources of his knowledge of African music, e.g., books by the Reverend A. M. Jones and by John Miller Chernoff; he also spent the summer of 1970 studying drumming in Ghana.)[22] The listening may also encourage the student to ponder the factors that possibly led this urban American, beginning in the 1960s, to seek musical roots in West Africa. Might it be relevant that, like most Americans of his generation, whatever their family background, Reich had grown up with much African-American music in his ears and nervous system? And how did his

interest in African music (and also Balinese music) relate to his process of reclaiming/constructing his own Jewish identity (perhaps seen as "foreign" and distinct from mainstream America), that he has, over the intervening years, worked out in some detail, not only in *Tehillim* (which sets verses from several psalms in the original Hebrew) but also in *Different Trains* and *The Cave*?

## The bottom line

It is probably best at this point to stress again that I have not actually put into practice the dozen or more "insertions" listed above (a few of which, in any case, relate to other eras than the Classic and Romantic). I certainly have never incorporated such a large number in any one semester-long course. Nonetheless, I find that including even a few can sharply reorient the listening patterns of the students, stimulate their thinking and shake them out of habitual value judgments. Each time that I try to broaden the students' understanding of what Leonard Bernstein used to call "the infinite variety of music," some of them react in ways that I have not anticipated. One particularly intense response I will never forget: gales of laughter in my undergraduate survey the first time I played the recording of the Alabama shape-note conventioneers. The Alabama singers' tense, untrained vocal style, their lack of "correct" choral blend, their "hillbilly" accent (as several students put it)—all of this made the students feel, instantly, that the recording was not worth listening to and could be treated with ridicule even while it was still playing through the speakers. Anxiety, I sensed, was feeding this reaction—the students' fear that they were not, in their own musical performances and in the ways that they present themselves in daily life, as utterly unlike the "uncultured" rural poor as they might imagine.

All in all, I decided, this recording was a keeper. It seemed to touch a raw nerve while also making good points about different conceptions of what is beautiful or desirable in a musical performance. Indeed, it raised questions about what is and is not a performance at all. (Is a fully participatory and social/functional event with no listening audience really a performance? How about a crowd of relatives, say, singing "For He's a Jolly Good Fellow" at grandpa's seventy-fifth birthday party?)

But, ever since that first time, I have preceded the Alabama recording with a few sentences of verbal framing. These are people, I instruct the students, who come together as a community for the pleasure of making music together; they stand in a square, beating the time with one arm and stomping with their feet. At the same time, singing for them is an energetically individual act, as we can hear in their lusty, sharply focused sound, with each trying to make him/herself heard above the general din. And, at least for many of them, the group singing connects them to Jesus (to whom the hymns are often addressed), to their neighbors and family members who are singing along or listening (or even just half-listening), and also to their ancestors, who sang many of these same hymns their whole life long. This, I add, is the sort of vital connection to music that is often missing from concert life today. In our class, we are privileged to be listening to this act of committed music making and to be witnessing the spirit that animates it.

The students still smile, some chuckle quietly, but they all listen. And I am quite sure that I see them thinking, too, about "high" and "low," "narrow" and "wide"—thinking about the art to which they have devoted their youth and first maturity.

*I would like to thank Ayden Adler, Rob Haskins, Gabriela Ilnitchi, Ellen Koskoff, James Parakilas, Michael Pisani, Martin Scherzinger, and Jürgen Thym for comments, challenges, pointers, and encouragement.*

## Notes

1    For example, the phrase "functional music" has the disadvantage of implying that concerts and other such performances are somehow pure, unsullied by social functionality, whereas, of course, people who participate in such events may be engaging in any number of not-strictly-musical functions, such as declaring their adherence to the tastes and values of a given social class, ethnicity, or age group. Furthermore, the act of listening, even within the Western idealist ("pure art") tradition, is often presented as functional in the sense that it ostensibly makes the listener in some sense better, more sensitive, less despairing, more empowered, more discriminating or thoughtful, etc.

2    Gerald Graff, *Beyond the Culture Wars: Teaching the Conflicts Can Revitalize American Education* (New York: W. W. Norton, 1992). Cf. *Teaching the Conflicts: Gerald Graff, Curricular Reform, and the Culture Wars*, ed. William E. Cain (New York: Garland Publishing, 1994).

3    The MacDowell and Billings examples here are my own. The report, entitled *Bringing American Music Home*, originally released as a booklet (now out of print), is regularly updated and can be accessed from musicologist J. Bunker Clark's web site, <http://falcon.cc.ukans.edu/~bclark>.

4    Elzbieta Wasowska, ed., *Mazurki kompozytórow polskich na fortepian: antologia ze zbiorów Biblioteki Narodewej*, 2 vols. (Warsaw: Biblioteka Narodowa, 1995). This repertoire, and its relationship to both folk music and Chopin, is discussed in Barbara Milewski, "Chopin's Mazurkas and the Myth of the Folk," *19th-Century Music* 23 (1999–2000): 113–35.

5    In addition, recent scholars have been pointing out that Chopin's floridity
     derives at least as much from keyboard traditions of the generation just before
     him as from operatic singing. See, for example, David Rowland, "The
     Nocturne: Development of a New Style," in *The Cambridge Companion to
     Chopin*, ed. Jim Samson (Cambridge: Cambridge University Press, 1992),
     32–49.

6    Oskar Kolberg's six collections (some multi-volume) and those of other
     researchers are listed in the bibliography to the "Poland" article in the first
     (1980) edition of *New Grove Dictionary of Music and Musicians*, ed. Stanley
     Sadie.

7    If one is going to use the A-major Nocturne, it seems to me worth pointing out
     to the students that it is quite odd in form: AB but then no return of A. I wonder
     whether all the scores of this Nocturne are simply wrong. This movement was
     first composed for piano and strings, as the first movement of a two-movement
     Divertimento. (The second movement is a rondo.) That version is included (and
     beautifully performed) in Oxford University Press's old *History of Music in
     Sound* LP recordings (the "Romantic" volume). Astonishingly, for anyone who
     has known the solo-piano version first, this version *does* go back to the A
     section after the B section ends. This inconsistency between the two versions
     could give an instructor occasion to draw the students' attention (once again,
     see the end of point 2 above) to the inherently problematic nature of musical
     scores and the sometimes unreliable character of textual transmission when it is
     entrusted to profit-making (and sometimes corner-cutting) publishers. There is
     much to be said for developing students' critical awareness that a given printed
     score (or part), which is set in front of them (e.g., at a college band rehearsal),
     may have been reworked by an (often uncredited) arranger.

8    [Various performers], *Pologne: Chansons et danses populaires*, ed. Anna
     Czekanowska, VDE-Gallo CD 757 (1994).

9    Alice Marriott, "*Beowulf* in South Dakota," *New Yorker*, 2 August 1952, 46,
     48–51. The author is the earlier of the two ethnologists, the one who *told* the
     Beowulf story to one of the tribal elders in 1936. The 1938 scholarly article by
     the other ethnologist (whom Marriott does not name) is "Occurrence of a
     *Beowulf*-like Myth among North American Indians." Marriott concludes wryly:
     "I have not yet [sixteen years later] solved the ethical problem that article posed
     for me" (p. 51).

10   Excerpt from his autobiographical entry in Mattheson's *Grundlage zu einer
     Ehrenpforte* (1740), as translated by Sam Morgenstern in *Composers on Music:
     An Anthology of Composers' Writings from Palestrina to Copland* (New York:
     Pantheon Books, 1956), 40. Also included in the revision of that book,
     *Composers on Music: Eight Centuries of Writings*, second ed. by Josiah Fisk,
     consulting editor Jeff Nichols (Boston: Northeastern University Press, 1997),
     26–27. Four works entitled "Polish" by Telemann—two sonatas, a concerto,
     and a *Partie* (i.e., Partita) *polonoise*, are performed energetically by Eduard
     Melkus and others on *Polnisch-hanakische Volksmusik in Werken von Georg*

*Philipp Telemann*, Deutsche Grammophon LP:Archiv SAPM 198 467 (released in 1967).

11   See the "Old Army March: 'Ceddin deden' (Your Forefathers)" on the CD *Turkish Military Band Music of Ottoman Empire*, King Records [Tokyo], KICC 5101 (1987). Further examples are available on: Kudsi Erguner, dir, *Les janissaires: musique martiale de l'Empire Ottoman*, Auvidis Ethnic B6738 (1990).

12   On the LP recording *White Spirituals from the Sacred Harp*, New World Records NW 205 (1977).

13   H. Wiley Hitchcock silently restores some syncopation to the folk tune when printing its first four measures in his *Music in the United States: A Historical Introduction*, fourth ed. (Upper Saddle River, NJ: Prentice Hall, 2000), 91, thereby making it seem more Hispanic/jazzy than the Gottschalk, rather than the reverse. The one surviving transcription of the tune from the nineteenth century that I have seen (reprinted in John G. Doyle's invaluable dissertation) states the fifth and sixth pitches as heavy and equal half notes.

14   "Christmas Party: Maria Magdalena," sung by Aña Iris Parilla on the LP recording *Folk Songs of Puerto Rico*, Asch Records AHM 4412 (1971).

15   The original fiddle versions and Grieg's piano adaptations (performed by Einar Steen-Nokleberg) are juxtaposed on: *Edvard Grieg: Slåtter (Norwegian Dances), op. 72 together with original fiddle tunes*, Simax PSC1O4O (1988), with performances (by Knut Buen) of the original tunes on Hardanger fiddle.

16   The original tune for no. 4 is imaginatively rendered by the Norwegian "folk revival" group Bukkene Bruse, on their CD *Åre*, Grappa GRCD 4100 (1995).

17   Camille Saint-Saëns, *Musical Memories,* trans. Edwin Gile Rich (Boston: Small, Maynard & Company, 1919), 270–71. This fact is almost never mentioned in the periodical or scholarly literature about Saint-Saëns's opera (e.g., in my own "Constructing the Oriental 'Other': Saint-Saëns's *Samson et Dalila,*" *Cambridge Opera Journal* 3 [1991]: 261–302). I thank Gregory Bloch (University of California, Berkeley) for bringing it to my attention. By the way, Saint-Saëns, like most of his contemporaries, called the military man in question "General Yousouf" (as if he were an Arab); the man's real name was Joseph Vantini. He was born to an Italian family on the island of Elba around 1810 and died in 1866, before Saint-Saëns had composed even half the opera.

18   Dimitri Pokrovsky Singers, *Les noces*, Elektra Nonesuch CD 79335-2 (1994).

19   *Hungarian Folk Music: Gramophone Recordings with Béla Bartók's Transcriptions*, a Hungaroton LP set, LPX 18058–18060 (1981).

20   See, for instance, Daniel W. Patterson, *The Shaker Spiritual* (Princeton: Princeton University Press, 1979).

21   Steve Reich, *Writings about Music* (New York: New York University Press, 1974).

22   Keith Potter, *Four Musical Minimalists: La Monte Young, Terry Riley, Steve Reich, Philip Glass* (Cambridge: Cambridge University Press, 2000), especially 204–7 (including transcriptions of Ewe drumming by Reich).

Chapter Four

# Teaching Music History (After the End of History): "History Games" for the Twentieth-Century Survey

*Robert Fink*

**Introduction: the "Collapse of the Master Narrative"**

*After the end of history*

Here is the problem in a nutshell: How do you teach music history after the end of history?

The end of (music) history might be considered one small consequence of what Jean-François Lyotard famously diagnosed in 1979 as *The Postmodern Condition:* "Simplifying in the extreme, I define *postmodernism* as incredulity toward metanarratives."[1] Lyotard's metanarratives are the overarching, often unexamined histories that intellectual disciplines like religion, philosophy, science, and (yes) musicology have used to legitimize themselves. His insight was that many of these "master narratives" (the rather melodramatic translation of *grands récits* that has become common coin in English) were in an advanced state of collapse. Modern science had already done most of the work, delegitimating all other narratives but its own; the postmodern era dawned when "scientific method," the final master narrative, itself began to show signs of wear. Recent counterattacks show that institutional science is well aware of the danger. The widely-publicized hoax perpetrated on the editors of *Social Text* by physicist Alan Sokal in 1996 was a new attempt to play a very old delegitimating card, in order to relegitimate the embattled truth-claims of modern scientific method.[2]

History (as we all learned in doctoral seminars) can also aspire to the scientific method—and this is nowhere more true than in the North American practice of *historisches Musikwissenschaft.* Ultimately, no aspect of historical musicology can remain unaffected by growing incredulity toward the metanarrative of music-scholarship-as-an-exercise-in-scientific-method; but most musicologists first encounter the "collapse of the master narratives" in the practical aspect of their work that deals in (what we hope are) masterful narratives: the quotidian but crucial work of building music history survey classes.

I think one could argue a "strong postmodern" position that would radicalize all survey teaching, but for the present, a weaker formulation will suffice. Do what you will with the Middle Ages—the twentieth-century survey poses uniquely self-reflexive historiographic problems. Even if we put aside any personal incredulity toward the metanarratives that legitimize us as historians, how are we to ignore the fact that "postmodernism," the collapse of these master narratives, happens within the period of music history that we are trying to teach? And that one of the narratives that collapses with the biggest bang is the self-congratulatory narrative of musical progress that twentieth-century musicians and composers have consistently mistaken for "music history" itself?

One sign of a postmodern attitude toward music (and music history) is a growing impatience with the modernist metanarrative that Christopher Williams has usefully labeled "techno-essentialism": the confident belief that musical history can be told (and musical works legitimized) solely in terms of the steady, inexorable development of purely musical technique.[3] We all know the tune: Beethoven was more "advanced" than Mozart, Brahms than Beethoven, Schoenberg than Brahms, and so on, through Webern, Boulez, Elliott Carter, and *(ne plus ultra?)* Brian Ferneyhough.

This techno-essentialist master narrative is most compelling, of course, when we construct histories of modern music. Given the embattled reception of the "difficult" music in the techno-essentialist canon, and the exaggerated Hegelianism of many pivotal musical modernists (Boulez: "The series is a logically historical consequence [and] a historically logical one"),[4] the tendency is for twentieth-century music historians to become emotionally involved advocates for a particular construction of musical modernism as heroic progress. The temptation is even more strong when the historian is, in reality, a composer and/or music theorist, rushing in where "official" music historians have often feared to tread.

But as the century draws to a close, the advocate's position is becoming more and more untenable. Forcing the appreciation of modernist music on unenthusiastic students as a moral duty ("This is the future of your profession!") has never been a good time; and after decades of postmodernism in all aspects of musical life, it is no longer good history either. Modernism has collapsed, taking with it the hegemony of the techno-essentialist master narrative. Uncomfortably enough, this appears to have happened right around 1965, in the middle of the twentieth-century historian's watch. The story turns out to be the fact that there *is* no story.

*History games*

If the preceding sounded like the throat-clearing before a ringing manifesto, a pronouncement on the principles of a new "postmodern pedagogy"—rest easy. The essence of a postmodern pedagogy is that it has no essence, and there is in any case something intolerably pedantic about a teacher lecturing other teachers on how to teach. Lyotard's strategy for the situation in which we find ourselves after the collapse of the great legitimating metanarratives is the proliferation of "language games": new and different ways of legitimating knowledge, pragmatic, self-reflexive, often involving complex performances of social interdependence, games that can complement the solitary game of detached, objective, "scientific" method.[5]

Accordingly, I would propose that we conceptualize what we are doing when we teach a twentieth-century survey as a species of *history game*: a complex, idiosyncratic, pragmatic, often self-reflexive performance of music history that foregrounds its own contingent nature. History games can introduce a lightness and flexibility to a genre of historical narrative often perceived by students as oppressive in its historical determinism (the *[sigh]* inevitable "collapse of tonality" followed by the *[yawn]* inevitable "rise of atonality"); they allow a style of teaching more resonant with the ludic sensibilities of many postmodern composers (Cage, Berio, Zorn); and perhaps most crucially, by making "the rules of the (historical) game" part of the survey class, they can engage students as players, not just spectators, in the ongoing game of telling stories about the past. Playing twentieth-century history games in front of a skeptical audience is certainly more risky than simply reciting the techno-essentialist master narrative for them. It is also more fun—for everyone involved.

In what follows I will refrain from telling others what to do, contenting myself with describing three of the twentieth-century musical history games I played (with some success) during the final decade of that century. I do not recall launching self-consciously into a grand postmodern teaching project; I now see that I was discovering that project on the job, as I tried to meet the immediate challenges of teaching an immensely complex subject—one that I myself often found confusing and overwhelming—to battle-weary conservatory undergraduates and distracted liberal arts majors. The three course syllabi I will annotate in the main portion of this essay outline my progress through three increasingly radical mutations away from the music-historical master narrative. They represent my attempts to master three increasingly tricky historical games. I adduce them here as three among many.

## Game 1. Collapse as history ("Music in Twentieth-Century History," Eastman School of Music 1992–1998)

*The modernist "parade" (of ideology)*

So ... how *do* you teach music history after the end of history? One possible strategy involves confronting postmodernism's "end of history" itself as history: the collapse of the master narrative becomes not just a historiographic, but a directly historical concern. The game is to teach the collapse of the master narrative *as* the narrative. As the syllabus for "Music in Twentieth-Century History" (Appendix 4.1) shows, this does not mean abandoning the hidden progress narrative of modernism: it means *foregrounding* that narrative as provisional and partial, as an artifact of intellectual history. Demoted from legitimating metanarrative to plain old narrative, techno-essentialism becomes "The Modernist Parade," my term for the self-conscious, totalizing, historical determinist line that runs from Wagner to Boulez. The first half of the class thus has a simple "plot": the parade grows (1860–1905), accelerates (1905–1932), generates a backlash (1932–1945), then sweeps (almost) all before it (1945–1960). The second half ... well, gets a little messier (see below).

But if we are not going to use the old progress narrative as a self-legitimating meta-historical construct, what in fact happens at the "meta"-level of the class? It is no accident that twentieth-century history surveys rely so heavily on a rigid linear metanarrative: as soon as I tried to put a syllabus together, I realized that the musicological scaffolding that usually supports teaching of earlier periods, like every vestigial social relation that survived those periods, had fallen to pieces under the assault of twentieth-century modernity. To paraphrase Marx, everything music-historical melts into air: each piece defines a new genre, each composer a new style; the very distinctions between music and the other arts, between music and the larger culture, between music and nature itself seem to collapse. What possible organizing principle other than incessant PROGRESS could there be? Almost in self-defense, and in a deliberate effort to get "up above" that progress-narrative of modernism, I chose to teach twentieth-century music history as *intellectual history*.

Thus I titled the class "Music in Twentieth-Century History," not "History of Twentieth-Century Music." The main focus—the replacement for meta-historical constructs like genre and style—was *ideology*: what my students and I came to know and love as the roller-coaster ride of the "-isms." The first part of the class took shape as a series of increasingly radical jumps between modernist positions on art as a cultural practice (symbolism, expressionism, fauvism, high modernism, etc.) considered in loose chronological order at the rate of one a week. (See Diagram 4.1 for the full list laid out graphically.) Some positions could be seen to "evolve" out of others, but more often the ideology of a given week flatly contradicted the one I had laid out with painstaking care the week before: Expressionism's spiritual abstraction condescended to Cubism's materialism; the New Objectivity then trashed Expressionism as old-fashioned bourgeois subjectivity; finally Socialist Realism sent the whole crew (except Copland and Shostakovich) packing. (I knew the strategy was working when a puzzled student exclaimed about five weeks in, "You don't believe in *any* of this, do you?" That is the sound of a master narrative collapsing.)

Here is what I *did not* teach: the death of the triad; the collapse of tonality; the liberation of atonality; the historical necessity of the twelve-tone row. These hoary musicological tropes were not only too determinist—they were too low-level, too technical, to operate in the absence of a legitimating metanarrative. I found myself talking about representation, about abstraction, about alienation-effects and mathematical lyricism, and letting issues of musical technique arise as logical consequences of composers' ideological choices. Schoenberg's dense chromatic webs, Stravinsky's "pictorial" use of clashing triads, and Weill's wheezing jazz clichés could all be seen as moves toward a modernist ideal(ogy) of abstraction, differentiated not by how "dissonant" or "atonal" they were, but by the radically new and different cultural goals they concretized in sound. In this broader context, it became quite natural to introduce some of the concerns of the "new" musicology: issues of gender, sexuality, and politics did not have to be shoehorned in, since they were often the very stuff of the "-isms" under discussion.

*The fragmented century*

Filling in the central box of Diagram 4.1—the parade of "-isms"—took up exactly half of a fourteen-week semester. Within that box were the fossilized remains of the traditional modernist master narrative, historicized and stripped of their power to mystify and legitimate. After the midterm, the task was to break out of the box and continue the story into the postmodern episteme. But first, it seemed necessary to lay some groundwork for the coming collapse by showing that even in its heyday, modernism was never the only avant-garde game in town. As the syllabus and Diagram 4.1 show, the next (risky) move in my history game was a sharp narrative reversal: after Boulez, not over to Cage (yet), but *back* to 1916, DADA, and the music of Erik Satie.

I proceeded to teach the first half of the class not once but twice again, both times from outside the modernist box. I presented two marginal narratives of the century, first tracing the DADA-Surrealist path from Satie to neoclassic Stravinsky (what German cultural critics call "the historical avant-garde"),[6] and then the American Experimentalist tradition from Ives to Cage. (These are the lines that snake down the page to the left and right of the modernist center in Diagram 4.1.) Increasingly radical attempts to delegitimate art music from these left- and right-wing "fringes"—culminating in the Zen anti-provocation of Cage's *4'33"*—helped students anticipate the eventual demise ca. 1965 of the entire legitimating metanarrative of music history.[7]

Collapse as music history—and the collapse of history represented in musical works—duly followed. Borrowing a prescient historiographic insight from Leonard Meyer, I postulated the late 1960s as the "End of the Renaissance": the end of musical teleology, and with it artistic subjectivity and historical determinism.[8] With sprawling, apocalyptic collage works like Lukas Foss's *Phorion* (1967), Arvo Pärt's *Credo* (1968) and Bernd Alois Zimmerman's *Requiem for A Dead Poet* (1969) as background, Luciano Berio's masterpiece of semiotic disintegration, *Sinfonia* (1969), served as a pivotal touchstone. Significantly, this moment of cultural upheaval was the first (and only) time popular music entered my narrative. I could not resist playing tape-collage pieces like "Strawberry Fields Forever" and "Revolution No. 9," even though there was no real socio-cultural context for these Beatles tracks in my art-music history. (Understanding the relation of pop and art music ca. 1968 would turn out to be a pivotal move in my next history game.)

The final three weeks of the syllabus dealt with the rise of various postmodernisms in music. A strong temptation was to present the twin trends of the 1970s—"postmodern" historical pastiche and minimalist process music—as two sides of a single redemptive trend: the "return of tonality" and the foreshadowing of a "new classicism."[9] (Especially since minimalism is my particular research specialty!) But the reappearance of triadic harmony (a question of low-level technique, after all) did not absolve our class from continued attention to the history of ideas. Postmodernists have ideology, too (modernism has no monopoly on "false consciousness"), and postmodern composers as ideologically divergent as George Rochberg, David Del Tredici, Steve Reich, John Zorn, and Thomas Adés submit to some new metanarrative of cyclic (r)evolution only under extreme duress.

On the contrary: the end of the class presented a stubbornly fractured musical landscape, with unrepentant modernism (Babbitt, Carter, New Complexity) sniping from the ruins at various grim postmodernisms, various attempts to survive the collapse at the end of history by repeating it. In earlier versions of the class, I finally succumbed to the pull of metanarrative and sketched a new historical dialectic in which minimalist reduction and postmodern pastiche, the two radically disjunct postmodern styles of the 1960s and 70s, began to resynthesize in the 1980s as "postminimalism" (see Diagram 4.1, bottom). This gave me occasion for a barn-burning final lecture on John Adams and *Nixon in China*—but I ultimately decided no single "masterpiece" could bear that much historical weight. Later versions of the syllabus tended to end with a frank portrayal of what Leonard Meyer had predicted over thirty years before: the "fluctuating stasis" beyond the end of the great narrative, perhaps even the heat-death of art music in the great pluralist wash of late-information-age capitalism.

*"If on a Winter's Night a Musicologist ..."*

A fragmented story for a fragmented century, each chapter a new beginning; a self-consciously deconstructed narrative that, returning again and again to its starting point, thematizes its own collapse: my first attempt at a twentieth-century syllabus ended up looking like some strange cross between a music history survey and a postmodern novel in the manner of Italo Calvino.[10] What were the pros and cons of this avant-garde pedagogical experiment?

I found that the clear and obvious attention I paid to historiographic questions was almost always appreciated. Students saw that I was taking responsibility for *putting a story together,* creating a lucid structure that, on the other hand, was complex and difficult enough not to violate their strong intuitive feeling that much twentieth-century art and music was deliberately confusing and alienating. My overt project to explain this alienation through cultural context and ideological critique made the class feel less like music-appreciation propaganda and more like "real" history. Students in Eastman's music history sequence often bridled at any attempts by musicologists to do technical analysis (they saw it as superficial replay of their music theory classes); but my insights about musical structure seemed less redundant when linked to contemporaneous beliefs about aesthetics, politics, religion, and sexuality.

The deliberate foregrounding of music as intellectual history gave me great freedom to introduce rich primary texts—not just those in the familiar Strunk anthology. It allowed me to find a way to teach the heart of the techno-essentialist canon without shilling for it, and to teach crucial repertories outside that canon whose ideological impact was, by the end of the century, finally too important to ignore: Satie, neoclassicism, Cageian experimentalism, minimalism. Perhaps most importantly, and most paradoxically, acknowledging the "end of history" allowed me to restart it. Not one of the smaller narratives in my syllabus has the grand legitimating sweep of the techno-essentialist story of progress. But some of them do have the incredible advantage of not seeming embattled or absurd—and not making the music historian feel both embattled and absurd—as we enter the twenty-first century.

On the negative side, an insistent focus on intellectual history did put a strain on those students for whom music had always been a uniquely intuitive pursuit. ("What does all this have to do with *the music*?") The pedagogical overhead for me was quite high, too: adding Schopenhauer, Levi-Strauss, Brecht, Mies van der Rohe, Picasso, and Andy Warhol to the syllabus, spending precious class time each week outlining "-isms," inevitably left less time for discussing and playing pieces of music. (The situation was exacerbated by extremely limited class time: two fifty-minute lectures per week.) Some major composers were sacrificed—Bartók, Ravel, Messiaen, Stockhausen—because their work, important and beautiful though it was, did not illuminate any important ideological shifts.

The sheer profusion of "-isms" made some students restless. The complex web of connections and disjunctions in Diagram 4.1 looked as daunting to undergraduates as one might expect, though I took care to assemble it systematically over the span of the class, and students came to rely on such diagrams quite heavily as they studied. There was also a real chance of fumbling the ball at the most gratuitously tricky narrative moment of the course: the complex looping back in Weeks 8–11 often confused students whose grasp of chronology and historical causality was intermittent under the best of circumstances. I had to deploy monstrous neologisms like "pre-postmodernism," and remind my class that Satie came *before* Boulez, year after year.

Finally, the complete absence of popular music, though perhaps barely justifiable within a classical conservatory context, no longer seems acceptable to me. It began to weigh on my conscience, and undermine my sense that all the crucial ideological issues around modern and postmodern music had really been raised. Was it enough to teach *against* the grand narrative by showing it in collapse? What about popular and mass culture—the "other" narratives it had crowded out for so long?

## Game 2. Other narratives/narratives of the other ("Modern and Postmodern Music 1948–2000," UCLA 2000–   )

*Meet the new boss, same as the old boss?*

My second game—exploring other, multicultural narratives in the space left by the collapse of the monocultural master narrative—is probably the one that leaps first to mind when a "postmodern" history is under discussion. In the absence of a single *grand récit,* should we not look for the *petites récits* that will supplant it—the "other" narratives—among the neglected "narratives of the other"? Does not the collapse of the grand legitimating narrative of "classical" music finally make room for the discussion of the *real* music of the twentieth century: the "popular" musics that have increasingly dominated our culture since the first outbreaks of "ragtime fever" almost one hundred years ago?

I confronted this question head-on as I put together my second full-dress twentieth-century survey syllabus, "Modern and Postmodern Music, 1948–2000." At UCLA the twentieth century is split into two intensive (four lecture-hours per week) quarters, and I was responsible for the postwar half only; I thus had forty hours to cover less than half the historical span I had sped through at Eastman in twenty-eight hours. On the other hand, the presumption was that this class would have a much broader scope, dealing with music within mass and popular cultures as well as the high-art culture of the West.

The temptation to impose a new master narrative was real: there is a romantic tendency to assume that by concentrating on popular music—especially music that owes allegiance to the African-American vernacular—we can somehow avoid the legitimation crisis so painfully obvious in "European classical" music. After all, people actually *like* this music! Why worry about ideology? But, in elevating vibrant vernacular musics over what the collapse of the master narrative has revealed to be a decaying art tradition, we run the risk of re-imposing that same utopian narrative on our "new" subject matter. The results often reproduce the worst power effects of the old pedagogy. (*Meet the new boss—same as the old boss.*) Henry Pleasants's 1955 *The Agony of Modern Music* set the pattern: follow a hatchet job on ugly modernism with a sentimental turn to vernacular and mass-culture music as the "new art music of the twentieth century."[11] Modernism may be a narrative of decline, but jazz can restart the narrative of progress. You know the tune: Armstrong is more "advanced" than King Oliver, Ellington than Armstrong, Parker than Lester Young, and so on, through Coltrane, Coleman, and *(ne plus ultra?)* John Zorn. And "classic" rock works even better, as the raw energy of rockabilly and Elvis gives rise to the increasing depth and technical control of the Beach Boys, Dylan, the Beatles, Genesis, and *(ne plus ultra?)* ... well, you fill in the blank.

I had already felt the pull first hand in my own teaching, essaying a Beatles seminar at Eastman during which every tired trope of the music history survey—genius, autonomy, difficulty, evolution, even techno-essentialist *progress*—had crept right back in to the classroom (*Revolver* is more "advanced" than *Rubber Soul,* etc., etc.). And I had no desire to construct for this new survey some omnivorous legitimating narrative on whose multicultural behalf I could guiltlessly propagandize.[12] In fact, I suspected that such a narrative would be so unwieldy as to be unteachable.

*Cross(over) relations*

On the other hand, the practicalities of the playing field *had* changed, and my game had to change with it. First: starting after World War II meant that the rise of modernism was no longer within the scope of the class—only its zenith and decline. This demanded that the long parade of squabbling "-isms" be replaced with some other meta-historical framework. Second: within this narrowed post-war perspective, the question seemed to be not so much the general impact of modernity and modernization since 1860, but the specific impact of post-war mass media and communications technologies—and the mass culture (with attendant culture industries) they helped create. The dialectical relation of high modernism and mass culture would thus become an alternative narrative strand of the class.

The basic "plot" of my Eastman survey—modernism, apocalypse, postmodernism—still operates within "Modern and Postmodern Music 1948–2000" (see Appendix 4.2); but there is now time to examine the collapse of modernism within a wider cultural field, and in slow-motion detail. Part One of the class, "Technocracy's End," postulates a three-stage process of disintegration: the disciplined *High* (1948–58) of post-war total serialism is gradually elbowed aside by a series of *Awakenings* (1956–67) in the culture at large (free jazz, experimental music; Elvis and the Beatles); Awakening then accelerates into *Unraveling* (1968–74), and liberation accelerates into chaos (Woodstock and Altamont; the White Album; Berio's *Sinfonia*).

Archetypal terms like "Awakening" and "Unraveling" have a nice mythic effect, but they also handily obscure political questions of high and low. Both John Cage's *4'33"* and Elvis Presley's 1956 recording of "Hound Dog" can be understood as music-cultural moments of "awakening"—but what about the fact that within the old master narrative only one of them really counts as "music"? My Eastman survey took on historical determinism; but it had little to say about the invidious hierarchies of musical culture that determinism was marshaled to support. How, then, to integrate vernacular music and mass culture—both of which interest me intensely as a scholar—into a wide-open survey of the later twentieth century?

Another self-reflexive history game seemed to be the answer. Rather than resolve prematurely the question of cultural hierarchy—either ignoring or exalting "low status" vernacular and commercial musics—I would *make the complex, evolving relationships between elite, vernacular, and commercial musical cultures into a narrative*, and play this narrative off against the end of the modernist parade. One can see at a glance in Diagram 4.2 (another (dis)orienting diagram I handed out to students) that the effect is quite literally to *de-center* modernism. The modernist box is pushed off to one side in the postwar period by a powerful new conglomeration of forces that I aggregated as "Mass Culture." Within the larger cultural field, "high" modernism can then be presented as a dialectical reaction to "Kitsch" and "Pop"—those novel transformations of traditional and folk musical cultures disseminated with overwhelming efficiency by new technologies (radio, LP, TV) and large-scale capitalization of the culture industries (RCA, NBC, MTV).[13]

The UCLA survey (Appendix 4.2) thus begins with a pair of introductory meta-historical lectures: one on cultural hierarchy, in which the post-war "mass culture" debate features prominently; and one on technology, in which I explain the choice of 1948 (the year of the first LP, the first solid-body electric guitar, and the first editable magnetic tape recording) as a logical starting point. The course then takes shape as a gradual intertwining of two distinct narrative strands, the awakening-unraveling-collapse story of modernist high culture becoming evermore entangled with increasingly explosive transformations in mass culture.

The dissolution of cultural hierarchy is thus built into the structure of the course. During the 1950s *High* (lectures 3–5), discussions of Boulez and Bill Haley's Comets proceed in complete mutual isolation. (I even allow myself a traditional evolutionary argument about the "birth of rock-n-roll" that makes no reference to high art ideologies.) The various 1960s *Awakenings* (lectures 6–10) do more than loosen modernist hegemony; they also outline a "New Sensibility," which exalts pure experience and rebels against rigid cultural boundaries. McLuhan, Sontag, and Mailer provide ideological constructs that for the first time try to deal with both "serious" and "popular" musics; the separate intellectual histories of jazz, rock, and experimental music begin to meld. Amazing cultural evidence came easily to hand: last year my transition between lecture 7 ("free" jazz) and lecture 8 (experimentalism) was a 1967 documentary film that cut back and forth between Rahsaan Roland Kirk improvising on multiple saxophones "in the key of Q" and John Cage rehearsing on a musical bicycle.[14]

Thus the *Unraveling* (lectures 12–13), the late Sixties apocalypse, becomes a much more complex scene of cultural crossover, of dissolution *and* reformation. Under the rubric of the "counter culture" I can parse the swirling counter-currents of mass and elite musical culture ca. 1968: the ménage of Yoko Ono and John Lennon leading the Beatles into Fluxus territory; Columbia Masterworks releasing Terry Riley's *In C* and Wendy Carlos's *Switched on Bach* in a desperate attempt to "get out of the classical bag"; Bernstein proclaiming "Mahler grooves!" and Boulez being sold with the bowdlerized street chant "Hell no, Boulez won't go (traditional)."

Part Two of the course, "Postmodernism" (lectures 14–18), goes on quite programmatically to efface the boundaries between elite and popular styles. The two opposing strategies of 1970s and 1980s post-apocalyptic art that figured in my first survey are generalized across the entire realm of musical production; along with the "art postmodernism" of Rochberg and Schnittke, we now consider a tradition of "vernacular postmodernism" that can trace its roots back to cartoon music and includes hip-hop and plunderphonics. Minimalism's stripped-down, impersonal repetition and emphasis on rhythmic process are found in Steve Reich and James Brown, Laurie Anderson and the Talking Heads; in disco, techno, and electronica.

In the end, a more nuanced historical picture of "postmodernism" emerges. The various postmodern strategies—resistance, reaction, capitulation—lining the bottom of Diagram 4.2 now appear as something more than just hopeless re-enactments (in a vacuum) of the end of (classical music) history; they also represent various resolutions of the tense negotiations between late modernism, the historical avant-garde, the realist tradition, and technologically-mediated mass culture. Whether it is the spirit of Fluxus mediating between avant-garde modernism and pop culture (Beck), or postmodern "traditionalism" appropriated by the most disruptive forces of late capitalism (Tan Dun)—any one of these possibilities offers, if not a way forward, at least a way out.

I have only taught "Modern and Postmodern Music 1948–2000" once, so it may be too soon to evaluate its strengths and weaknesses. It is no less complex for students than my previous survey, and the emphasis on intellectual "superstructure" is even greater. Classically-trained performers were not uniformly convinced that musical hierarchies are now obsolete; and—new problem—the handful of jazz performance majors were even more jealous for their own baby master narrative. Still, this syllabus has the great advantage of engaging with what I have come to believe are the fundamental music-cultural issues of our time: postmodernism, cultural hierarchy, mass culture, mediation and technology, late capitalism. As it does so, the modernist master narrative is not just shattered, it is dwarfed within a survey class that truly surveys the full sweep of postmodern culture. (The "box" takes up much less space in Diagram 4.2.) Justifying his own turn away from modernist orthodoxy, Steve Reich may have said it most pithily: "In the real context of tailfins, Chuck Berry and millions of burgers sold—to pretend that instead we're really going to have the dark-brown Angst of Vienna is a lie, a musical lie."[15] It is also a music-*historical* lie—one that my twentieth-century surveys, whatever their merits, will no longer perpetuate.

## Game 3. Music history on shuffle play ("Music Now," UCLA 1999–  )

*"The Lexus and the Olive Tree"*

Finally, a brief overview of a truly freestyle music history game, played outside the practical constraints of a course for the undergraduate performance major. "Music Now" is my deliberate attempt to reconceptualize what the general-enrollment music history elective might look like after the end of history. Many cultural critics argue that postmodern subjects inhabit a perspectiveless "eternal present"[16] where—to dramatize the problem/opportunity for music historians—the young Louis Armstrong and the aging Elton John can jam in a Coke commercial, Hildegard of Bingen is reborn as "timeless" world music, and the Allegri *Miserere* can mingle with Minnie Ripperton inside an ambient chill-out room.

Field observation of UCLA undergraduates tends to support this conclusion: except for a small subset of obsessive collectors and amateur historians, they prize eclecticism and tolerance of a wide spectrum of sounds over any mastery of tradition. This may be the age of the channel-surfing "zapper," whose legendary short attention span has led to a cultural style dominated by fragmentation and sampling; but it is also the era of Napster, multiple CD changers, and Shuffle Play. Many of my students now seem drawn to an endless and omnivorous circulation of all the tracks that are "out there" at any given time, not because they are bored and immature, but because they see no reason to follow someone else's Baedeker through the bazaar. My training as historian still impels me to throw narratives over the wall to these determinedly ahistorical consumers of culture; but I am enough one of them to shy away intuitively from stories that subordinate the present to the past. It is a thankless task—and perhaps a fool's errand—to deflect interest from the synchronicity that everyone already knows to the diachronicity that enshrines disciplinary and cultural power. (To use the terms of Thomas Friedman's influential study of globalization, it is of little use to offer the music-historical olive tree to students accustomed to driving Lexuses.)[17]

This is not to say that traditional "histories" cannot work in this environment, especially if they deal with musicologically underrepresented subjects. UCLA currently enrolls literally thousands of students in classes with titles like "History of Rock and Roll," "History of Jazz," and (my own addition) "History of Electronic Dance Music." But "Music Now," as its name suggests, is designed as a direct music-historical response to teaching in postmodernity's eternal present.

### Back to the future

Thus "Music Now" (Appendix 4.3) has no overarching narrative. As the course description promises, its fundamental organization is synchronic, not diachronic, a "free-wheeling attempt to use musicological, historical, and cultural perspective to illuminate some representatively chosen current events in the postmodern musical scene." The large-scale division of the class into topical "Units" was done purely for convenience; within each unit the individual weeks were given the epistemologically neutral designation "Item." An Item could be a physical object (the Sony "Soundtrack for A Century" box set), a piece of music (the NBC "Mission" Theme), an artist (Beck), or some complex situation of music in culture (ad campaigns by the Gap and Dean Witter). Some of the items covered lent themselves to purely synchronic, almost ethnographic surveys, for instance, the discussion of music in ad campaigns; in these weeks the class left the domain of "music history" behind altogether.

But in most of the class, the Item under consideration served as the spur to the construction of a (loosely) historical narrative. But these genealogies of the present (as I imagined them) bore little resemblance to the linear progress narratives of music history. Diagram 4.3 (which I built up systematically around Item 3, the music of Beck) differs radically from its predecessors, not the least in its resolutely non-linear tangle of intersecting lines and absence of a clear center. And, as you will immediately see from the sequence of dates at the side of the page, I taught the class *backwards*. The weeks' lectures took the form of multiple excursions back from the present moment into various possible historical contexts and ancestries. The game here was relatively explicit: to use the self-conscious artifice of a historical narrative, turned upside down, to range as widely and as promiscuously as possible through the entirety of the de-historicized eternal present. How far could I get before the given ideological construct broke down?

Far enough. As Diagram 4.3 demonstrates, starting from Beck and moving through several discrete genealogies of "fragmentation" (distinguished on the page by different typefaces), I was able to introduce a large class of non-music majors to works as "difficult" as Cage's *Williams Mix,* Berio's *Sinfonia,* Schaeffer's *Symphonie pour un homme seul,* and Satie's DADA ballet *Relâche*—and make them see the connection to things they already knew, like James Brown and Public Enemy; and things they did not know they knew, like Carl Stalling's cartoon music and John Oswald's plunderphonics.

*Only connect*

Alert readers will recognize this swath of music as identical to the art/vernacular "postmodernisms" I outlined for my music majors. But unlike those students, who still have a legitimate claim to be taught some kind of discriminating narrative about classical music (it is, after all, what many of them are devoting their lives to), my general enrollment students do not really worry that much about high and low, about the "authentic," the "classical," the "serious" and the "popular." In the eternal present, connecting Beck and Berio is no big deal—so I was emboldened, week by week, to stretch the web of discourse ever wider and thinner.

From the NBC Nightly News to Wagner's *Ring;* from the DeBeers diamond commercials to Mahler's Fourth; from Queen's "Bohemian Rhapsody" to the castrati of the Vatican; "Music Now" floats quite free of legitimating *and* delegitimating approaches to "classical music," and this is its strength, as well as its weakness. Not every press of the "Shuffle Play" button will work, but we can no longer play the A-side and then the B-side of music history and be done with it. We can no longer proceed as if the best way to teach twentieth-century music still is, as the title of Paul Griffiths's 1995 survey makes it, *Modern Music and After.*[18] What happens when the master narratives are gone, and "after" is all you can see? Now that we have lost the guiding thread, all we have left is the sheer immensity of the web, and its myriad of connections. Perhaps—as we invent the history games of the next century—that will be all we need.

> *Only connect! That was the whole of her sermon. Only connect the prose and the passion, and both will be exalted, and human love will be seen at its height. Live in fragments no longer ...*

—E. M. Forster, *Howard's End*

## Notes

1    Jean-François Lyotard, *The Postmodern Condition: A Report on Knowledge,* trans. Geoff Bennington and Brian Massumi (Minneapolis: University of Minnesota Press, 1984), xxiv.

2    See Alan Sokal, "Transgressing the Boundaries: Towards a Transformative Hermeneutics of Quantum Gravity," *Social Text* 46–47 (Spring–Summer 1996): 217–52; and also Alan Sokal and Jean Bricmont, *Fashionable Nonsense* (New York: St. Martin's Press, 1998). Sokal himself has collected many of the key texts at <http://www.physics.nyu.edu/faculty/sokal/>.

3    Christopher Williams, "Of Canons and Context: Toward a Historiography of Twentieth-Century Music," *repercussions* 2, no. 1 (1993): 31–74.

4    Pierre Boulez, *Notes of an Apprenticeship,* trans. Herbert Weinstock (New York: Knopf, 1968), 275.

5    Lyotard, *The Postmodern Condition,* 53–67. Lyotard borrows the term "language games" from Wittgenstein (see *The Postmodern Condition,* 9–11).

6    See, for instance, Peter Bürger, *Theory of the Avant-Garde* (Minneapolis: University of Minnesota Press, 1984).

7    An undeniable myopia of this class was its deliberate disregard of the persistent *conservative* critique of modernism: no Pfitzner, no Rachmaninov, no Barber, no Rorem.

8    See Leonard Meyer, "The End of the Renaissance?" (Chapter 5), *Music, the Arts, and Ideas* (Chicago: University of Chicago Press, 1967), 68–86.

9    Conservative revisionism was rampant in the popular press at the turn of the millennium—thus Terry Teachout's attempt to reinstate a very old master narrative of tonal tradition in his three-part survey of "Masterpieces of the Century: A Critical Guide" *Commentary* (April–June 1999): 46–50. This right-wing settling of scores should have little effect on professional historians. A more tempting redemptive reading of the century is proposed in Kyle Gann's *American Music in the Twentieth Century* (New York: Schirmer, 1997). Gann, a practicing experimental composer, argues that hardcore minimalism

represents a "pre-classic" style, a new tonal beginning, which foreshadows an eventual progress through classic and mannerist phases.

10   For instance, the brilliant novel whose title is parodied in my section heading: Italo Calvino, *If on A Winter's Night A Traveler,* trans. William Weaver (New York: Harcourt, 1982).

11   Henry Pleasants, *The Agony of Modern Music* (New York: Simon and Schuster, 1955).

12   For a more extended discussion of battling canons and the "death of classical music," see Robert Fink, "Elvis Everywhere: Musicology and Popular Music Studies at the Twilight of the Canon," *American Music* 16, no. 2 (Summer 1998): 135–79.

13   This relation was conceptualized and thoroughly explored by Andreas Huyssen. See *After the Great Divide: Modernism, Mass Culture, Postmodernism* (Bloomington: Indiana University Press, 1986).

14   Dick Fontain, *Sound??* UPC# 7 4547580563 (1967, re-released on video by Rhapsody Films, 1988).

15   Conversation with Edward Strickland, 1987.

16   See Frederic Jameson, *The Seeds of Time* (New York: Columbia University Press, 1994), 15–19 and 72.

17   Thomas Friedman, *The Lexus and the Olive Tree: Understanding Globalization* (New York: Doubleday, 2000). The Lexus, the shiny modern product of a globally decentralized manufacturing chain, stands for the homogenizing and integrating tendencies of global capitalism and the "eternal present"; the olive tree (Friedman was a specialist in the Middle East) stands for the stubborn attachment to particular histories and places.

18   Paul Griffiths, *Modern Music and After* (Oxford: Oxford University Press, 1995). This short book, a revised edition of Griffiths's *Modern Music: the Avant-Garde since 1945* (1981), simply disintegrates after 1970 or so; classical music historiography in crisis.

# DIAGRAM 4.1
## Graphic Representation of Music Game 1

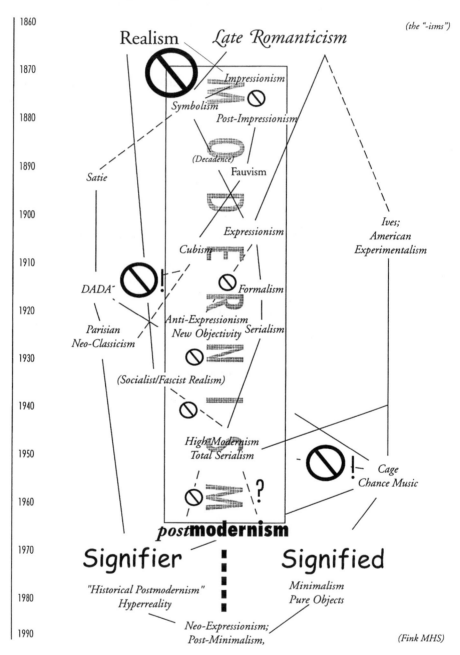

*(the "-isms")*

1860

Realism     *Late Romanticism*

1870
                    *Impressionism*

*Symbolism*
1880           *Post-Impressionism*

        *(Decadence)*
1890            Fauvism

*Satie*

1900                                    *Ives;*
                                        *American*
            *Expressionism*            *Experimentalism*
        *Cubism*
1910

*DADA*        *Formalism*
1920
            *Anti-Expressionism*
*Parisian*   *New Objectivity* *Serialism*
*Neo-Classicism*
1930

    *(Socialist/Fascist Realism)*

1940

            *High Modernism*
1950        *Total Serialism*
                                    *Cage*
                            ?       *Chance Music*
1960
        *post*modernism

1970
Signifier  ▮  Signified
           ▮
1980 *"Historical Postmodernism"*  *Minimalism*
     *Hyperreality*                *Pure Objects*

     *Neo-Expressionism;*
1990 *Post-Minimalism,*              *(Fink MHS)*

# DIAGRAM 4.2
## Graphic Representation of Music Game 2

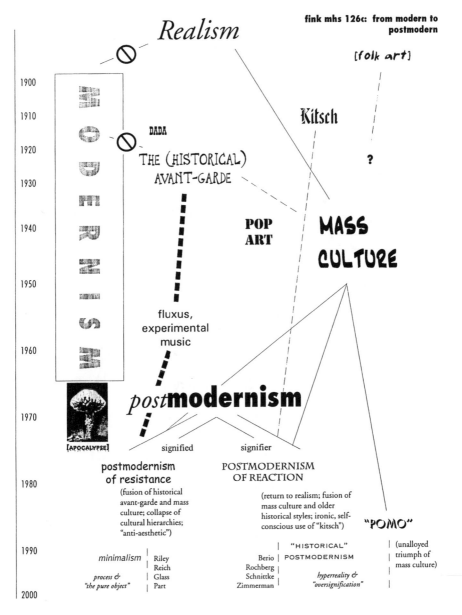

# DIAGRAM 4.3
## Graphic Representation of Music Game 3

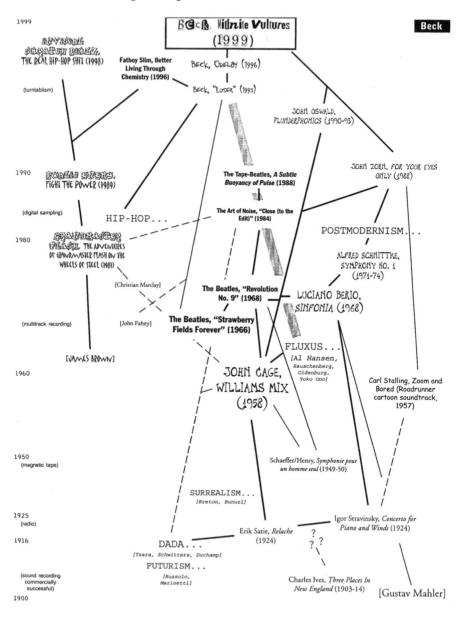

# APPENDIX 4.1
## Representative syllabus from "Music in Twentieth-Century History," Eastman School of Music 1992–1998

PART I: THE MODERNIST PARADE

Week 1: "WHAT IS *MODERN*?"; "Erklärung" vs. "Verklärung"
   Schopenhauer, Wagner's *Tristan und Isolde,* and the Roots of Musical Modernism
Week 2: SYMBOLISM
   *Esotericism, Mystery and Symbol*: Representing Nothingness
Week 3: PRIMITIVISM (from Fauvism to Cubism)
   *Abstraction, pt. 1*: Representing the Geometric Structure of (outer) Reality
Week 4: EXPRESSIONISM 1905–1914
   *Abstraction, pt. 2:* Representing the Psychic Structure of (inner) Reality
Week 5: FORMALISM and Anti-EXPRESSIONISM 1916–1933
   *The Alienation-Effect:* Representing the Social Structure of (political) Reality
Week 6: SOCIALIST REALISM
   *"Engineers of Human Souls"*
Week 7: HIGH MODERNISM
   Mathematical Lyricism in "The Age of Science"

PART II: OUT OF STEP: ON THE TRAIL OF THE POSTMODERN

Week 8: "WHAT IS *POSTMODERN*?"; DADA
   *Art as Anti-Art:* Eric Satie and DADA
Week 9: STRAVINSKY, COLLAGE, and Post-Modernist NEOCLASSICISM
   *Art as Cut-and-Paste*
Week 10: AMERICAN EXPERIMENTALISM, Ives to Cage
   Tinkerers: *Music, Anti-Music, and Noise*
Week 11: THE SIXTIES and "The End of the Renaissance"
   *Apocalypse Now:* the Self-Destruction of Modernist Technocracy
   (or, *How I learned to stop Worrying and love the Bomb*)

PART III: POSTMODERNISM, OR, MUSIC AFTER MEANING

Week 12: "POSTMODERNISM," 1965–1980
   *"Even Better than the Real Thing"* the Music of the Signifier
Week 13: MINIMALISM, 1965–1980
   *Pure Objects*: the Music of the Signified
Week 14: POST-POST-POST ... ? (Music in the 1980s and 1990s: the Death of "Classical Music"?)
   Hypertonality; "Post-Minimalism"; the Death of "Classical Music"?

## APPENDIX 4.2
### A representative syllabus for "Modern and Postmodern Music 1948–2000," UCLA 2000

INTRODUCTION: MUSIC(S) IN THE AGE OF MASS CULTURE(S)

1. Music, History, and Cultural Hierarchy
2. Technology and Music History (LP-Stereo *[exotica]*, Magnetic Tape *[musique concrète]*, Electric Guitar *[R&B]*

PART I: TECHNOCRACY'S END (1948–74)

*High (1948–58)*
3. The Composer as Specialist (Total Serialism, Electronic Music)
4. High Modernism and Its Discontents (The "International Style")
5. Sounds of the Country/Sounds of the City (Country Music, Rhythm-and-Blues, and the Birth of Rock'n'Roll)

*Awakenings (1956–1967)*
6. The New Sensibility (Meyer, Sontag, McLuhan, Mailer)
7. The Shape of Jazz to Come (Miles Davis, John Coltrane, and "Free" Jazz)
8. Avant-Garde and Experimental Music I (DADA to Cage)
9. Avant-Garde and Experimental Music II (Cage and Beyond—Fluxus, Scratch, Eno, etc.)
10. Elvis, Beatlemania, Bob Dylan

11. MIDTERM

*Unraveling (1968–74)*
12. "The Sixties" (Music, Culture, and Politics from the Summer of Love to Watergate)
13. Apocalypse Now! (Berio's *Sinfonia* and the Implosion of the Classical Mainstream)

PART II: POSTMODERNISM (1965–PRESENT)

*The Music of the Signifier ("Postmodernism," Collage, Sampling)*
14. Art Postmodernism (Rochberg, Schnittke)
15. Vernacular Postmodernism (Hip-Hop, Sampling, and Collage from Bugs Bunny to Beck)
16. Within the Context of No Context (John Adams, *Nixon in China*)

*The Music of the Signified (Minimalism, Repetition, Trance)*
17. Art Minimalism (Riley, Reich, Glass, Pärt)
18. Vernacular Minimalism (Funk, Disco, Punk, New Wave and other repetitive musical idioms) *Paper Due in Class I *

CONCLUSION: TOWARD THE POST-CANONICAL ERA

19. Back to the Future (The Early Music Movement, 1890–1990)
20. Current Trends

# APPENDIX 4.3
## The syllabus for "Music Now," UCLA 1999

This course will be a free-wheeling attempt to use musicological, historical, and cultural perspectives to illuminate some representatively-chosen current events in the postmodern musical scene. The emphasis is on synthesis, not analysis. I hope that the musical and intellectual histories we build together will give students an appreciation for the rich sonic culture that surrounds all of us at every moment. No musical training is necessary to participate in this class. Through an oversight, the class does not carry official General Education credit, but the Musicology department encourages any student enrolled who needs GE credit to petition for it.

Class Schedule at a Glance

UNIT 1: WHAT IS MUSIC HISTORY NOW?

Item 1: "SOUNDTRACK FOR A CENTURY" CD COLLECTION *(It's Sony's World We Just Listen to It)*

UNIT 2: SOME LATE TWENTIETH-CENTURY ARTISTIC STRATEGIES

Item 2: MARILYN MANSON *(Freedom and the Urge to Transgression)*

Item 3: BECK *(Fragmentation, or Living Close to the Edit)*

Item 4: THE DEBEERS DIAMOND MUSIC *(Fakery, Simulation, and Hyperreality)*

MIDTERM EXAM

UNIT 3: MUSIC IN THE CONSUMER SOCIETY

Item 5: GAP KHAKIS/DEAN WITTER ADs *(Advertising, Retro-Culture, and Hip Consumerism)*

Item 5A: VANESSA-MAE *(Classical Crossover and Marketing)*

UNIT 4: MEN AND WOMEN

Item 6: ANDREA BOCELLI *([P]opera and the Myth of the Tenor)*
\* REPORT DUE in class \*

Item 7: NBC "MISSION" THEME" *(Musical Representation of Corporate Masculinity)*

Item 8: R-E-S-P-E-C-T *(Music and Feminine Empowerment)*

Item 9: Music at the Superbowl *(The Society of the Spectacle)*

# Teaching Non-Majors: The Introductory Course

Chapter Five

# Interdisciplinary Approaches to the Introduction to Music Course

*Maria Archetto*

As many college professors of music are aware, the "Music Appreciation" or "Introduction to Music" course for non-majors is one of the most challenging courses for an instructor to teach and often a very problematic humanities course for the undergraduates who enroll in it. I recall a conversation I had several years ago with a colleague in another field whose grandchild had taken a college music appreciation course. She lamented that the course had turned out to be much more difficult than the young man had anticipated, and she was amazed that a music course could have been so difficult. I was not surprised by her story. For the past several years I have been thinking about the problems that my non-major students have with music appreciation, and I have come to the conclusion that there are good reasons for them. This essay highlights some pedagogical problems often encountered in teaching music appreciation and also presents some suggestions for teaching strategies that may help in overcoming them. My experience has led me to believe that we ought to try some new approaches to teaching this type of course. Recently, I have used an interdisciplinary approach with some good results. A brief analysis of the preparation of students entering our classes reveals why this approach can be successful.

While many students enter the introductory music course with some experience in listening to their favorite popular music, relatively few of them have had much experience with scholarly study in the discipline of music such as music history or theory. Unlike the academic preparation our students receive in English, history, or the sciences, their previous school work in music (if there has been any at all) is not likely to have been geared toward giving them the intellectual tools necessary for developing an appreciation of music history, criticism, or analysis. Perhaps even more important, only a minority of students enters class with much experience in making their own music, alone or with others, either by singing or playing an instrument. Relatively few have had private vocal or instrumental lessons, and it is a rare student who has studied composition.

In the "Introduction to Music" course both students and teachers are faced with several difficult problems simultaneously. Most music appreciation instructors have several goals that exist at different levels of pedagogical theory. I think of my course goals in two levels, those of foreground and background. The foreground goals are skill-oriented and can be measured by observation and examination. The background goals are broader and not so easily measured but are equally important. My foreground goals for the course include:

1.  Attentive listening to music.

2.  Verbal and written description of music using appropriate vocabulary.

3.  Formulation of questions about music.

4.  Critical analysis of music at a basic level (isolating and describing the "elements of music" in a composition).

5.  Construction and defense of rational arguments, oral and written, about music.

My background goals are:

1.  Making of aesthetic judgments.

2.  Development of reason and imagination.

3.  Careful use of verbal and written language.

4.  Increased self-awareness

5.  Increased interest in and curiosity about the world.

In seeking to achieve these multiple and rather complex goals, the teacher and students are confronted by several difficulties. First, the vast literature of Western art music is mostly unfamiliar to our students. Whether the instructor takes a traditional Western art music "canonical" approach to the course repertoire, or whether he or she goes beyond the canon to include women's music, or popular, folk, ethnic, and traditional musics, the basic problem of unfamiliarity with the musical repertoire(s) remains.[1]

Second, the music of the Western tradition is formulated in various stylistic languages. Most of these styles are no longer current and many of them appeal to a highly musically educated few. Many stylistic languages, especially those of early music and twentieth-century music, are likely to be quite unfamiliar and even unpleasant to the uninitiated student.

Third, musicians have a specialized vocabulary for describing, analyzing, and critiquing music, as well as a specialized symbolic language for writing music. The descriptive/analytical vocabulary (beginning with such basic terms as melody, rhythm, harmony, and texture) and the symbols of written music are usually unknown to the student who has not had private music lessons or participated in a school music ensemble. Besides this, the vocabulary of music contains many terms in languages foreign to a majority of students.[2]

Finally, the intellectual processes of today's college students have been nurtured in the era of television and film, which has fostered the development of mental habits that are not necessarily conducive to attentive and concentrated listening or to detailed analysis of the kind with which trained musicians are familiar.[3] In addition, as Brian Mann has pointed out, the students who choose to enroll in music appreciation classes are likely to resist considering music intellectually because of their experience with popular music.[4]

Given this set of problems, college teachers need to develop some new strategies for teaching music appreciation. One strategy, which has worked for my students and myself, is the interdisciplinary approach. The approach outlined here is based on my experience in teaching music appreciation, music history, art history, and interdisciplinary courses in the humanities at a small liberal arts college for several years. I have found that students without much previous knowledge of *musica disciplina* respond well when their music course material is combined with the study of topics that relate music to other fields of study.

I have designed and taught several instructional units for my music appreciation course in which topics involving disciplines outside of music are explored in order to form intellectual "bridges" to specifically musical topics. In this way I try to take advantage of the experience and preparation that my students have had in other disciplines, while leading them to apply some of that experience to the study of music. Each unit is taught in the context of a one-semester course in which the students have a music appreciation textbook with a correlated set of compact disc recordings. Supplementary readings from the other disciplines are also assigned. The units are introduced in the second half of a semester, after students have made a basic study of the elements of music including melody, rhythm, dynamics, timbre, harmony, tonality, genre, and form. The following are descriptions of three sample units, one interfacing music and art history; another combining music, drama, and philosophy; and a third drawing on music and psychology.

**Sample Unit I: the concept of style in art history and music history**

The teaching of general concepts in art appreciation may be appropriately and successfully integrated with the teaching of musical concepts. Because of their cultural conditioning, students are often more quickly comfortable with a new visual experience than with new listening experiences when these are the focus of analysis and discussion in an introductory class. I have noticed that when faced with a new visual image, beginning students are often more willing to participate in a class discussion than when they are presented with an unfamiliar piece of music.

After students have had some experience in defining and recognizing the basic elements of music, introducing the concept of style provides a framework for the discussion of music history. The foreground goals of the art history/music history unit are:

1. Students will be able to articulate orally and in writing a definition of style in art and music.

2. Students will know the names and dates of the Classic and Romantic style periods, and will recognize and describe some representative musical works of each era.

3. Students will be able to articulate orally and in writing some basic aesthetic principles underlying the artistic and musical works of the Classic and Romantic style periods.

4. Students will recognize the style period of an unknown musical work as Classic or Romantic and will be able to explain why it is so classified.

I begin by presenting the concept of style to the students using examples from art history. A series of art images from each style period under discussion is shown to the class. At first it is useful for the students to view images on similar themes or from similar genres. For example, one may choose to use a series of paintings of either landscapes, portraits, or narrative scenes. In an instructor-guided class discussion, students are asked to analyze and compare the images from the two style periods. They are encouraged to observe and to discuss the differences they can see in color, form, light and shade, line, pattern, shape, space, and surface. They then are asked to begin to develop a definition of "style." Following more class discussion, students reach a definition of style as the total aesthetic character of a work of art based on the way in which the artist has treated all of the visual elements under discussion.

Having developed a basic definition of style in art history, students are ready to view varied images from each of the two style periods. At this point paintings and sculptures on various themes as well as examples of architecture are introduced. This time the task of the student is to describe the similarities in the visual elements among the images from the same style period. Further class discussion helps them to clarify, understand, and articulate some of the underlying aesthetic principles forming the basis of style in each period.

I then apply the same procedure that was used in examining works of art to the examination of musical works from the same two style periods. Several musical works are selected from each style period, and students are asked to isolate and describe a number of essential elements of each including melody, rhythm, harmony, dynamics, timbre, texture, and form. The students are then guided to follow the same method they have used in analyzing the works of art. They compare the musical selections and provide descriptions of the similarities in the elements of music among works from the same style period. Then they must articulate in writing some basic aesthetic principles for each style and compare the principles they have deduced with those deduced for the art works. Finally, students listen to an unknown piece of music and determine whether it is based on Classic or Romantic principles of composition. Feedback from my students has indicated that they both enjoy and appreciate the use of visual images to introduce concepts that can be applied to musical study.

## Sample Unit II: music, drama, and philosophy in early opera

The study of opera provides a good opportunity to explore the relationships among music, drama, and philosophy. Since undergraduates are often taking their first philosophy courses, a focus on the birth of opera gives them the opportunity to see how the interest of Renaissance scholars in ancient Greek philosophy affected the course of development of late sixteenth-century music. The unit is intended to introduce the class to the genre of opera by having the students focus on the intellectual context for its creation in the late Renaissance. The foreground goals of the unit are:

1. Students will be able to articulate the nature of the influences on early opera found in Greek philosophy and drama.

2. Students will be able to articulate some of the basic aesthetic principles of the opera theorists and composers of late sixteenth-century Italy.

3.  Students will be able to describe and analyze Monteverdi's *Orfeo* (1607) in terms of its sources in Classical philosophy and drama and its classification as an example of the new genre of opera.

The students begin this unit by reading excerpts from ancient sources in translation. These include writings by Plato and Aristotle on the philosophy of music, a Greek tragedy, and the myth of Orpheus. We discuss Greek thought on music and analyze the general dramatic style of Greek tragedy. Students then read excerpts from the works of Florentine scholars and musicians who were inspired by ancient Greek drama and, as a class, we discuss the aesthetics of the creators of opera. Finally, we move to an analysis of Monteverdi's *Orfeo*, focusing on its poetry, dramatic elements, and music.[5]

## Sample Unit III: physics, psychology, and music

At my particular institution, many undergraduates are engaged in the study of the sciences and are naturally interested in the ways in which studies in the natural and social sciences interface with the arts. Given this degree of interest, an instructional unit organized around some of the unanswered questions about human cognition, musical creation, and musical perception has been valuable in focusing student attention on music. The foreground goals of this unit are:

1.  Students will read and critically analyze some of the current scientific literature concerning the perception of music by the human brain.[6]

2.  Students will be able to articulate and explain current theories of human musical perception.

3.  Students will prepare class presentations on music perception issues.

The music and psychology unit has resulted in some interesting class presentations including one in which a student, inspired by reading about Evelyn Glennie, succeeded in recreating for the class a means of musical perception employed by the deaf. Another student presented the results of an experiment in which he played excerpts of program and absolute music for schoolchildren with an attempt to measure and compare their intellectual and emotional responses to each type. The resulting discussions brought the classes to a new understanding of acoustical, physiological, and cultural factors in the human perception of music.

Attempting to apply an interdisciplinary approach in the music appreciation course may be considered risky by some. Indeed one does spend valuable time on questions and issues that are not "purely musical." I have found, however, that forays into other disciplines are worth the effort. Once students are given interdisciplinary bridges to deeper musical listening and analysis, they often change the way they think about the subject of music. In class, students often begin to consider such questions as "What is happening in the music?" or "What does this musical experience mean?" or even, "What is music?" in new and more profound ways. Students who entered the class with the ideas that the humanities are "fluff" and music is purely a form of light entertainment often find that they have entered a realm of study with serious ramifications for the expansion of mind and spirit.

## Notes

1    We would not expect a student to arrive in a college English course without ever having read some works of Shakespeare, but we are not surprised when our students are unfamiliar with music by Handel, Beethoven, or Wagner, except for the bits used in television advertising or film scores. Peter Kivy has referred to this problem (as well as to the problem of defining what the "basic" literature of Western music is or should be) in *The Fine Art of Repetition: Essays in the Philosophy of Music* (Cambridge and New York: Cambridge University Press, 1993).

2    As the reader might expect, I am sympathetic to Peter Kivy's view that in order to teach music appreciation in a meaningful way, we must teach students to read music and to master some analytical language. As Kivy states (*The Fine Art*, 30), "the way we teach music to humanities students is much like trying to teach the nineteenth-century novel to people who cannot read."

3    The view that exposure to television programming is detrimental to critical thinking and analysis is presented forcefully by Neil Postman in *Amusing Ourselves to Death* (New York: Penguin Books, 1985).

4    Brian Mann, "A Response to Kivy: Music and 'Music Appreciation' in the Undergraduate Liberal Arts Curriculum," *College Music Symposium* 39 (1999): 87–106.

5    Supplementary readings for this unit include excerpts from Plato's *Laws* and *Republic* and Aristotle's *Poetics*, *Politics*, and *Rhetoric*; as well as excerpts from the writings of Caccini, Peri, and Monteverdi edited in Oliver Strunk, *Source Readings in Music History* (New York: W. W. Norton, 1965). Students listen to excerpts from *Orfeo* and view the complete opera on video.

6    Some examples of the supplementary reading for this unit are: Bennet Riemer, "Music as Cognitive: A New Horizon for Music Education," *Kodály envoy* 20, no. 3 (1994): 16–17; and Wanda Wallace, "Memory for Music: Effect of

Melody on Recall of Text," *Journal of Experimental Psychology: Learning Memory, and Cognition* 20, no. 6 (1994): 1471–85; and Justine Sergent et al., "Distributed Neural Network Underlying Musical Sight-Reading and Keyboard Performance," *Science* 257 (1992): 106–9.

Chapter Six

# The "Why" of Music: Variations on a Cosmic Theme

*Marjorie Roth*

*I give you the end of a golden string*
*Only wind it into a ball,*
*It will lead you in at Heaven's Gate*
*Built into Jerusalem's wall!*

William Blake

## Introduction

When organizing the type of departmental service course traditionally known as the "Music Appreciation Class," the instructor confronts head-on the array of pedagogical tensions that arise whenever the task of teaching "music history" to non-majors is at hand.[1] The practical realities of presenting the basic tenets and repertoire of Western classical music to students who have little experience with the subject—and in many cases, little genuine interest in it—impose what often feel like crushing constraints upon decisions as to course content, presentation, and evaluation. To work within the restrictions dictated by an audience of non-musicians creates at the very least a crisis of method, if not also one of conscience. How does one maintain the integrity of the repertoire while still making it palatable to an obviously captive and potentially resistant audience? What is the best way to introduce and insist upon use of the specialized vocabulary required for the discussion of art music without arousing feelings of intimidation or suspicions of elitism? Since the majority of the students enrolled will not be able to read music, how does one effectively highlight the fine points of music-analytical aesthetics without recourse to the written score? And finally, how should the course be structured as a whole: in lecture format, group discussion, or some combination of the two? Of all the possibilities available, which would prove the most effective way to organize and present largely unfamiliar concepts to an audience possessing little background in or cultural preparation for the subject at hand:[2] by genre? masterwork? performance medium? cultural context and function? or the old reliable standby, chronological development?

These and many more difficult questions unite to create a daunting pedagogical dilemma for the teacher of music appreciation. All the basic assumptions that underlie the structure and content of introductory courses for music majors are missing from the service-course equation: that the students will be interested in the material, that they will understand how the class fits into the overall scheme of their education and career trajectories, that they can read music, make music and will be willing to listen attentively to it, that they will have more than just a passing familiarity with classical styles, media, and genres. The absence of these reassuring structural pillars prompts a serious reconsideration of the true goals of a music appreciation course, and the formulation of a new set of assumptions from which to proceed. Not an easy task, but on the bright side, this "all bets are off" atmosphere offers the professor a rare opportunity for pedagogical creativity and freedom. Released from seeing to it that students master a fixed body of repertoire, terms, and concepts, the music appreciation teacher has room to pick and choose from among favorite pieces, to offer up those minor jewels of the repertoire that have something distinct, important, and often very personal to say, but which generally fall outside the "canon" that must be rigorously addressed when training professional musicians. Moreover, the informal setting of the music appreciation course affords ample opportunity for leisurely group exploration of those "peripheral" but nonetheless fundamental questions about the cosmic nature of music and the musical nature of mankind for which there is, alas, no time or place in the crowded curriculum of the average music major.

Other essays in this book offer a variety of excellent strategies as to *how* a teacher can meet the special challenges of working with non-musicians. My contribution, as its title suggests, is geared more toward addressing the *why*-related aspects of the task, those common intuitions and all-too-often unspoken convictions about music—*any* music—that are the real force behind the fact that my non-majors and I stand face to face over the CD player.

## The Nazareth College environment

Before going on, it might be best to describe the environment in which I have been able to develop and refine my ideas about teaching music appreciation. For the past several years, I have taught studio flute lessons, music history, musical analysis, and basic ear training to music majors, as well as flute lessons and music appreciation courses to non-majors at Nazareth College of Rochester in Rochester, New York. Nazareth is a relatively small, private liberal arts college, founded in 1924 by the Sisters of St. Joseph, originally as a women's college. Although Nazareth was secularized in 1967 and became a coeducational institution in 1973, the student body is still predominantly female and there remain a significant number of clergy on the faculty and in administrative positions. Unlike many colleges and universities today, Nazareth maintains a serious academic and financial commitment to the arts, and the music department has grown continually in terms of numbers, quality, resources, and reputation since its inception. Undergraduate degrees can currently be earned in music theory, music history, and music performance, but by far the largest proportion of our music majors are enrolled in music education and/or music therapy programs. Recently, a graduate certificate in music education has been added to the department's offerings.

We also maintain a variety of "service" courses for non-majors.[3] During my time at the college, I have had the opportunity to teach the "Master Composers" course (a "life and works" format organized around a selected group of major composers), "The Way of Music" (a chronological survey of repertoire, stressing elements of musical style and genre), and the "Women and Music" course (an integration of the repertoire and historical contexts of music history into the format of an introductory Women's Studies course). I generally break the ice on the first day by asking the students to fill out a "Musical Tastes and Experiences" questionnaire, which we then take the remainder of our class time to discuss.[4] Predictably, the most common reasons for taking the course are neither encouraging nor are they particularly flattering: "Because it was required" and "Because it is the only thing that will fit into my work schedule" are two of the favorites. Somewhat more ambiguous and only marginally less deflating is the caveat some kind-hearted students see fit to include, explaining that they felt a music course would be "less boring" or "less scary" than a poetry class or something in the visual arts. There are always a few, though, who seem genuinely interested and who exhibit a certain nostalgia about a previous brush with classical music in their past; these students have often participated in high school band, orchestra, or choir, and are finding that they miss both the tangible (social) and intangible (harder to describe) elements those musical organizations contributed to their pre-college days. Finally, there are the ones in every group who display a grudging and somewhat hostile attitude toward the fine arts in general. These students have usually had either no prior contact with classical music, or else the contact they did have was in some way intensely negative. They are not naturally drawn to the sounds or genres, and are openly suspicious of "art music" as a concept. They resent the aura of exclusivity the term "classical" seems to imply, and rebel against what they perceive to be a tacit criticism of their own favorite, non-classical music and its use.

And what are their favorite musics? In response to the "Listening Tastes" question students cite any number of popular, folk, jazz, and/or ethnic musics, and they become noticeably animated when asked to describe the reasons their music is important to them, the ways in which it both shapes and conforms to their social, emotional, and physical requirements. Music is a stimulant, a narcotic, an inspiration, or a soothing accompaniment to daily routines ranging from driving and dusting to dancing and dating. For some, music defines the perimeters of their social groups, articulating shared beliefs and underscoring the perks of self-esteem and acceptance that are part and parcel of group identification. Conversely, music is for others the very thing that sets them apart from any established group, highlighting a much-valued sense of independence and individuality. Depending on taste and temperament, music is "mind candy" or genuine "food for thought." Opinions vary, but it is rare that a student will claim to have no opinion at all and to live a life entirely devoid of music.

Our initial class discussion serves not only to acquaint me with the particular group of people in front of me, but it also furnishes the cornerstone upon which I build the entire course, the guiding assumption that generates all details of content, presentation, and evaluation. Whatever their background or reasons for taking the class, I have found my non-majors at Nazareth to be on the whole cooperative, intellectually curious, well prepared for college-level study, and open to the assimilation of new ideas. They are usually upperclassmen, several years into their chosen field of study, with a very clear picture of the careers that lie ahead. These young people have no illusions; what Nazareth College claims they "need" in terms of a solid humanistic education is one thing, while what they know they will "need" in order to get by in the real world is quite another. Despite the good intentions displayed by registering for "The Way of Music," my students and I know from the outset that the thirteen weeks we spend together may well be the only time their lives intersect in a meaningful way with whatever it is that classical music has to offer.

## Common ground

What are my intentions on that first day? First and foremost, I consider it my greatest responsibility to offer the students not only my knowledge of classical music, but also my passion for it. And while acquainting them with the unfamiliar repertoire, terminology, and ideas that will help them access that passion, my larger-scale aim is to help them connect their own musical experiences to mine, and to those of individuals and cultures far removed in time and place. Our initial discussion almost always begins with an articulation of the differences among our various musical worlds, but toward the end of class I steer the conversation toward potential similarities. For my own part, I proceed methodologically from the assumption of a "common ground" among us when it comes to music, a belief that we share a bond of involvement and curiosity, and a deep intuition that music is much more than just sounding entertainment. To the study of this intuition I have dedicated a large portion of my life, they, a small number of their elective credits—and these individual choices have led us to the joint experience of the next thirteen weeks. I ask them: What shall we do with our time together? What does it mean that we find ourselves here in this classroom, prepared to listen to music, to talk about it? Why does music exist in the first place? Why the abiding human interest? What need does it answer in our lives? in the lives of those who came before us and of those who will come after us?

Within these questions lies the antidote to the lost structural pillars mentioned earlier in connection with teaching non-majors. An assumption of common ground overrides the effect of those missing elements, since the main goal of the class is less a thorough assimilation of names, periods, and pieces than it is the development of an ability to successfully locate classical music—along with their own musics—into some much greater cosmic scheme. My task is to offer them a set of tools for this integration, and to highlight the ways in which classical music entered and continues to enrich my life. No, they will most likely not be terribly interested, at least not at first; but since they are invariably interested in *some* music, that fact is more than sufficient as a point of departure. Certainly for the majority, classical music will play an insignificant role in the external details of their future careers and personal lives. But what of the potential for a lasting *internal* impact? How might exposure to classical music expand their thought processes, enhance their enjoyment of the music they already love, and influence the ways they will choose to spend their future free time and money? The answers rest, of course, within each individual student, and with what he or she chooses to take away from the course. But there is no doubt that it offers the chance to acquire a potent means by which they can explore, evaluate, and expand at least one aspect—the "harmonic" aspect—of their humanity, for as long as they live.

I tell my non-majors at the outset that developing a "feel" for classical music is a long process, one that will certainly extend far beyond the temporal borders of any single academic semester. It will require patience, persistence, and a willingness to meet the music halfway. I tell them that they will find some of the repertoire we study immediately attractive, while some will take a bit longer to work its magic in them. Some concepts and contexts will be clear and make perfect sense; others will require a stretch of their historical imaginations and a suspension of their natural disbelief. I ask them to trust my choices of repertoire, learn what I think is important about the music I present to them, and then use that information as a model for comparison and critique as they continue to expand their listening tastes in the future. But I remind them always to bear in mind the image of their own music, their first love, and the way it makes them feel; and I suggest the possibility that a similar affection for the classical repertoire might grow during the journey we have before us. They have taken the first steps by signing up, and showing up. I see it as my part of the bargain to pick up the thread, and make it worth their while.

## *Musica mundana* in the classroom

> *How sweet the moonlight sleeps upon this bank!*
> *Here we sit, and let the sounds of music*
> *Creep in our ears; soft stillness and the night*
> *Become the touches of sweet harmony.*
> *Sit, Jessica. Look how the floor of heaven*
> *Is thick inlaid with patines of bright gold:*
> *There's not the smallest orb which thou behold'st*
> *But in his motion like an angel sings,*
> *Still quiring to the young-eyed cherubins;*
> *Such harmony is in immortal souls ...*

> *... For do but note a wild and wanton herd,*
> *Or race of youthful and unhandled colts,*
> *Fetching mad bounds, bellowing and neighing loud,*
> *Which is the hot condition of their blood;*
> *If they but hear perchance a trumpet sound,*
> *Or any air of music touch their ears,*
> *You shall perceive them make a mutual stand,*
> *Their savage eyes turned to a modest gaze*
> *By the sweet power of music ...*

> *... The man that hath no music in himself,*
> *or is not moved with concord of sweet sounds,*

*Is fit for treasons, stratagems and spoils;*
*The motions of his spirit are dull as night ...*

William Shakespeare
*The Merchant of Venice*, Act V, Scene 1

So right he is, Shakespeare's young Lorenzo, as he sits in the moonlight with his ladylove, listening to distant strains and rhapsodizing on the power and magic of music. He is certain the heavens are singing, and he senses the connection between the soft harmonies his ears perceive and the melody he knows his own soul spins out in answer to the stars. When I read this passage to my students, they instantly make the connection, immediately grasp that Lorenzo's musings relate directly to that introductory talk in which we took our first tentative steps into the realm of cosmic music. The scene from Shakespeare's *Merchant of Venice* quoted above highlights the three concepts that form the topic of our second class meeting and serves to reinforce, contextualize, and expand the assumption of common ground already established: *musica instrumentalis* (the sounding trumpet), *musica humana* (the motions of the spirit), and *musica mundana* (celestial music, the "Harmony of the Spheres"). Having suggested Universal Harmony as the source of our common intuitions about music on day one, I spend the next very enjoyable class period reviewing the ways in which that concept has played itself out historically, to plant the magic of the idea in their imaginations and to give it an increased sense of historical depth and validity.

Whatever their level of experience with music, almost all class members are familiar with the concept of the musical scale, *do re mi fa sol la ti do*. I ask them: have they ever wondered where the Western musical scale comes from? How is it we arrived at the collection of pitches from which we draw all melody and harmony? In partial explanation, I read them the muddled and mysterious recipe for the World Soul's divisions contained in Plato's *Timaeus* and tell them of the singing planetary "rims" glimpsed by one lucky mortal in the famous *Myth of Er*. The ancient Chaldeans also believed in a music produced by the revolution of celestial bodies; their oracles called it "sounding light," the very stuff of the human soul, and the conduit by which it could reach the supercelestial world. And what about "chords," a concept with which most students are at least marginally familiar? How do we determine which notes will sound well together and which will not (a perfect opportunity to introduce the important subject of consonance and dissonance)? The answer lies in Pythagorean proportions, the very simplest ratios of sacred geometry that reflect the mathematical structure of the Universe and give us a mirror in which to perceive the face of God through sounding number.

As a group we have already established that music profoundly influences our moods. Have any other cultures or individuals in history also noticed this transformative property? Well, yes, as a matter of fact the Greeks had fairly strong opinions about modal ethos, and Plato himself expended a good deal of effort explaining the mechanics of sympathetic vibration. During the Renaissance we find Marsilio Ficino's magical songs, which were used to attract celestial forces, Pietro Bembo's neoplatonic convictions about the nature of words and music that inspired an entire genre, and Robert Fludd's fantastic monochord, rendering all the Cosmos on a two-octave string. Near the end of the period, we encounter the Florentine Camerata and their fierce commitment to solo song as the true means by which to reach and alter the human soul. And subtly underpinning these specific examples is the doctrine of hermetic similarity and its related science of alchemy, both fundamental precepts of the early modern period that do not fail to acknowledge the power of music. As a famous illustration from Heinrich Khunrath's *Amphitheatrum sapientiae aeternae* of 1602 shows us, a proper alchemist's laboratory contained space on the right for his *labor* (his ovens, alembics, coal, and tongs), space on the left for his *oratory* (his altar), and space in the center of the room for musical instruments, the tools through which work and prayer become one, and the door to the Cosmos stands open to all.

My presentation of this material is supplemented by recordings and illustrations and is greatly enhanced by the lively questions and comments of the class. There is no set content for this lecture, and no telling where it will go once the students start to respond. But however the hour unfolds, by its end my general aims have been achieved and the tone of the class established for the rest of the term. We have developed the habit of speculating aloud and have become comfortable with the idea that *musica mundana,* the Harmony of the Universe, is a far more potent force than the mere details of genre and style that set our earthly examples of *instrumentalis* at odds with one another. And also, we know that we are in good company, that we share the same instincts and responses to music that have occupied some of the most creative and sensitive minds in human history. From this operational vantage point, we are now ready to move on to the nuts and bolts of our music appreciation course—the genres, styles, and repertoire of Western art music—with an open mind and a sense of camaraderie.

## The chronological format

In terms of overall organization, I find the chronological approach to be both the most simple and the most congenial to my personal aims and tastes.[5] A majority of the standard music appreciation texts adopt this format, and it has the added advantage of corresponding to traditional "Western civilization" courses, which will already have established a set of historical and political "pegs" upon which students can hang the accouterments of musical culture. I will suggest here that with only slight adjustments, the materials and methods of a music appreciation class need not differ significantly from a historical survey course for undergraduate music majors; it is only a question of focus and degree of emphasis. Even non-majors must develop a working vocabulary of technical terms and a set of functional concepts from which all subsequent study of classical music can proceed: What are the main historical periods? What are the canonical works of the repertoire? What are the genres, forms, and styles of these works? Under what cultural conditions and for whom were these works composed? Who are the composers, and when did they live? What are the rudiments of music theory and what is the basic terminology needed to describe and discuss art music intelligently?

In all my service courses, I insist upon a reasonable level of demonstrated expertise in these areas. But I make it clear that complete mastery of these facts is not our end goal, that students will not be expected to engage these questions with the same depth and intensity required of a music major, and that my evaluation procedures will reflect this attitude. Because I am blessed with relatively small classes, my exams can include a substantial component of short and long essays in addition to the standard "drop the needle" and "term definition" sections. This type of exam holds a definite appeal for my non-majors because it reflects a comfortable balance between concrete detail and thoughtful reflection. Students who are more at home with facts and figures can do well enough, at least to pass, simply through rote memorization of musical themes and term definitions. Other students, perhaps less facile with technical detail but more willing to engage imaginatively with the "big picture," can skimp on the facts but make up for it with interesting comments and speculations. In any case, my emphasis on *why* we define terms and memorize themes, and *why* we need to develop the skills to communicate our ideas about musical repertoires and contexts has the effect of smoothing out individual differences in experience and varying learning styles while still demanding a reasonable level of technical competence with the material. Under these relaxed conditions, it is sometimes astonishing to me how much my liberal arts students actually take in, and the aesthetic depth with which they process the information.


## Monteverdi's *Orfeo*

I would like to close with an example of the ways in which I use the idea of *musica mundana* to bind the structure and content of a typical lecture in my music appreciation classes to the underlying liberal arts agenda outlined above. The work I have chosen to discuss here is one of my favorite pieces of music, the elaborate strophic variation aria "Possente spirto" from Monteverdi's *Orfeo* of 1607. I always conclude Unit I (Medieval/Renaissance) with *Orfeo* because although this wonderful *favola in musica* undoubtedly stands as the herald of the Baroque period, it also represents a full flowering of the genres, styles, and ideas born during the Renaissance. By the time we reach *Orfeo*, my students and I have made a fairly good survey of medieval and Renaissance music history and literature, and the class has acquired the basic skills necessary to understand the music, the cultural context, and the expressive force of the work. For many, *Orfeo* is their first encounter with opera, and so I take special care to make the experience as pleasant and meaningful as possible. There is usually a bit of resistance when the subject of opera arises, a suspicion that they will not like the genre, tinged with a stoic resignation to put up with it (because it is clear from both the syllabus and my enthusiasm that there is no way out). To combat their initial reservations, I promise them a love story (not unproblematic) packed with romance and adventure, fantastic characters, spectacular costumes, exotic locations, elegant words, passionate emotions—and truly amazing music, of course. We take time to learn the details of the plot, to meet the characters individually, and especially we take notice of Orfeo's extraordinary nature: his strengths, his weaknesses, and his unique existence as a Being half god and half human.

When it is time to listen to the music we focus on Act III, Orfeo's dramatic arrival in the Underworld, accompanied only by his harp and his Hope. To guide students through the act, I provide an extremely non-technical handout containing some basic historical facts about the work, a sequence of the unfolding dramatic/musical events, and a few details of character and instrumentation that will help them follow the action as they listen to the music (see Figure 6.1).[6] Highlighted on this graph is the strophic variation aria "Possente spirto" which, after an initial viewing of Act III in its entirety, we study in greater depth in order to learn how Orfeo's magical song eventually persuades the gods of the Underworld to bend the natural laws of life and death. Beginning with the text alone, we analyze what the demi-god says and exactly how he says it. (Figure 6.2 is the translation I give to the class, including the strophic divisions and rhyme scheme of the text.) Although great suffering is eminently clear in his words, the general consensus is usually that words alone could not have done the trick. To accomplish such an extraordinary feat, some amplification of Orfeo's situation is clearly required, and so we move on to a closer examination of the persuasive power of words when combined with music.

Figure 6.3*a* is a simple "roadmap" of the piece, an unsophisticated line-diagram providing text incipits, ritornello instrumentation, the tonal focus for each of the six strophes, and a summary of the dramatic transformation Orfeo undergoes as he sings. "Roadmaps" like this one are my usual solution to the problem of presenting the fine points of analytical music aesthetics to people who do not read music. The essential point to be made about "Possente spirto" is that the composer's choice of form is not an accident, not simply the use of a conventional formula upon which to map abstract and unrelated elements of melody and harmony. By choosing the strophic variation form for this particular moment in the story, Monteverdi not only provides his main character with a perfect vehicle for his legendary musical talent, but he also exploits the potential of that musical structure to serve as a mirror of dramatic progression and character development. In Monteverdi's hands, the simple strophic song form becomes a complex and detailed representation of Orfeo's fluctuating emotional/psychological condition, revealing much more to us about his dual nature than words alone could ever convey.[7]

How is this done? We begin by identifying the specific words and phrases that are emphasized through the madrigalistic device of tone-painting. For example, there is the wandering melodic line at the opening of strophe three, which convincingly projects the image of Orfeo groping blindly through the darkened Underworld. Among other instances, there is the crushingly dissonant appoggiatura at the end of strophe five when Orfeo begs for relief from his suffering, the cascading melodic gesture in strophe three at the mention of Euridice's beauty ("Tanta bellezza"), and the edgy intimidation implicit in the active accompaniment and jagged rhythms of the vocal line when he makes his name and his intention to transgress known to the gods in strophe four. Next, we examine the musical details that mark the seams of the strophic form itself. The first three stanzas (each with its own varied instrumental ritornello) consist of Orfeo's initial appeal to the Underworld, a narrative description of his terrible loss and emotional devastation. He attempts to draw sympathy, to flatter; but also he clearly means to impress his audience with the potency of his supernatural gifts. The instrumental ritornelli and internal interpolations serve as a subtle and mildly threatening subtext to the helplessness his petition would seem to imply. There can be little doubt of Orfeo's power to summon all the magic of music to his aid as first the strings, then the winds, and finally the harp gather around him, lending a regal authority to the pathos of his situation, a nobility befitting the sadness of a god—but also confirming the presence of a will that is not to be ignored. Thus through the simple technique of creative orchestration, Monteverdi positions a veritable army of celestial forces behind Orfeo's strophic song, making it almost inconceivable that his plea should go unanswered.

And yet it does. Astonishingly, at the end of strophe three no one is moved to let Orfeo pass, and he is compelled to adopt a more straightforward approach. The elaborate accompaniments disappear with strophe four, and he comes straight to the point: he is Orfeo! Only a demi-god, perhaps, but still enough of a god, and one determined to breach the gates of Hell in the interest of his great passion. As mentioned earlier, the force of Orfeo's personality is palpable in the tone-painting of strophe four, yet in the following stanza his resolve gives way completely to a wave of tenderness as his mode of address shifts from the gods of the Underworld to Euridice herself. The melodic range expands upward momentarily (at a reference to the life-giving light of her glance), and the tonal focus shifts correspondingly from a grim G minor to a joyous B-flat major.[8] By this point in the aria we have passed with Orfeo through the crucible of his power, his pain, and his desire—but to no avail. The Thracian singer stands defeated before a silent and immovable Plutone, his musical forces exhausted, his god-like status denied.

But in this last and decisive moment, it is the one aspect of Orfeo's nature that has yet to be developed in the music that finally causes the Underworld to yield. At the outset of strophe six, all blustering reference to supernatural power and divine status is abandoned: the bass line returns to its unornamented version, the melodic line becomes comparatively plain, and the accompaniment consists only of simple chords in the strings. Orfeo's grand and god-sized passion is revealed to be little more than an inconsolable and very mortal pain. Both textually and musically, the demi-god has been brought to his knees and for the first time in the aria, his helplessness, his humility, and—most important—his humanity rise to the fore. "Sol tu, nobile Dio." Only you, noble God, can help me now. In this final and desperate plea to recover the body and soul of his beloved Euridice, Orfeo at last relinquishes control of the situation and entreats the Underworld not to fear his song, for although it embodies a force that is divine, it works in the service of a love most human.

Thus the simple diagram of figure 6.3*a* not only articulates the formal structure of a strophic variation aria in a way that is easy for non-musicians to follow, but it also clarifies the compositional process by which Monteverdi exploits that form to reveal the humanity that lies within divinity, and both emphasize the mutual dependence of the one upon the other. The line of demarcation between Heaven and Earth is all but erased when Orfeo sings, and it is music that manifests the trans-substantiation. From Orfeo's experience we learn that song is the key to both realms, and that one single Being is capable of embodying that sacred space in which the things of God and the things of Man join and are purified in the combining. So too in our music appreciation classroom, our academic crucible, our little musical microcosm. *Solve et coagula*. "My" music and "their" musics unite, dissolve their differences, and re-combine to form a single, multi-faceted entity, one golden string in the fabric of the Cosmos.

## Conclusion

At the end of Unit I, we have met Orfeo and found that He is Us. Music is a tool for magical transformation, a means to awaken the divine within the human: the ancients believed in it, Orfeo proved it, and we, since that first day of class, have become increasingly aware of a similar force within ourselves. To develop and preserve that awareness is the ultimate goal of my music appreciation courses. I have no doubt that ten years after graduation, very few of my "non-musicians" will retain much of the technical and historical details we covered in class, nor will they possess more than a dim recollection of Beethoven's Ninth should it float past their ears on the car radio after work. But equally, I am certain that the seed of Orfeo will remain embedded deep within some soft fold of their souls, and will continue to work its magic from that silent place. My Destiny as their Fine Arts Requirement will have been fulfilled completely if, when attending some concert of the future, my former students look up from their programs and see a familiar image in their mind's eye, attend to the message of his song in their hearts. Whatever they may or may not have forgotten about "The Way of Music," the "Why" of music—of all music—which stood as the foundation of our time together will be with them forever. Once met, Orfeo is not easily forgotten. He will be their talisman, their guide, and their reminder that no music is beyond their reach, their understanding, and their deepest, most fully-human "appreciation." All they need do is listen, and pick up the thread … .

**Notes**

1     The title "Music Appreciation" is rarely used in course catalogs today, having been replaced by any number of trendier and more user-friendly designations. Whatever the class is called, however, its origin and function remain the same: it is the music department's contribution to the pool of undergraduate elective classes designed to broaden a student's base of knowledge beyond that of his or her own discipline and to encourage the kind of humanistically based thinking that is the ultimate goal of a liberal arts education.

2     This question in no way implies that non-majors have no interest in music; on the contrary, most of my music appreciation students speak eloquently about the music they know and care about most. The overwhelming majority, however, claim they have had next to no significant and/or positive prior contact with classical music. It is a sad fact of American culture, and one we address at length during class discussions, that the sound- and idea-world of Western art music is largely inaccessible through the regular channels of cultural transmission in the United States.

3     In addition to three music appreciation courses, Nazareth's music department has offered several other service courses in the past, reflecting the varied interests of our faculty. These include: "America's Music," "Music and Poetry," "Introduction to Opera," "Literature and Music of Germany," and "Celtic Music." In this essay I will discuss only my experiences with "The Way of Music," but suffice it to say that my basic assumptions as to what a music class for non-majors should be remain the same for any service course I teach.

4     I am fortunate at Nazareth in that these courses are rarely larger than twenty-five to thirty students. I find this size quite manageable in terms of class discussion, and it also allows me to include a sizable component of essay writing in their examinations.

5     I should make clear here that the choice to organize a music appreciation class chronologically is completely a matter of personal taste. Any method of organization—as well as any repertoire the teacher might choose—is suitable for the kind of course I outline in this essay. The key is not so much the method of presentation as it is the manner, the instructor's enthusiasm about the music, and his or her ability to embody and convey the nature of that enthusiasm to the students.

6     I use the 1984 EMI CD recording of *Orfeo* with Nigel Rogers as Orfeo when we are focusing just on the music and the 1988 Harnancourt/Ponelle video with Philippe Huttenlocher in the title role when we want to get the big picture. Despite the problems of vocal style and performance practice in this video, there is no getting around the dramatic impact of the production and its rate of success in overcoming the last shreds of resistance to opera among my students. After having watched many fine opera videos over the course of the semester, a

surprisingly large number of my students say at the end of the term that *Orfeo* remains their favorite in terms of plot, music, and visual spectacle.

7     Figure 6.3*b* illustrates exactly what is "strophic" about Orfeo's aria. We spend a little time discussing what we traditionally think of as strophic form, and the class comes up with any number of folk songs or nursery-rhyme settings to illustrate the concept. "Possente spirto," of course, does not appear to be strophic until we take a close look at figure 6.3*b*, which reveals the underlying formal organization provided by the strophic bass line. Even students who cannot read music are capable of understanding that strophes one, two, three, and six make use of the same bass line (simply by noticing where the black note-heads fall on the staff), while strophe four is an ornamented variation of it, and strophe five at least cadences in the same place.

8     In my music appreciation classes we do not fuss with the subtleties of correct modal terminology when it comes to describing harmony. For our very broad and general purposes, a clear distinction between the affect conveyed by a "minor" harmony as opposed to a "major" harmony is more than sufficient.

## FIGURE 6.1
### *L'Orfeo: favola in musica*

| | |
|---|---|
| Composer: | Claudio Monteverdi (1567–1643) |
| Librettist: | Alessandro Striggio (1573–1630) |
| Text sources: | Myth, Ovid, Virgil, Dante |
| Date & Place: | Court at Mantua, 1607 |
| Occasion: | Carnival entertainment |
| Structure: | Prologue and five acts |

*Act III*

Characters: Orfeo (tenor); Speranza (soprano); Caronte (bass); Choro de Spirti

| Character/number | Text form | Instrumental forces | Tonal center |
|---|---|---|---|
| Fanfare sinfonia | — | regal, cornetti, trombones | G |
| Orfeo | recitative | harp and basso continuo | c →G |
| Speranza | recitative | lute and b.c. | B-flat |
| Orfeo | arioso | harp and b.c. | a/A |
| Caronte | aria | regal | F/d |
| Procession sinfonia | — | not specified | g |
| *Orfeo* | *strophic aria* | *organ, harp, violins, cornetti, strings and b.c.* | *g/(B-flat)* |
| Caronte | aria (reprise) | regal | F/d |
| Orfeo | arioso | harp and b.c. | g |
| Procession sinfonia | — | viola da braccio, harp and b.c. | g |
| Orfeo | recitative | organ and harp | G |
| Fanfare sinfonia | — | regal, cornetti, trombones | G |
| Chorus | madrigal | full ensemble | G |

## FIGURE 6.2
### "Possente Spirto": Strophic Variation Aria *(terza rima)*

Strophe one
*Possente spirto, e formidabil nume,* A Powerful spirit, formidable god,
*Senza cui far passagio a l'altra riva* B without whom no soul, cast from its
*Alma da corpo sciolta invan presume.* A body can hope to gain passage to the opposite bank,

Strophe two
*Non viv'io, no, che poi di vita è priva* B I am no longer alive, since my dear wife is deprived of life,
*Mia cara sposa, il cor non è più meco,* C My heart remains no longer with me,
*E senza cor com'esser può ch'io viva?* B And without a heart, how can it be that I am still living?

Strophe three
*A lei volt'ho il cammin per l'aer cieco,* C I have made my way toward her through the dark air,
*A l'inferno non già, ch'ovunque stassi* D Yet not to Hell, since anywhere there is
*Tanta bellezza il paradiso ha seco.* C as much beauty as hers is paradise.

Strophe four
*Orfeo son io, che d'Euridice i passi* D I am Orfeo, who follows in the steps of Euridice
*Segue per queste tenebrose arene,* E through these shadowy wastes,
*Ove già mai per uom mortal non vassi.* D where mortal man has never set foot.

Strophe five
*O de le luci mie luci serene,* E O serene light of my eyes,
*S'un vostro sguardo può tornarmi in vita,* F If one glance from you can restore life to me,
*Ahi, chi niega il conforto a le mie pene?* E Who can deny me comfort in my suffering?

Strophe six
*Sol tu, nobile Dio, puoi darmi, aita,* F You alone, O noble god, can give me relief
*Né temer dei, ché sopra un'aurea cetra* G Nor should you be afraid, since my fingers are armed
*Sol di corde soavi armo le dita* F with nothing more than the sweet chords of a golden lyre
*Contra cui rigida alma invan s'impetra.* G Against which even the hardest of souls is powerless to resist.

**FIGURE 6.3a**
**"Possente Spirto"**
**Roadmap**

| Strophe | one & rit. | two & rit. | three & rit. | four | five | six |
|---|---|---|---|---|---|---|
| Text | "possente spirto" | "non vivo" | "a lei" | "Orfeo son io!" | "O de le luci mie" | "sol tu, nobile Dio" |
| Ritornello | violins | cornetti | harp | – | – | – |
| Tonal focus | g minor | g minor | g minor | g minor | B♭ major | g minor |
| Topic | narrative | | | assertion of power | reference to Euridice | surrender of power |

**FIGURE 6.3b**
**Strophic Bass Line**

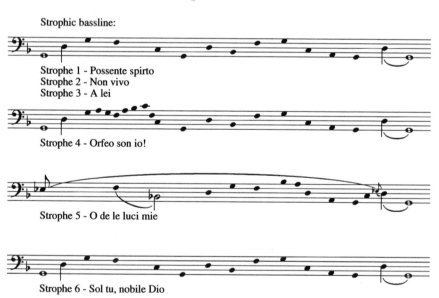

Chapter Seven

# *First Nights*: Awakening Students' Critical Skills in a Large Lecture Course

*Noël Bisson*

In the spring of 1995, *First Nights*: *Five Performance Premieres* was offered at Harvard for the first time. I was a third-year graduate student just beginning to teach, and, along with an assortment of other graduate students, I was recruited by Professor Thomas Kelly to join the teaching staff of his new course. Professor Kelly had taught *First Nights* to music students at Oberlin College prior to his coming to Harvard in the fall of 1994, but the Harvard version of the course was newly conceived for students with little or no background in music. All of us involved in that first rendition of *First Nights* felt that we were part of an exciting venture. The premise of studying performance premieres drew us in immediately, and we were certain that the students would react favorably. No one was sure how many students would decide to take the course, but it was anticipated (correctly) that the enrollment would be fairly large, certainly over 200 students. Since its first go-round at Harvard, *First Nights* has become one of the most heavily enrolled courses, and a large proportion of the Harvard undergraduate population takes the course before graduation. The tremendous success of the course has also spawned several side projects, including the creation of a detailed, interactive web site, and a book on writing about music.

*First Nights* is not a typical "music appreciation" course in that it is not a survey of a wide span of music history, nor is it an introduction to a particular period of music history. However, in at least one respect it certainly falls into the category of the big music appreciation course that non-majors often take at universities or colleges: *First Nights* generally attracts an enormous number of students—sometimes close to 800. In addition, the majority of the students who take this course have very little background in music.

Professor Kelly adapted the format and philosophy of *First Nights* to fit into Harvard's undergraduate program. The course is not offered through the music department but is instead given as part of the Core Curriculum. The Core program functions in much the way that "distribution requirements" work at other schools: Harvard undergraduates are required to take a certain number of Core courses in specially designated subject areas, depending on a student's choice of major. However, whereas non-majors at most schools will satisfy distribution requirements by taking introductory or survey courses within particular departments, often along with students majoring in that field, Harvard undergraduates must satisfy distribution requirements by taking Core courses that are not intended to satisfy departmental credit. (So, a Harvard undergraduate majoring in music would usually not take a music Core course, but would instead begin his or her course of study with a music department entry-level course.) Courses offered in the Core program should not be survey courses, nor should they focus on a narrow body of knowledge. They are instead intended to introduce students to "major approaches to knowledge" with an emphasis on teaching "a particular way of thinking," as stated in the Core guidelines.

In short, Core courses generally attract students with very little background in the subject. Music Core courses, on the other hand, like any big music course designed for non-majors at any school, tend to be a bit more complicated in this regard since many students with strong music backgrounds, but who happen not to have chosen to major in music, often need to take these courses to satisfy Core requirements. Thus, one of the many challenges of teaching a course such as *First Nights* is figuring out how to teach the course in a way that will not terrify and alienate students with no background in music and, at the same time, will not bore those who happen to have had years of piano and theory lessons.

*First Nights* looks at five important works in the Western classical canon: Monteverdi's *Orfeo*, Handel's *Messiah*, Beethoven's Symphony No. 9, Berlioz's *Symphonie fantastique*, and Stravinsky's *The Rite of Spring*. These works were chosen in part because each has a well-documented premiere. The course looks at these works in their cultural contexts and as timeless pieces of art. *First Nights* teaches techniques of musical listening in addition to addressing the numerous historical questions that surround each of the works. At the end of the course, after studying the reactions of listeners and critics at the premieres of each of these five works, the students are then asked to document their own reactions to a new piece of music. For this purpose, a piece is commissioned each year from a local composer, and the students are required to attend the premiere of the piece (which takes place during the last lecture of the semester) and then to document their reactions.

In studying the premieres of these five works the students learn not only about the pieces themselves but about reception history, performance practice, and about the importance of an audience's response to a piece of music. The students are taught to interpret contemporary criticism of the works and are encouraged to imagine how they themselves might have reacted to the premieres of each of the works. In this way the students begin to form an understanding of the works as cultural artifacts. Thus, even though the students do a fair amount of musical analysis along the way, the course is in fact much more than an analytical survey of the five works.

The materials required for the course currently include: a two-volume book of the complete score of each of the works and a textbook, which contains pictures, narrative, and readings (translated into English),[1] many of which are original source materials relating to the first performances. Although most of the students cannot read music very well (or at all) when they begin the course, by the end most feel comfortable (or at least familiar) with the scores. The students are expected to read extensively in the collection of documents and to mine the material there for use in their papers and section assignments.

Because *First Nights* has become one of the most popular courses offered in the Core, each year an army of teaching assistants is required. Such a large teaching staff (sometimes as many as fifteen teaching assistants) necessitates that the course be tightly organized with constant contact among the teaching assistants and with Professor Kelly. Regular staff meetings are essential. In addition, one teaching assistant takes on the role of Head Teaching Fellow and is responsible for the many organizational details that arise in a course of this size. The Head TF is often the liaison between Professor Kelly and the rest of the teaching staff; he or she also maintains the enrollment lists and divides the students into discussion sections.

*First Nights* presents many of the challenges that are inherent in a course of this type and size:

1. Reaching all of the students equally well when so much of the course takes place in a large lecture format.

2. Making sure that the students feel they can ask questions and speak directly to the professor and to the teaching assistants despite the large number of students in the course.

3. Conveying meaningful analysis of music in a way that is intelligible to the many students who have had no prior musical training.

4. Maintaining control of the substance of the course when the bulk of the teaching takes place in sections taught by a large teaching staff of varying backgrounds, interests, and experience.

5.  Maintaining continuity from year to year when the majority of the teaching staff changes.

6.  Making sure that every section leader is following, more or less, the same lesson plan, while still allowing for some variation resulting from individual teaching styles.

7.  Maintaining consistent grading standards across all the sections.

8.  Maintaining consistent grading standards when the students have such varied musical backgrounds ranging from no exposure at all to classical music to conservatory-trained students who have already had several years of music theory.

9.  Making sure that each student is encouraged to participate in the course to his or her fullest potential and that no student is lost in the shuffle.

*First Nights* is built around fifty-minute lectures that occur twice a week. The lectures are given by Professor Kelly and often incorporate live performances. Kelly's engaging and energetic approach to the pieces never fails to draw in the students. His obvious love for the music is infectious and helps to build the confidence of even the most timid students. Kelly's first lecture provides a pithy summation of the course with examples of some of the more well known passages from the five works. He also discusses the reasons for studying these works and how a piece of music can be viewed as a piece of culture. Most importantly, the lecture serves to draw the students in and to stress that the course, and, ultimately, these five pieces and the musical worlds from which they originated will be accessible to the students, even those with little or no musical background. One of the goals of *First Nights*, and, indeed, one would think of any music course designed for non-majors, is to open a new world to the students and to do it in such a way that the students' lives will be forever changed.

Although the lectures take place in a large lecture hall and Professor Kelly is up on a stage, he likes to maintain a certain informality, thereby giving the students the sense that they too are a part of the lectures. Kelly often throws out questions to the students, and someone will usually shout back an answer. After the lectures he is usually surrounded by students asking him questions. His incorporation of live performance in many of the lectures helps to break the barrier between stage and audience since many of the performers are the students' peers. The students become even more engaged and enthusiastic when they learn that a fellow undergraduate is about to perform. Kelly also maintains regular office hours and encourages the students to come find him. Although the students still deal mainly with their section leaders, Kelly's openness helps to dispel the shyness of many of the students who might otherwise feel too self-conscious to speak to a professor.

To begin a course for non-majors by looking at a work such as *Orfeo*, and then, a few short weeks into the semester, to require the students to write a paper on this work, is a tall order. Even those students with no familiarity with musical notation are required to plunge right in and look closely at the score of the opera. For *Orfeo*, the students are provided with the early seventeenth-century print, which throws off even those students with some security in reading scores and at first generates a large amount of bafflement and even fear. However, the old print provides the means to teach certain key elements of the course that would not be so easily learned through examining a modern transcription. In particular, the score offers a good lesson in issues of performance practice. Even those students who cannot read a note of music understand the idea that the score, as a representation of the music, must be interpreted by the performer. A live performance of Act II of the opera in class at the end of the unit on *Orfeo* illustrates many of the questions of performance practice that Kelly stresses in his lectures. For instance, the students hear the continuo section embellishing a passage with notes that do not appear in the score. Even if they are unable to read the actual notes, the students usually quickly understand the concept of ornamentation and can make the connection to the passage of music in the score. Kelly's lectures on *Orfeo* help the students to place the work historically and introduce them to the music. However, most of the close analysis of the music and the preparation for the paper takes place in the discussion sections.

In addition to the twice-weekly lectures, students are required to attend weekly fifty-minute section meetings. Much of the work of the course takes place in the sections, and here students are expected to discuss the material and participate in the various section assignments. At the end of the first week of the course, students are asked to fill out a brief questionnaire describing their familiarity with music and their musical training, if any. On the basis of these forms the Head TF then assigns each of the students to a section. The sections usually fall into one of two levels: "A" for students with the least musical experience, with little or no musical vocabulary, and little or no ability to read music, and "B" for the more advanced students, many of whom are very advanced indeed. Some students will, of course, fall somewhere in between the two extremes, and, depending on the composition of each section, some "A" sections will tend to be a bit more advanced than others are, while some "B" sections will need to do a bit more remedial work.

Although this system of sectioning tends to work fairly well with music Core courses, there are still a number of problems with it. Students often simply do not know how to rate themselves; I have encountered some students who acknowledge having had several years of piano lessons and a little theory, for instance, but feel that they "didn't learn anything" and therefore should be in a beginning section; similarly, some students over-rate themselves, often unintentionally. The brunt of sorting out section placement falls on the Head TF who must track down students with questionable section forms. Placing hundreds of students in sections, trying to accommodate specific scheduling requests while also being sure to place students in the correct level (in addition to making certain that there is a balance of male and female students and that no section contains, for instance, fifteen seniors and one freshman), is a logistical nightmare. Although Harvard has been working on its computerized sectioning system to allow it to work with the complexities of scheduling music Core courses, I have found that the best way to do sectioning is still the old tried-and-true method of sorting the piles by hand on my living room floor.

Over the five years that *First Nights* has been offered at Harvard, there have been a small number of teaching assistants who have taught the course several times. They have become an essential part of the teaching staff, taking new teaching assistants under their wings. Continuity in teaching staff is a great help in recreating the course each year, and, in order to facilitate this process, last year, in consultation with Professor Kelly, I wrote a manual for new *First Nights* staff. The manual outlines the various things that are expected of anyone teaching in the course and then offers teaching strategies and scenarios for the first-time teacher trying to develop an approach to teaching each of the five pieces in the sections. The manual has now been expanded from its original form to include a large supplement of all the teaching materials, handouts, and quizzes used by many of the teaching assistants who have previously taught the class.

The success of the course depends in large part on the success of the individual sections, for it is here that the students begin to develop a musical vocabulary by participating in weekly discussions and assignments. For this reason, it is essential that each of the teaching assistants be aware not only of the trajectory of the course and of how one section assignment should lead to the next, but also of the particular needs of the individual students in each section. Some students in some sections will need more remedial help with basic theoretical terms than other students, and the section leader must take these extra requirements into account. Moreover, it is essential that the section leaders know enough about their students to be able to anticipate and deal with a problem, should one arise. In a course that often has more than 500 students, it is impossible for the professor, or for anyone else, to keep tabs on each of the students. It is important that the section leader connect with each of his or her students right away from the first section—learning names and establishing a teaching style—so that the students know what to expect. The small section is the only place where real face-to-face contact happens, and the section leader holds great responsibility for keeping track of his or her students; taking attendance at each section is essential to make sure that no student is slipping through the cracks. I have found that in a course such as this the students depend greatly on their teaching assistant for guidance and, when necessary, for reassurance. For those students for whom the lecture hall is large, anonymous—and even scary— the section is a safe place for airing ideas.

Discussion of teaching strategies and of more and less successful approaches to the material dominate staff meetings. In such a large course, it would be easy for some sections to deviate from the norm. Although teaching assistants are always encouraged to be creative in their approaches to the material, and no single way of teaching is ever required of the section leaders, it is still important to make sure that all the staff are essentially working toward the same goals.

In order to narrow the gap between those students with some background in music and those students with little or none, the teaching staff offers a series of workshops in the first two weeks of the course. These fifty-minute workshops cover everything from the basics of staff notation to more advanced theory, such as basic harmonic progressions. All students are encouraged to attend as many workshops as they can. Of course a student with no musical training at all cannot be expected to pick up a working knowledge of music theory by attending a few workshops, but many of the basic questions about terminology can be answered here, saving valuable time in the section later in the semester. Students who attend these workshops come to their sections with at least a bit more knowledge than they might have had before.

The students in *First Nights* also have another resource, which is the course's web site. This site, password-protected so that only *First Nights* students have access, offers synopses of each of the five works along with interactive links providing musical examples where appropriate (for instance, where the text discusses a ritornello in *Orfeo*, the student can click on the highlighted word "ritornello" and hear the passage). More complicated links allow a student to isolate a passage of music, listening first, for instance, just to the rhythm of the passage, then to the melody, and then putting the two together. In addition, the site has a glossary of musical terms, again with interactive links, and a newly created theory tutorial. Numerous past and present teaching assistants have helped to create the site, and it is added to every year. The site is one of the most intricate of any associated with Harvard courses and has attracted much attention from people, both within and outside Harvard, interested in the educational uses of the web. Feedback from students has been positive, with many of them telling us that the interactive links have clarified several points that had come up quickly in lectures and sections. One of the greatest values of the site is that it allows a student to listen repeatedly to a passage in isolation from the context of the piece; a student having difficulty understanding the concept of meter, for instance, will find several examples of meter at the web site. The site also allows the students to post messages to the teaching staff and to Professor Kelly and encourages dialogue about the music and the course.

Although the level of musical discourse among the students in *First Nights* is usually lower than one would probably find among a group of music majors, the students in this course achieve a surprisingly high level of expression of musical ideas by the end of the semester. The students are certainly not expected to understand the complexities of music theory, nor are most of them even expected to fathom the intricacies of an orchestral score; they are, however, expected to be able to talk in fairly specific terms about the music itself. The assignments in the course are intended to build this fluency in discussing increasingly complicated notions of musical analysis.

From the very first lecture on *Orfeo*, the students are introduced to the idea of musical form. Monteverdi's use of ritornelli is something that everyone can hear, as is the structure of a strophic aria. In the sections the students further explore this idea of form in the opera. Some of the teaching assistants like to ask the students to come up with a list of all the different musical forms in one of the acts of the opera. Most of the students are unable to identify all the forms correctly, but this exercise accomplishes the much more important task of making the students listen actively to the music, requiring them to decide where one piece ends and another begins and to notice differences in musical style.

The technique of actively listening to music is one of the most difficult to teach, and much of the emphasis in sections in *First Nights* is given to developing this habit. Students with no musical training, and even those with some training, often have no idea of how to listen to a piece of music. For most of these students, music has generally constituted pleasant background noise. However, even those who seem most perplexed by the sudden demand that they discuss what they have heard can usually sing all of one of their favorite pop songs. Often, then, I have found that making an analogy to the music that these students know best works wonders in the early weeks of the course. I point out that if a student can sing the words of a favorite song he or she is clearly taking in some of what he or she is hearing. Many of these students feel intimidated by the idea of having to listen to classical music, and, thus, it is often useful to design an in-class exercise in which the students listen to, say, a Beatles song. Using this more familiar medium, I ask the students to listen to the song as I would have them listen to a passage from *Orfeo,* listening first, perhaps, for formal structure, then instrumentation, then for the melody, then the accompaniment, and, finally, the work as a whole. An example taken next from *Messiah* often works well too, since the style of the music is a little more familiar than is Monteverdi; this example also allows the students to feel competence in listening to a piece that they will later need to learn. It has been my experience that students with little familiarity with classical music tend to grasp vocal music more easily than purely instrumental, and in *First Nights* we are fortunate that the first two works are primarily vocal. The accessibility of vocal music may be due to the fact that there is text to follow in the score, which enables the less-skilled score readers to follow more easily, or perhaps to the fact that texts, at least in the pieces that appear in *First Nights*, are usually set to prominent melodies that allow for clear formal analysis.

Listening for formal divisions in the assigned works is stressed continuously during the semester; this technique is often the simplest for the students to apply, until, that is, they encounter Stravinsky. (The last movement of Beethoven's Ninth also leads to interesting discussions of form, especially in the advanced sections.) It is particularly important that the students practice listening for large structural patterns since the pieces become more complicated as the semester progresses. Of course, the students are also instructed to listen for other elements of the music as well. Always, however, the idea of comparing and contrasting, within a passage, within a work as a whole, or among two or more of the five works, is stressed: is this melody higher or lower than what came before? louder or softer? more angular? how does the instrumentation change? how has the mood changed? etc. The questions are endless, but always the students are asked to listen to a specific element of the music. Often I have found that when a particular passage stumps the students, as soon as I contrast the passage with another one—playing the two passages one after another—they are suddenly full of interesting observations. In this way, students are taught to use structured listening, that is repetitive listening that involves focusing closely on one element of the music at a time.

Although the focus and format of each section changes from week to week, the unifying emphasis is on clarity in talking about music. The students are taught that the listening skills they are developing are key to being able to talk about the music in a way that others will understand. But the big leap for most of the students is from speaking about the music to writing about it. Many of the section assignments, especially in the early weeks, are geared toward bridging this gap. All of the section leaders devise their own assignments, but a common type of assignment is to have the students write a short descriptive exercise about a particular passage of music. These short exercises allow students to develop the skills for writing longer analyses.

To facilitate this process of developing writing skills, *First Nights* uses a pamphlet, developed in the course, called *Writing about Music*. This pamphlet was largely written by a group of veteran teaching assistants and was revised and edited by Elizabeth Abrams, formerly of the Expository Writing program at Harvard. The pamphlet leads the students, step by step, from the initial stages of hearing a piece, making sense of what one hears as one gets to know the piece, beginning to come up with thoughts about the piece, writing a brief analysis, and, finally, taking several approaches to writing a long essay. In addition, students are able to work through and listen to the examples given in the book by visiting a web site that is tied to the pamphlet. Although we certainly do not expect the students to develop good writing skills simply by reading a pamphlet, many teaching assistants have found the exercises provided in *Writing about Music* to be useful and instructive. Also many students have found that working through the pamphlet on their own has helped reinforce the ideas that have come up in their sections. Most importantly, using the pamphlet helps make the point that good writing about music can develop only through consistent practice. Once the students understand this fact, the anxiety levels about producing the main written work for the course diminish markedly.

In spite of this, however, the papers the students must write for this course still produce a great deal of anxiety, and for this reason it is all the more important that they be well prepared for writing. I believe that the worry that *First Nights* students feel when confronted with their first writing assignment is typical of that felt by most students taking a music course for the first time. "How on earth do I begin to write about something as ephemeral as music?" they ask. Compounding the fear in *First Nights*, however, is that the two paper topics seem at first to be impossibly difficult to novice music students. The first topic is about *Orfeo* and requires the students to draw specific examples from the music to support their arguments; the second paper is a personal account of the new work commissioned for the course and heard for the first time in the lecture at the end of the semester. Here again the importance of the section comes to the fore because it is there that the students gain the confidence necessary to make their first forays into music analysis.

The papers are not entirely analytical, however, and reflect the other equally important element of the course—the idea of audience response to a piece never before heard. In the first writing assignment, the students are asked to compare their own reactions to *Orfeo* with the reactions of an imagined contemporary listener hearing the premiere of the work. The students must use specific evidence both from the work itself and from the original documents provided in the textbook. The second assignment goes a step beyond the imagined response to *Orfeo* by requiring the students now to become the critics of a new work. The challenge here is that the students will hear the work performed only once (they also hear a warm-up rehearsal); they have no access to a score of the work and must rely entirely on their listening skills, so carefully developed over the previous two and a half months. The students are generally extremely worried about this second paper, since there is little preparation they can do for it. Most rise to the occasion, however, finding the process of listening to the piece and then reporting on it to be a wonderful challenge and even a liberating experience after spending the semester reading about other people's reactions to the five main works in the course. Often students take great delight in being able to say categorically that the new work is "good" or "bad." The better students have learned that such statements need to be supported with strong evidence from the piece itself.

The question of how to grade a paper that is a subjective assessment of a work of music always comes up in staff meetings. Indeed, grading this final paper is sometimes difficult for the teaching assistants (who do all the grading in the course). Maintaining parity between sections and within sections is one of the great challenges of any course of this size. How to compare a beginning-level student's paper with a paper written by a more advanced student and then how to assign grades are also thorny questions. Despite different musical backgrounds, however, both authors can be held to the same standard of clarity of writing. One should expect the more advanced student to be able to use more sophisticated analytical vocabulary, but both students should be able to write a carefully organized and clearly argued essay. Some of the most thoughtful and perceptive papers that I have read in music Core courses were written by students with the least musical background.

Although much has been said here about the difficulties of teaching such a large number of students, I cannot finish without mentioning some of the many advantages afforded *First Nights* by virtue of its size. Some of the disadvantages of such a large teaching staff were listed above, but in fact the size of the staff can also be advantageous. The weekly staff meetings usually include substantial discussions of teaching strategies, and in these meetings each teaching assistant is asked to describe what he or she did in a section and to assess what worked well and what did not; often new approaches to the material emerge in these discussions, and the fresh pool of teaching assistants each year allows for numerous new approaches. These meetings are also often attended by a consultant from the Derek Bok Center for Teaching and Learning, which provides various kinds of support for teachers at Harvard including individual, private consultations with any teacher who wishes for some feedback on his or her teaching style. The Bok Center, affiliated with Harvard's Faculty of Arts and Sciences, works with anyone teaching Harvard undergraduates, but usually only particularly large courses, such as *First Nights*, attract a consultant to the staff meetings. The size of the course also has allowed for the marshaling of resources that smaller courses probably cannot manage. The course's web site continues to grow thanks to several grants, as do *Writing about Music* and the teaching assistant manual. The course's size and innovative approach have attracted collaboration with the Expository Writing Program at Harvard, and a consultant from that program also regularly attends staff meetings.

*First Nights* is offered each fall at Harvard and will likely continue to attract another 500 or so students, eager to be initiated into the magical world that the course creates and, at the same time, apprehensive about taking a music class for the first time. For many, *First Nights* will be their only taste of the academic study of music. It is these students in particular that the course strives to touch. Although some who take *First Nights* may never again listen to the five works that are the focus of the course and may never attend a concert of classical music again in their lives, it is hoped that for a great many more the course will serve as a catalyst for future forays into the world of music. For many students, the course leads to newfound interest in the field, and several of my beginning-level students have gone on to take entry-level courses in the music department. Many other graduates of the course begin to go to concerts given by the Harvard-Radcliffe Orchestra, Boston Symphony Orchestra, Handel and Haydn Society, and the many other music groups at Harvard and in the Boston area. It is a wonderful feeling, as a veteran teaching assistant, for me to run into a former student in the classical music section of one of the local record stores in Harvard Square. I hope that *First Nights* will spawn a whole generation of new lovers of music.

**Note**

1     Thomas Kelly, *First Nights: Five Musical Premiers* (New Haven: Yale University Press, 2000).

# Topics Courses

# Chapter Eight

# Teaching "Women in Music"

## *Mary Natvig*

What and how we teach reflect what we value, either as individuals, a profession, or a culture. Most of us (including our students) have been taught music history in a traditional way—by examining a canonical repertory of "masterworks" by male composers. Because I appreciate, enjoy, and in many cases adore that body of works, I am not sorry that my students receive this information. However, I have come to value the presence of others in the musical story: of women, minorities, amateurs, etc. In order to teach with integrity, I find myself compelled to include these "others" in my courses.

Several years ago the director of the Honors Program at Bowling Green State University asked me to teach an undergraduate honors seminar. The course could be on any musical topic and should have an interdisciplinary focus; it would enroll both music majors and non-majors and he predicted there would be fifteen to twenty students in the class—a luxury for me since I was used to at least fifty to sixty students in my survey courses. Thus, the "Women in Music Seminar" was born and the first obstacle facing a course of this kind—how to establish its presence in an otherwise crowded curriculum—was serendipitously avoided.

Although the class is not a part of our prescribed music curriculum, it does enroll several music majors each semester it is offered, and non-honors students may take the class with permission of the instructor. Therefore, any student who is motivated and competent can enroll. In this way, the class sneaked in the back door of our curriculum; it is there for students as an elective and its very presence validates the study of music from a perspective other than the one offered by the standard music history surveys.

Given the paltry coverage of women in most music history textbooks, one would think that an overabundance of material would not be a problem in this course. Over the last ten years, however, the field has grown so much that it is now difficult to decide what to include on the syllabus. Women in classical music? Women in jazz? Non-Western music? Popular music? Women as patrons, performers, scholars, composers, educators? Gender issues or feminist analysis? Each of these alone could form the basis for an entire semester. My own choice has been to develop seven categories of varying and flexible lengths: (1) Music and power, (2) Where are the women? (they've all gone crazy), (3) History of women in classical music, (4) Changing roles, (5) Women from a cross-cultural perspective, (6) Women in popular music, and (7) Introduction to feminist criticism. Each time I teach the course, I choose two or three of these units to emphasize, including the others in the syllabus but in far less depth. The resulting flexibility easily reflects my own strengths and changing curiosities as a teacher and scholar, the availability of my colleagues who graciously appear as guest lecturers, and the strengths and interests of my students.

## Women and power

For this unit I have the students read "Difference and Power in Music" by John Sheperd, "Gender, Professionalism and the Musical Canon" by Marcia Citron, and "Gender and Power in Music" by Ellen Koskoff.[1] Here we try to define power, observe its presence in our own sub-cultures and identify the kinds of power music has in those cultures. We examine the concept of a canon, how it upholds the power structure in Western society, and what kinds of music have subverted or could subvert that structure. At first the students are rather reluctant to assign any significant kind of power to music, a "harmless entertainment," after all, until I tell them how I *did not* see The Beatles on their first appearance on the Ed Sullivan Show because of how they were then perceived by the conservative "establishment." My father, in fact, forbade us to watch them, as he thought their music was dangerous and that John, Paul, George and Ringo, with their "long" hair, were hoodlums. I am sure my father thought that rock'n'roll was the end of Western Civilization as we knew it. In fact, in the early 1960s there was a change in Western Civilization as *he* knew it and music helped to signify the shift. With this anecdote, the students can then see how their own experiences with music have sometimes meant more than they realized. Once the idea that music may hold cultural or political power is realized, students begin to share their own encounters with music and commercialism, music as a cultural delineator, and music as a political force.

## Where are all the women (they've all gone crazy)

This unit examines the idea that creative women who veer from mainstream roles are often perceived as odd, crazy, and even clinically mentally ill. It provides fertile ground for comparative studies with other artistic disciplines. I have the class read Linda Nochlin's article, "Why Have There Been No Great

Women Artists?" that explores various reasons for the lack of women painters.[2] We keep these reasons in mind when studying the lives of female musicians and inevitably find similarities. Then we examine what happens when women's creativity is suppressed. A New Zealand poet who is forced to be a teacher finds her despair misdiagnosed as schizophrenia and must live much of her life in a mental hospital (*Angel at My Table* [1990], a film about Janet Frame). A writer is unsuccessfully domesticated to the point of being subsumed by the suffocating, monstrous vines in "The Yellow Wallpaper" (a short story by Charlotte Perkins Gilman).[3] And Margaret of Scotland (fourteenth century) dies from consorting with her women attendants who "keep her up all night writing *rondeaux* and *ballades*."[4] Sometimes the students see their mothers or grandmothers in this unit—not crazy, we hope—but unhappily forced into roles they would not have chosen if other options had been available.

## History of women in classical music

I consistently choose this unit as one to emphasize since it corresponds to my interests in monastic women and my own training as a historical musicologist. We use Karin Pendle's venerable *Women and Music: A History*[5] but, like the variable time spent on each unit, the amount of emphasis on each chapter is flexible, depending on the semester. For each section we cover I have the students choose one of various supplemental reading assignments so that each person has an area of "expertise" to bring to the discussion. Here I present my own research and interests on women in convents. I concentrate on the process of my investigation rather than the results, which engages the students far more critically than a formal presentation. It also sets the stage and piques their interest for the study of women and music in the Middle Ages and Renaissance. If possible, for the units on the common practice era, I ask music students to perform in class; and for contemporary music I invite my colleague, composer Marilyn Shrude, to speak to the class about her works, compositional process, and life experiences. The students are often quite surprised to realize that "classical" music is still being composed, especially by someone who lives within a mile of the campus. Shrude's description of composing at the kitchen table at three in the morning (after feeding her babies—one of whom is now a BGSU student) illustrates the challenges still faced by women professionals in a far more personal and vivid way than any lecture or reading I could possibly assign.

## Changing roles

This topic embraces any number of concepts. Because both our tuba teacher and our university orchestra director are women, I usually concentrate on women's positions as conductors and symphony musicians. Kay Lawson has written an article on women conductors in *The Musical Woman*,[6] and I also have the class read Carol Neuls-Bates's article on women's orchestras.[7] Both of my colleagues generously come to class and share their experiences in two of the last bastions of male domination (in music). We have also followed the controversial ban on women in the Vienna Philharmonic with great interest and incredulity on the part of all of us. Finally, this is the unit where we watch Jack Lemmon and Tony Curtis disguising themselves as "girl" jazz musicians in *Some Like it Hot* (1959). As the impostors limp along in high heels in frantic pursuit of the band's sexy singer (played by Marilyn Monroe), the movie outrageously illustrates nearly every gender stereotype imaginable—and it is great fun to watch.

## Women from a cross-cultural perspective

We are fortunate at my university because we have a Balinese gamelan, an Afro-Carribbean dance and drumming ensemble, and summer workshops to both Bali and Ghana—all of which I have participated in. With these resources we are able to offer hands-on experience for the unit on non-Western women. According to student evaluations, the most captivating session of the course is when the class takes a "field trip" to the gamelan room to learn a simple piece. In order to prepare for studying music from a "foreign" culture, however, I ask them to think about the place of music within their home of origin. Some students come from strongly ethnic backgrounds and are able to speak cogently on how music's role in their home was distinct from that of other families. Even if music or ethnicity was not prominent in a student's background, he/she can still talk about family religious and holiday rituals and/or cultural assumptions that differ from those of college friends. Other students come from musical cultures that highlight different aspects of popular culture (Mom listened to jazz and Dad liked country) and these, too, are cross-cultural as we find out when the Rave fans in the class begin to interact with the Christian rock followers. All of these explorations lead to a self-awareness that is the first step toward cultural awareness. Once we have examined our own cultural "baggage," we can more easily examine the musical traditions of more distant cultures. Thus, our trip to the gamelan room or our donning of authentic

African cloth (which I bring in) and dancing to *Ewe* drumming patterns is seen as a natural expression of another culture, rather than something weird. (One of my fondest memories of this class is the time the Honors Director, a rather buttoned-down English professor, decided to observe me on the African dance day. We wrapped him in cloth and had him dancing *Agbadja*, a dance from Ghana, which to the uninitiated looks strikingly similar to the *Funky Chicken*.)

## Women in popular music

In this unit we read excerpts from Reynolds's and Press's *Sex Revolts: Gender, Rebellion and Rock'n'Roll*.[8] I show a powerful (though now dated) critique of the misogyny on MTV called *Dreamworlds: desire, sex, power in rock video*, [9] and we analyze clips from several Madonna videos to prepare for our debate: "Is Madonna a feminist?" I usually have to assign students to take the negative side but it is a good exercise for them; and first we have to define what a feminist *is*—not an easy task and it often differs from class to class. (Madonna can, of course, be replaced by other, more contemporary female artists, but as long as she remains current in the minds of the students I think she works particularly well for this exercise.)

Most of the students choose to do their final papers on women in popular music, so this unit expands enormously at the end of the semester with presentations on women artists not covered in class. This is fortunate for me for it is admittedly my weakest area, though I have learned so much from my students, and over the years of teaching this course have even expanded my pop CD collection by nearly 100 discs.

## Introduction to feminist criticism

This unit focuses on opera, which I think is the most approachable way to introduce critical theory, especially to non-music majors. Here we read sections from Susan McClary's writings[10] in addition to the chapter in Pendle's book, "Recovering Jouissance: An Introduction to Feminist Musical Aesthetics."[11] We examine a video of *Carmen* in light of McClary's remarks and we attend the university's opera production (whatever it may be) as a group, keeping in mind questions of gender depiction in text/drama, music, and the director's interpretations. For most of my students, this will be the first live opera they see.

## Music majors vs. non-music majors

One of the advantages of teaching a course on women in music is the incredible availability of materials on the world wide web.[12] I have benefited greatly from posted syllabi and discussions on teaching women in music on various professional lists; I have found that one of the main concerns of most instructors is how to develop a course that includes both music majors and non-majors. Some instructors screen students to make sure they have at least nominal music reading ability. Others accept anyone and have no reading or analytical skills required. Still others have varying expectations and requirements of the different majors.

I do not assume that the students in my class can read music (though of course, some do). In my experience the mixture of music and non-music majors has advantages and disadvantages. The obvious drawback is that most of the non-majors, in addition to not reading music, have had little, if any, background in either music history or theory. (Although many students who are attracted to the course have participated in their high school band, orchestra, or choir, others have had no musical background or exposure to music other than pop or country.)

On the other hand, students from other majors usually enliven our discussions as their attitudes toward music, especially classical music, are quite different from the music majors. Also, they are often more adept at referring to literature, science, philosophy, etc. than our music majors, whose curriculum is limited almost exclusively to music courses. For the first few class periods the non-music majors seem nervous about their perceived lack of musical preparation. They soon find out, however, that neither group knows much about gender issues or women in classical music, and most of the time the non-music majors know more about women in popular music than many of the music majors. I try to be sensitive to these issues at the beginning of the course in order to keep the playing field even between the two groups of students.

Only once in the course do I consciously use specific music theory terms to present a topic; this demonstrates to the music majors how to apply what they have learned in their theory classes and introduces the non-majors to simple analysis and the technical side of music. In the unit on Romantic music I bring in a sentimental favorite of mine, Clara Schumann's *Liebst du um Schönheit,* and show how the song is structured in conjunction with the text.[13] Here I ask the music majors to talk about specific chords and tonal relationships, phrases, rhythms, and melodic characteristics that delineate the form. I ask the other students to discuss the text. Both groups learn well from each other and realize that, regardless of their major, everyone is able to contribute to the class in some way. Once in a while there will be a music major who wants a more musically analytical experience in the course. Because the course content is flexible, I can either include that in a unit (depending on the abilities of the class) or give the student extra credit for exploring the topic independently.

## An inclusive classroom

Just as the subject matter of the course implies inclusion and validation of a traditionally marginal group, I try to model those same principles in the classroom atmosphere. My goal is to encourage everyone in the class to contribute and use his or her knowledge and gifts to enhance the group's learning. bell hooks's ideas have informed and inspired my own classroom style. She writes,

> As a classroom community, our capacity to generate excitement is deeply affected by our interest in one another, in hearing one another's voices, in recognizing one another's presence. Since the vast majority of students learn through conservative, traditional educational practices and concern themselves only with the presence of the professor, any radical pedagogy must insist that everyone's presence be acknowledged. That insistence cannot be simply stated. It has to be demonstrated through pedagogical practices. To begin, the professor must genuinely *value* everyone's presence.[14]

To this end I work for a non-hierarchical classroom: we sit in a circle, I lecture as little as possible, we have numerous discussions with guests and each other, and I freely admit that I will learn as much from them as they will learn from me. I establish ground rules at the beginning of the course regarding inclusive language and what I call language parallels. In other words, if males are referred to as men (boys or gentlemen) then females are women (girls or ladies)—not men and girls, or even worse, men and ladies. It may seem like a trivial concern, but the difficulty the students have at first referring to females as *women* (rather than ladies or girls) confirms the inherent sexism in our choice of language. In addition, while most students would never refer to Mozart in their papers as "Wolfgang," they usually refer to women composers by their first names ("Clara played the piano and Schumann [Robert] composed"), so gender equality must extend to the students' writing as well. After I set the ground rules I find it is most effective to let the students monitor each other's lapses; since these are difficult habits to break, we generally approach the whole matter with a sense of humor rather than dogmatically. Interestingly, I find that the men who elect a class on women in music are far more sensitive to inclusive language and sexist behaviors than many of the women. (These are issues that may not pertain to every situation. BGSU attracts many rural students, some of whom are the first in their families to go to college. Their level of awareness, sophistication, and family backgrounds vary widely.)

The other classroom etiquette I insist on is no "male-bashing." This is not to protect the men in the class, but to uphold the idea of equal value between the sexes rather than dominance on anyone's part. This usually leads to a discussion of patriarchy versus matriarchy and the inherent flaws in each, from a feminist perspective. I like to introduce the term "partnership model" borrowed from Riane Eisler's *Chalice and the Blade*, in which she describes a society where men's and women's roles may historically have been different but equally valued.[15] With partnership rather than power as our classroom goal, we can then seek to understand the cultural atmosphere that creates "-isms," in particular sexism, with less animosity toward men in general who may or may not be personally responsible for sexist behavior. (A few of my women students have told me that this classroom style is more conducive to their learning than the sometimes abrasive tone they encountered in some women's studies courses.)

One has to remember, however, that anger, and often anger toward men, can be a normal part of a women's growing awareness of historical and culturally inherent sexism. It is a natural and expected stage of consciousness. Most of my women students begin the course claiming they have never experienced, or seen in others, any discrimination based on their sex. As the semester progresses many students, male and female, begin to look at these issues more critically and often there are personal emotional ramifications. One student, who adamantly maintained at first that she had never been discriminated against, shared with the class her agony in high school where, since she had a mature voice and body, she was the victim of false rumors that alleged sexual misconduct with the school choir director.

While I encourage students to share their epiphanies with the class, in some cases it can be necessary to talk to them in more depth privately. The classroom is not a place for therapy. To that end, it is important to know when teaching ends and counseling begins, in which case the student should be referred to a qualified professional. While personal issues sometimes do arise in other kinds of courses, I have found that this class is particularly ripe for them. I keep a drawer in my desk full of pamphlets from Counseling Services, the Rape Crisis Center, and the Women's Center on campus. When student evaluations come back with "I will never look at the world or fit in the world in the same way," I realize that I have a greater than usual responsibility toward these students. This course, then, is about much more than content. Because my values compel me to expose my students to a different world view and to encourage them to recognize, critique, and assess their own values, the course can be unsettling at one extreme, overwhelming at the other. While the students and I are ostensibly examining "women in music," I find that we are really exploring our place in the world, and this is where the real learning begins.

### Notes

1    John Sheperd, "Difference and Power in Music," in *Musicology and Difference*, ed. Ruth Solie (Berkeley: University of California Press, 1994), 46–65; Marcia Citron, "Gender, Professionalism and the Musical Canon," in *Journal of Musicology* 8 (1990): 102–17; and Ellen Koskoff, "Gender and Power in Music," in *The Musical Woman* 3 (1990): 669–788.

2    Linda Nochlin, "Why Have There Been No Great Women Artists?" in *Art and Sexual Politics: women's liberation, women artists, and art history*, eds. Thomas B. Hess and Elizabeth C. Baker (New York: Collier, 1973), 1–43.

3    Charlotte Perkins Gilman, *The Charlotte Perkins Gilman Reader: The yellow wallpaper and other fiction*, ed. Ann J. Lane (New York: Pantheon Books, 1980), 270–82.

4    Paula Higgins, "The 'Other Minervas': Creative Women at the Court of Margaret of Scotland," in *Rediscovering the Muses: women's musical traditions*, ed. Kimberly Marshall (Boston: Northeastern Press, 1993), 172–3.

5    Karin Pendle, *Women and Music: A History* (Bloomington: Indiana University Press, 1991).

6    Kay Lawson, "Women Conductors: Credibility in a Male Dominated Profession," in *The Musical Woman* 3 (1990): 197–219.

7    Carol Neuls-Bates, "Women's Orchestras in the United States, 1935–45," in *Women Making Music: The Western Art Tradition 1150–1950*, eds. Jane Bowers and Judith Tick (Urbana: University of Illinois Press, 1986), 349–69.

8    Simon Reynolds and Joy Press, eds., *The Sex Revolts: Gender Rebellion and Rock 'n' Roll* (Cambridge, MA: Harvard University Press, 1995).

9    Sut Jhally, *Dreamworlds: desire, sex, power in rock video* [videorecording, n.p.], 1990.

10   Susan McClary, "The Undoing of Opera: Toward a Feminist Criticism of Music," Foreward in Catherine Clément's *Opera, or the Undoing of Women* (Minneapolis: University of Minneapolis Press, 1988) and Georges Bizet,

*Carmen: Cambridge Opera Guide*, ed. Susan McClary (Cambridge and New York: Cambridge University Press, 1992).

11     Pendle, *Women and Music*, 331–40.

12     There are many, but the two I use most often are the links provided on the web pages of the American Musicological Society and the Society for Music Theory.

13     See James R. Briscoe, ed., *Historical Anthology of Music by Women* (Bloomington: Indiana University Press, 1987), 172.

14     bell hooks, *Teaching to Transgress* (New York: Routledge, 1994), 8.

15     Riane Eisler, *The Chalice and the Blade* (San Francisco: Harper Collins Publishers, 1987).

Chapter Nine

# Teaching Film Music in the Liberal Arts Curriculum

*Michael Pisani*

In many undergraduate curricula, courses such as American music, world music, and film music are offered as liberal arts electives rather than as credits toward a degree program. Music majors often are not expected to take these, nor can they in many circumstances, when their course loads are filled to capacity with required surveys of Western art music, theory, sight singing and keyboard skills, and private lessons, etc. At my educational institution, Vassar College, such is the case when it comes to "Music in Film," a course I have developed over the last three years. My focus in this essay, therefore, will be on teaching film music to non-majors, students with little to wide-ranging musical backgrounds, though many of the ideas can be adapted to a class of music majors.

Students are generally enthusiastic about studying film music because many already have a personal connection through favorite films and soundtrack recordings. The course at Vassar is designed to expand students' knowledge of what film music is, its variety, how it is created, how it functions, what its historical traditions have been, and to some degree what exceptional works have been written. While some of the best film music is often stylistically indebted to other musical media—folk, non-Western, and particularly the classical symphonic genres of the nineteenth and early twentieth centuries—film music is undoubtedly popular music. But understanding film music as a genre also means recognizing its formal connections to the technical apparatus of the film medium. This class is designed to emphasize and explore these connections.

From a musical standpoint, it would be possible to teach the rudiments of theory, listening skills, dictation, and style, all from the vast array of film music. In fact, it may seem that for those students with little background in music one would have to spend much class time on basic musical terms and concepts. Some traversing of rudimentary principles is necessary (especially since it is extremely difficult to talk about music without using a shared vocabulary of some kind). The technical vocabulary of most conservatory-trained musicians, however, is too technical, too context-laden for the non-musician. The search for accurate and meaningful terms that do not dilute concepts provides a continuous challenge. The challenge is doubled in a course on film music because one often has to teach entirely without the usual guideposts of written music. Scores or excerpts may not be available or easily accessible without foresight and advanced planning. (More about this later.) From the instructor's point of view, this can seem a remarkable disadvantage, since most of us are used to teaching with scores and transcriptions. One advantage, however, is that the whole problem of notation and the ability to read music does not get in the way of communication about music as sound. Under these circumstances, I have to rethink nearly every musical term that is second nature to me and in the process must find new means of conveying essential musical information. Sometimes standard music terminology works just fine, as long as I take the time in the right instance to explain simply and vividly what individual terms mean. I usually wait for a context where there is not a more appropriate word and at that point introduce the technical term ("accent," "dissonance," or "chromatic," for example). The students seem receptive to learning terminology this way, for they have an immediate grasp of its usefulness as a tool of communication, rather than as a linguistic sign with too many foreign or cultural associations. Gradually, many of the students with little or no musical background find themselves talking more freely about the fundamentals of music and doing so in ways that sometimes allow for interesting readings to emerge.

## Choosing the repertory

One of the goals of the course is to introduce students to the wide range of musical styles and aesthetic approaches used in narrative film. For this reason, I try to include examples from European, Russian, and Asian film, and American experimental as well as Hollywood movies. Invariably, however, the bulk of films that we study nearly always consists of mainstream English-language cinema. This still allows me the opportunity to explore an enormous variety of Western and non-Western classical and popular styles in film music. Major film composers' styles also vary considerably, and we study examples from Miklos Rozsa to Bernard Herrmann, from Henry Mancini to Lalo Schifrin, Duke Ellington to Quincy Jones, Erich Wolfgang Korngold to John Williams, William Walton to Rachel Portman, Danny Elfman to Hans Zimmer, and Aaron Copland to John Corigliano. In fact, the choice is so great that one can easily feel at sea when choosing a balanced repertoire of films. Is there a "canon" of film composers we should be teaching, I ask myself? Or, if not a canon of composers, is there a body of significant films that have historically important scores? Even if the answer from the film music scholars were a decided yes, a historical approach may not be an ideal pedagogical solution for this genre. Most of the current textbooks on film music address these questions differently and with surprisingly little overlap.[1]

In May 1999 it was possible to find online a well-maintained site dedicated to film music that listed the "fifty major film scores of all time" (called "the Essential Collection").[2] One tends to find in such compilations a number of recurring films, among them, *King Kong, Laura, Psycho, To Kill a Mockingbird,* and *Patton.* Each of these works pioneers new techniques in film music:

Max Steiner in *King Kong* (1933)—the first use of the through-composed dramatic score by a single composer for a feature-length sound film;

David Raksin in *Laura* (1944)—the use of a pervasive (almost hypnotic) theme song in a jazz style;

Bernard Herrmann in *Psycho* (1960)—a non-standard use of orchestral instruments (strings) to convey abnormality, insanity, and terror;

Elmer Bernstein in *To Kill a Mockingbird* (1962)—for music that expresses a young girl's vision of a complicated adult situation; and

Jerry Goldsmith in *Patton* (1969)—for his combined use of varying motives, subtle orchestration, and electronic enhancement to suggest the complex temporal relationships between past and present that motivate the actions of the hero-general.

One consistency among most texts is an emphasis on the so-called classical scoring tradition that predominated in Hollywood cinema from 1930 to about 1960. During these years, composers such as Alfred Newman and Franz Waxman wrote under contract for a single studio in return for being granted the freedom to develop a signature style. While studio composers had to face the addition of a few dialogue and sound-effects tracks, these generally did not threaten the integrity of the personal dimension that their score added to the film. Today, composers are often hired on contract and there is more pressure to produce a product in line with the studio's idea of a successfully marketable film. Moreover, producers and sound engineers use hundreds of tracks, several for dialogue, sometimes dozens or even hundreds for sound effects and music.

The whole mix is often referred to as "sound design." The product is shaped not solely by the vision of director and composer, but also by the sound editor, the sound mixer, the foley (or sound-effects) artists, and the sound engineer—in other words, by a large creative team. Most published studies dealing with music in film have yet to unravel the sound/music synthesis that film theorist Michel Chion calls the film's "superfield."[3] In addition, detailed studies of individual film scores are rare. In their coverage of the 1980s and 1990s, most textbooks offer little more than lists of information on composers and films. But even for the period 1927 to roughly 1980, authors do not seem to agree on a canon of films beyond a handful of titles such as those mentioned above.

The lack of consensus, on the other hand, affords an opportunity to shape a course to suit one's own teaching strengths and to take into account the skills and interests of the students. The search for "canonic masterpieces" in this genre may in fact pose more problems than it solves. Film music, unlike that of other music media, is first and foremost functional.[4] It assumes a subordinate role to the film's diegesis (or "story space"). Even from this position, music may overwhelm the images given its range of emotional possibilities. An example can be seen and heard in Michael Curtiz's *Mildred Pierce,* a 1940s *film noir* melodrama starring Joan Crawford, with music by Max Steiner.[5] This is not the type of score that is likely to appear on a top-fifty list. As many students have discovered, however, it is a masterpiece of the genre. Unlike Thomas Newman or James Newton Howard working today, Steiner wrote for an existing Warner Brothers studio orchestra in an emotive style, essentially rubber-stamped by the studio heads. But he also knew that much of his underscoring of plot exposition would otherwise be submerged under dialogue in the mixing stage. In typical artisan fashion he provided plenty of work-a-day functional music in addition to several truly soaring moments. As head of the music staff at Warner, however, Steiner also enjoyed a certain prestige within the studio system. His direct influence in the post-recording sound mix allowed his music to emerge as more than functional. It surges forth at crucial moments of emotional catharsis projecting, even more than the dialogue and sound effects, a kind of "third dimension" to the two dimensionality of the film image (a quality of emotionalism Chion calls "added value").[6] Some of my students in their papers have gone so far as to say that the real drama of the film was actually in the music. And yet many of the students after their first viewing could not recall that there even *was* much music, so subtle was its operation. Though functioning to serve the film's diegesis, the music works at levels of sublimation that only become evident under close scrutiny. The film as a total visual/aural experience succeeds on an artistic level partly because of Steiner's music and his crucial dramatic sense.

One of the surprises encountered in studying film music is the discovery one inevitably makes of the range of musical invention that took place in the twentieth century outside the concert hall. The medium is rich with examples of composers' creativity in using thematic material, in developing musical ideas, and in shaping drama. My own first close encounter with this genre probably occurred at age ten when, in front of Sunday-afternoon television, I found myself transfixed by Korngold's magical sonorities and heroic motives in *The Prince and the Pauper*, Herrmann's cavernous organ-harp combinations in *Journey to the Center of the Earth,* and Alex North's stark evocation of "primitive" Egypt in *Cleopatra*. I later came to realize that I, as an incipient musician, had found films such as these emotionally gripping largely *because* of their music. The structure of my course and selection of films no doubt reflect my attraction to thematic scores, especially those large musical canvases that incorporate themes, motives, and musical characterization on many complex levels.[7]

A film such as Baz Luhrmann's 1996 *Romeo and Juliet*, on the other hand, uses the compilation technique, where songs and other musical numbers by several artists impose structure onto the drama but are not related to each other thematically. Since films such as Mike Nichols's *The Graduate* (1967) or Dennis Hopper's *Easy Rider* (1969), compilation scores drawn from popular music proved a compelling alternative to the thematic film-scoring technique of the earlier studio composers. Their marketability as soundtrack recordings has made the use of compilation scores an attractive commercial venture for large film studios.[8] Both types of scores survive in the present market, in the cinema as well as in soundtrack bins of music shops. The bulk of the emphasis in my course, however, is on thematic or "through-composed" music. For many students, this is "classical" music that they enjoy and feel comfortable talking about.

## The functional role of film music

The course contains three units of different lengths. The units are: (1) a study of music's functional roles in film; (2) an examination of the technical aspects of composing, orchestration, recording, mixing, and synchronization; and (3) a few studies of complete films. I like to involve the students immediately in the rich sound-world of film music and to get them thinking about why it is there, what it is doing, and what effect it has on them. In the first unit, we view a wide variety of clips from different films in varying styles and isolate the importance of a primary function in each. (In many cases there may be several functions in operation at once.) As early as 1949, Aaron Copland had listed "a number of ways in which music serves the screen."[9] Copland's five functions need to be considerably enlarged, qualified, and refined to account for the technical and stylistic developments of the last fifty years. The presentation of functions in the outline below (figure 9.1) has also been influenced by "Sound in the Cinema," in David Bordwell and Kristin Thompson's *Film Art: An Introduction*, as well as by separate publications by Claudia Gorbman, Michel Chion, Roy Prendergast, Fred Karlin, George Burt, Larry M. Timm, and from film-score reviews and published interviews with composers.[10]

In this outline I have grouped diverse functions into four broad categories. The first includes those that specifically relate to cultural identification of the film's subject matter. The second includes those that work principally to render audiences susceptible to the fictive experience. The third identifies functions that work more subtly to add psychological complexity to various characters and situations. The fourth contains functions that contribute to the formal and dramatic unity of the narrative. The presentational order of these functions allows the class to probe deeper aesthetic issues with each successive function. In very few cases is a music cue *simply* functional. But identifying the predominant function of specific cues provides us with a basis for a more sophisticated narrative analysis of the film score as a whole. One key aspect in which my list differs from some others is that I do not make a distinction here between the two spatial levels of film music, that which operates within the film's diegesis ("source music") and that which operates outside the film's diegesis ("non-source music"). Either level can serve the same function.

Choosing examples from films that best illustrate each of these functions involves a lengthy, though rewarding, process. Short of a video anthology of excerpts, which is not likely to happen in the foreseeable future (given copyright restrictions), the method I use is to choose examples from films that I know and think will be most effective for my students.[11] (Depending upon available resources, it might be possible to access a large number of clips by downloading them onto a hard drive or, perhaps soon, onto rewritable DVD, although I have not pursued the legality of such a procedure.)

Music used in the service of numbers 1–7, figure 9.1, is usually expository and is often, for audiences, some of the most memorable in the film. This typically foregrounded music usually contains many immediate cultural references—the sound of a distinctive rock group or a specific opera aria. These sometimes function as "markers" or "signifiers" of genre, time, place, character, and mood.[12] One of the most important and immediate signifiers in film music is that used for the film's main title. When used traditionally it immediately signals genre (westerns, gangster dramas, *films noir*, romantic comedies, etc.) and therefore suggests a rich universe of semiotic associations. The associative power of music can be easily demonstrated at this point through a process of "commutation"—borrowing the music of one genre film and replaying it along with the image track of another. The effect may range from the comical to the disturbing.[13] I show the opening credits to Alfred Hitchcock's *North by Northwest* (1959) using the opening of Gershwin's *Second Rhapsody* (1931) instead of Herrmann's "Fandango." (Reportedly, it was *Gershwinesque* "New York" music that MGM's producers asked Herrmann to write.) It is important for students to begin examining critically some of the networks of musical associations they bring with them to the cinema, both at the conscious and subconscious levels. Main title music as well as music for identifying specific characters or character types usually relies upon networks of what I call "external associations"—conscious or subconscious responses to styles and traditions drawn from outside the film itself. The function is to signal the audience even before it has entered the characters' story world and to establish a cultural context for the situations that follow. (The term "extratextual" is sometimes used for this concept.) In our discussion of musical style and characterization, I draw attention to the composition of the sound, especially the components of texture, volume, and instrumentation.[14]

For numbers 5 through 9, I like to emphasize that the role music plays in spectator receptivity is related anthropologically to the experience of participating in a social event. For examples of number 5 (*creates a sense of spectacle*), I use the "Parade of the Charioteers" from William Wyler's *Ben-Hur* (1959) and the first desert-crossing scenes from David Lean's *Lawrence of Arabia* (1962), both of which transport the spectator to settings in which the vastness of the diegetic space is only partly conveyed by the image. To demonstrate the way music personalizes and creates a sense of identification with a character (number 6), I like to show an excerpt from Peter Yates's *Breaking Away* (1979). The sequence uses sonic space in a variety of ways and also employs both source and non-source music. While the seventeen-year-old Dave has gone off to serenade an unattainable sorority girl in what he thinks is a typical Italian standard of courtship, his mother puts on a recording of an opera aria ("M'Appari" from Flotow's *Martha*) to entice her husband to bed. This is recorded music heard in a limited diegetic space (the parents' bedroom). Dave then sings the same song (with much awkward charm) to the accompaniment of his friend's guitar, strumming outside the sorority house. This is "live" diegetic music in a larger, outdoor space (but still contained within the visual space of the film). Then, as Dave and Katherine go off on his bicycle, the same operatic melody, now lushly orchestrated and played by an invisible studio orchestra, passes to the (nearly infinite) non-diegetic space on the soundtrack. The spectator is enveloped in the sonic world that inhabits Dave's romantic imagination.

In addition to identifying cultural attributes of genre, setting, and character, music can work in the background to reinforce a dramatic turning point or underscore a key event or emotional development. This is where a score can have its finest moments, although these are likely to be least noticed by the audience if they are working effectively. The more subtle application of music in film is the focus of numbers 10 through 12, and I draw on examples from Irving Rapper's *Now Voyager* (1942), Robert Mulligan's *To Kill a Mockingbird* (1962), Franklin Schaffner's *Patton* (1969), and Peter Weir's *Witness* (1985).[15] In key narrative moments, music can communicate at deep psychological levels (and often deep semiological levels as well). Music uses its ability to unfold developmentally over time to transform emotion and to convey meaning. Pure visual images cannot quite accomplish this on their own, or at least do so differently. The essentially tenseless quality of the motion-picture frame is overcome by logical juxtaposition with other frames into the composition of a shot. But music in its temporal medium offers no possibility for such contrivance. Its continual transformation is actual rather than illusory and is therefore interpreted by the audience as perhaps more "honest" in what it conveys. (View with and without Elmer Bernstein's music the conclusion of the courtroom scene in *To Kill a Mockingbird* where Atticus Finch quietly packs up his papers after losing Tom Robinson's case.) Music's associative richness and its apparent transgression of the boundaries of time (compared with a series of edited shots that parse time) lend it significant influential and transformative power on the soundtrack of a narrative film. During our analyses of music's psychological implications, I assign readings that address some of these issues in depth, among them: Bordwell and Thomson's *Film Art*, Hanns Eisler and Theodor Adorno's *Composing for the Films* (the standard Marxist criticism of Hollywood film music as bourgeois propaganda), Claudia Gorbman's *Unheard Melodies* (which identifies and examines critically many of the functions in the second and fourth categories above), as well as Royal S. Brown's *Overtones and Undertones*, Michel Chion's *Audio-Vision: Sound on Screen*, Jeff Smith's *The Sounds of Commerce: Marketing Popular Film Music*, James Buhler, et al., *Music and Cinema*, and Anahid Kassabian's *Hearing Film*.[16] In addition to addressing aesthetic issues of function and technique, a few of these writings isolate important aspects of film music that defy categorical designation. Brown analyzes the dramatic and psychological effectiveness that some directors achieve by exploring the interplay between source and non-source music. Burt includes an excellent essay on "the function of silence": when a sequence of film is most effective *without* music.

We then turn to music's role in defining form and structure (figure 9.1, numbers 13 through 16, beginning with examples of music for cuts, wipes, montages, and changes of time and locale). While there are literally thousands of possible examples for each of these, two remarkable early examples are Steiner's "Paris Montage" from Michael Curtiz's *Casablanca* (1939) and Herrmann's "Breakfast Montage" from Orson Welles's *Citizen Kane* (1941), the latter using the form of theme and variations. For music that creates emotional contour throughout an entire film sequence (number 15), we study the opening homecoming from William Wyler's *The Best Years of Our Lives* (Hugo Friedhofer, 1946) and the climactic scene from Elia Kazan's *East of Eden* (Leonard Roseman, 1955), both of which are substantively analyzed in Burt's *Art of Film Music* (with complete scores in piano transcription). For a more recent example, I also like to use the launching sequence from Ron Howard's *Apollo 13* (1995). I play the entire scene for the class without sound, reading the dialogue from a script. The sequence involves complex continuity editing between the interior and launch pad of the ship and Mission Control in Houston and takes us from the astronauts' final preparations for departure to the ship's take-off and clearance of earth's gravity. I ask the students to imagine the kind of music they would write, when it might stop and start, and the kinds of instruments they would use. I ask them if they would vary the tempo. Would they use music to "comment" on the action? Would they change style and mood with each character and location, etc.? They each sketch a short outline during a second showing of the clip. Afterward, we discuss various possible solutions, and it becomes evident that the range of choices varies widely. I then play the clip again with the soundtrack. Composer James Horner chose to underscore this ten-minute sequence initially with slow-moving music, in counterpoint to the nervousness of the characters but more in harmony with the "weightiness" of the spaceship and the matter at hand. The music begins with a solemn, hymn-like character, played with a noble and warm tone by the French horns and trombones, which imparts a sense of grandeur to the scene. (For their effectiveness, these musical devices rely on the spectator's awareness of their external associations.) Musical changes occur gradually, from the quiet entry of a military snare drum as the men are sealed in the capsule to the addition of a new violin motive suggesting the heroism implicit in the mission, to the increasing complexity of the underlying rhythmic motion as one of the ship's five rockets fails and a decision must be made whether to continue the mission, to the eventual falling away of the lower instruments of the orchestra and the prominence of a wordless chorus as the ship successfully releases its boosters and enters a state of weightlessness. In contrast to this type of through-composition, we examine the use of a highly formulaic pop song to bridge complex editing where, in Mike Nichols's *The Graduate* (1967), several stanzas of Simon and Garfunkel's "Mrs. Robinson" provide formal continuity over a long sequence collapsing time and distance and serving to propel the action toward the climax of that film.

Unlike functions that rely principally on external associations, many film scores are unified (figure 9.1, number 16) through the use of various "internal [musical] associations": recurring theme songs or themes and leitmotifs for characters or concepts. Max Steiner unified *Casablanca* musically with "As Time Goes By." We hear Herman Hupfeld's 1931 song as "source music" (Dooley Wilson plays and sings it in Rick's Cafe). But the melody is also woven into the non-source music as well, sometimes appearing in fragmentary form to remind us of the passion that still persists despite the anguished circumstances in which Rick and Ilse unintentionally find themselves.[17] Korngold's music for *The Adventures of Robin Hood* or *The Sea Hawk* or Williams's music for the *Star Wars* cycle, for instance, are more elaborate examples of motivic saturation. Throughout our discussion of film music's contribution to the structure of a film, I begin to introduce more technical terms such as phrase, cadence, ostinato, motive, counterpoint, and [musical] sequence.

**Technical aspects**

Because the functions of the film score are closely connected to the mechanics of the genre, I devote the second unit of the course to an investigation of how the technical medium of film shapes the character of the music. (In my course this unit is shorter than the first, but it might be expanded given available technical resources. Some teaching environments may have sound labs for demonstrations or may be located near a film studio where a recording session could be observed.) I introduce students to examples of directors' and composers' timing, breakdown, and spotting notes, as well as music editors' cue sheets.[18] As an example of how these relate to the finished score, I use a metronome and Korngold's timing notes to a scene in Michael Curtiz's *The Sea Hawk* to simulate how a variable click track works. In our process of isolating and identifying exactly where and why Korngold chose to use slight tempo modifications to underscore the escape of Errol Flynn and the English prisoners from the galley of a Spanish ship, the crucial relationship between tempo and film scoring becomes evident. The subtle shifts in tempo are critical to the dramatic effectiveness of the scene. In modern film-scoring, professional digital editing programs such as Auricle add what are called "SMPTE time codes" to the image track and compensate for much of what was done mechanically to synchronize sound to image in the 1940s. But the click track and punches and streamers, devised by Steiner and Newman in the early stages of classical Hollywood scoring, are still a part of the technology. Now, however, exact frame-by-frame information has been computerized and can be manipulated with the same precision on video as on film stock.

Another important development in the last thirty years is the increasing sophistication of the "temp track," the director's and music editor's temporary synchronization of preexisting music to the film before the composer has finished writing and recording the score. Stanley Kubrick's *2001: A Space Odyssey* (1968) is particularly effective in demonstrating how a temp track influences the composer's choices. In this infamous case, Kubrick decided to lock his "temporary" classical music into the final cut of the film, rather than dub in Alex North's commissioned music. North's score has recently been recorded and can be synched to parts of the film for comparison. This process of commutation reveals how aesthetic aspects of the film beyond the dialogue and visuals are imposed on composers and often limit the originality of their contribution. (Compare North's "Sunrise," for example, to that of Richard Strauss's *Also Sprach Zarathustra*, used at the opening of the film.)

We also touch upon the recording and mixing process. It would be easy, and certainly misleading, for students to draw the conclusion that film music is better today simply because there are more sophisticated methods of recording and playback. I illustrate the problem of studio mixing in the earlier decades of sound film first by using a sequence from Joseph Mankiewicz's *Julius Caesar* (MGM, 1953) with some truly remarkable music of Shakespearean breadth and insight by Miklos Rozsa (even though much of his original score was heavily cut in the final editing of the film). We watch the sequence of Caesar's entry into the Roman forum as it is currently available on video transfer, where the nondescript "movie music" appears to buzz annoyingly beneath the sound effects of crowd noise.[19] The recording of the score by Bruce Broughton and the Sinfonia of London, however, reveals that the ineffectiveness of the music on the soundtrack is due to the manner in which the relatively flat mono tracks were further reduced in dynamic range when mixed with the dialogue and sound-effects tracks in the studio editing process.[20] Only when the range of dynamics and color of Rozsa's music is revealed—a heavy military march seething with dark, explosive terror and orchestrated with snarling trombones and ripping tam-tam—is it possible to experience the full impact of this "musical subtext" underpinning Caesar's ambitious nature. A few film scores have been remixed in cases where original recorded tracks have been preserved (as is the case with *Vertigo* on DVD). As one successful example of the daunting task of entirely rerecording a score, we view in both versions the opening of the "Battle on the Ice" from Sergei Eisenstein's *Alexander Nevsky* (1938). In this case, the full color and dynamic range of Prokofiev's "reconstructed" orchestration renders this scene absolutely riveting.[21]

After covering some of the technical aspects of how a film is spotted for music and how a score is composed, orchestrated, recorded, mixed, and dubbed, we analyze sequences from films that demonstrate some of the functions listed above, but in which the technical aspects of synchronization are highly concealed. For one sequence in George Lucas's *Star Wars* (1977), for example, we listen to the music on recording several times before we turn to the film. The students have the outline in table 9.1 below, but I ask them to cover the descriptions of the film sequences. Most of the students recall the scene in the film when Ben Kenobi dies, and Luke Skywalker, Princess Leia, Han Solo, and Chewbacca escape in the Millennium Falcon, followed by Han and Luke's battle with the TIE fighters. But while students recall the events in the film, they do not generally remember specific details of the music. This scene is one of the most remarkable examples of compression in all film music. The two continuous music cues (labeled M32 and M33) last under four minutes. But the sequence seems much longer since so much visual information occurs during this time.[22]

The music of these cues adheres precisely to a steady beat (though not always the same tempo) as Williams is conducting to a click track for precise synchronization of music and action. The varying pulse of each section affects mood as well as conveys the illusion of time passing more quickly or slowly. Structurally, Williams chose to use only three internal themes—Ben's theme (also called "the Force"), Leia's theme, and the rebel fanfare. The rest of the music is indigenous to the cue. Since three important themes serve to relate this sequence to the rest of the film, we discuss both their internal and external associations. Key external elements are: the constructions of heroism in the rebel theme, evocations of lyricism and the "feminine" but also striving in Leia's theme, and the emphasis on the mystical but also poignancy in the harmonic setting and instrumentation of Ben's theme. We also discuss external associations of the indigenous music—similar devices used in earlier battle music, for example. We review the musical terms in the outline (which in this case are my own, not the director's, sound editor's, or composer's) and then play the example again so that verbal descriptions connect with sound. The piece is exciting in its own right, but many of the musical gestures do not in themselves make formal sense (for example, the big cadence at 3:01 and the "spiraling" French horns that follow). When we see and hear the sequence in the film, however, meaning in these gestures is nuanced and enriched. The cadence implies a sense of relief—Luke's joy at having wiped out one of the TIE fighters. But Luke's inexperience as a warrior is signaled musically (and deceptively) by a strong cadence that manages to avoid a sense of conclusion. A feeling of relief at this point would be premature and, for Luke and his friends, potentially lethal. Leia's sharp warning that there are two more attacking fighters—underscored by the spiraling horns—refocuses his (and our) concentration on the fight at hand.

### Studying complete films

After studying a few cues at this level of detail and analyzing the functional and technical aspects of music, I ask each of the students to prepare spotting notes for a film of their choice, to discuss briefly each cue and its primary functions, and conclude his or her paper with a close reading of one cue. We then use the final weeks of the course to examine three or four films in their entirety. My choices vary from year to year and tend to be idiosyncratic rather than based on a scholarly consensus of historical or stylistic importance. Among those that have yielded interesting analyses are: *High Noon* (Dmitri Tiomkin, 1952), *Vertigo* (Bernard Herrmann, 1957), *To Kill a Mockingbird* (Elmer Bernstein, 1963), *Charade* (Henry Mancini, 1963), *Goldfinger* (John Barry, 1964), *Planet of the Apes* (Terry Goldsmith, 1968), *Jaws* (John Williams, 1976), *The Empire Strikes Back* (John Williams, 1980), *Altered States* (John Corigliano, 1980), *Blade Runner* (Vangelis, 1982), *The Natural* (Randy Newman, 1984), *The Color Purple* (Quincy Jones, 1985), *The Mission* (Ennio Morricone, 1986), *The Last Emperor* (Ryuichi Sakamoto, David Byrne, and Cong Su, 1987), *Glory* (James Horner, 1989), *Edward Scissorhands* (Danny Elfman, 1990), *Dances with Wolves* (John Barry, 1990), *Age of Innocence* (Elmer Bernstein, 1993), and *Beyond Rangoon* (Hans Zimmer, 1995).[23] The study of complete films offers an opportunity to tie in many of the functional and technical aspects presented in the course, as well as allow for a deeper understanding of how external/internal associations contribute significantly toward enriching the film-viewing experience. For students with advanced music-reading skills, more complex formal and tonal analyses of the film score as a whole could be encouraged. Here it would be helpful to have access to the composers' scores, or at least sections of them if possible. Scores for films before the 1980s are sometimes available for consultation in various libraries, and a list of these can be found in H. Stephen Wright, *Film Music Collections in the United States: A Guide*, published by the Film Music Society.[24]

## Conclusion

After teaching this course in a liberal arts environment, I have developed a personal philosophy about music for film. It seems that the best film music is written when the composer is wholly dedicated to the medium, not when motivated by potential sales of soundtrack recordings or possible future concert adaptations. Composers' musical choices are shaped and limited by the edited film. Some composers manage better than others to exploit these limitations and, in doing so, reach extraordinary levels of creativity. While this subordination of the composer's autonomy to a higher goal might seem to render this music somehow less artistic than other compositional venues, film music's unique qualities emerge only when we "listen" to a film critically. This means asking ourselves questions the composer is likely to have asked him or herself: Does the emotion of the scene need reinforcing here? To what degree? Would this important event be enhanced by being personalized or more universalized? Should the music stay out of the way of certain dialogue, or should it flow in counterpoint to the dialogue's timbres, shapes, and rhythms? What can music suggest that would add meaning rather than further mystify gestures or expressions (for example, those of Cary Grant's squint-eyed wariness or Eva Marie Saint's coy smile in *North by Northwest*)? Should the underlying music suggest emotional ambivalence?

Another important goal for a film-music course—one that goes along with developing students' listening skills—is to convey enough information so that students in a liberal arts environment are prepared to consider musical questions at this level of inquiry. When film music itself provides successful answers to these questions it excels as an art form, especially in the emotional richness and complexity it is able to convey in connection with the film's diegesis. As the students in my class have discovered, film music may often be thrilling on its own, but heard in context it becomes an important artistic genre well worth our time to study.

*I am grateful to members of the Film Music Society in Hollywood, California and to composer-orchestrator Warren Sherk at the Academy of Motion Picture Arts and Sciences for helping me find my way through the initially daunting world of the film music industry. I would also like to thank several scholars who teach film music, among them Claudia Gorbman, Neil Lerner, Martin Marks, Katherine Preston, Lawrence Leviton, Gary Uhlenkott, Linda Schubert, composer Fred Karlin, and music editor Roy Prendergast, all of whom have been generous with their time in discussing technical aspects of film music and in sharing ideas and syllabi. Special thanks also to my colleagues at Vassar, among them Sarah Kozloff and Ken Robinson in the film department, for their advice on earlier drafts of this chapter.*

## Notes

1   Main textbooks on film music currently in print are: Roy Prendergast, *Film Music: A Neglected Art*, second rev. ed. (New York: W. W. Norton, 1992); Kathryn Kalinak, *Settling the Score: Music and the Classical Hollywood Film* (Madison: University of Wisconsin Press, 1992); George Burt, *The Art of Film Music* (Boston: Northeastern University Press, 1994); Fred Karlin, *Listening to Movies: The Film Lover's Guide to Film Music* (New York: Schirmer Books, 1994); Larry M. Timm, *The Soul of Cinema: An Appreciation of Film Music* (New York: Simon and Schuster, 1998); and Nicholas Cook, *Analysing Musical Multimedia* (Oxford University Press, 1998). Laurence E. MacDonald's *Invisible Art of Film Music: A Comprehensive History* (New York: Ardsley House, 1998) is an interesting decade-by-decade survey rather than a textbook.
2   <http: //www.movietunes.com/>.
3   Michel Chion, *Audio-Vision: Sound on Screen*, ed. and trans. Claudia Gorbman (New York: Columbia University Press, 1994), 150–52.
4   Film music was identified in 1929 as a "functional" genre by Paul Hindemith at his Donaueschingen Festivals of New Music. As one of the four original types of *Gebrauchsmusik*, it remains today the most viable.
5   Claudia Gorbman uses *Mildred Pierce* as her case study of "classical" film scoring in *Unheard Melodies* (Bloomington: Indiana University Press, 1987). This book is currently out of print.
6   Chion, *Audio-Vision*, 8–9.
7   Elmer Bernstein's score to Martin Scorsese's *Age of Innocence* (1993) is one recent example.
8   Jeff Smith analyzes 1960s and 1970s films and the commercial potential of film music in *Sounds of Commerce: Marketing Popular Film Music* (New York: Columbia University Press, 1998).
9   Aaron Copland, "Tip to Moviegoers: Take Off Those Ear-Muffs," *New York Times*, 6 Nov. 1949, sec. 6, p. 28, revised and incorporated in *What To Listen For in Music* (New York: McGraw Hill, 1988), 252–63. Prendergast elaborates in his *Film Music* upon Copland's five functions by providing specific examples from films from the 1940s to 1960s.

10    David Bordwell and Kristin Thompson, *Film Art: An Introduction*, fifth ed. (New York: McGraw Hill, 1997); Gorbman, *Unheard Melodies*; Chion, *Audio-vision*; Prendergast, *Film Music*; Karlin, *Listening to Movies*; Burt, *The Art of Film Music*; and Timm, *The Soul of Cinema* and from film-score reviews and published writings of composers (such as those in the periodical *Film Music Notes* from the 1940s to 1950s) or interviews with composers in *The Cue Sheet* (published by the Film Music Society; see n. 24).

11    Although I often use recordings in class, I almost always prefer to use the film (usually in a remastered format) and to maintain the connection between image and sound. In the classroom I have three non-celluloid formats, VHS, laser disc, and DVD, each hooked up to one projector and one sound system.

12    The functions in numbers 1–4, therefore, correspond to Gorbman's concept of "referential cueing." Here music communicates directly to the audience through the semiotic apparatus.

13    Claudia Gorbman applies the linguistic term "commutation" to film music with some examples in *Unheard Melodies*, 16.

14    Though generalized categories for types of instrumentation may often be difficult to define, I find it beneficial to acknowledge that most scores before 1980 or so may be grouped roughly according to five types of recording ensembles: (1) a standard symphonic studio orchestra of winds, brass, strings, and simple percussion—can include harp and sometimes chorus (especially prominent in the 1930s to 1960s); (2) "concept" scores with variations on the studio orchestra (either the addition of non-studio instruments to the "standard" symphonic ensemble: i.e., piano, harpsichord, ondes martenot, theremin, percussion instruments other than timpani, bass drum and cymbals [such as temple blocks, mark tree, etc.], or non-standard combinations of instruments such as Herrmann's use of winds, harps, and organs for *Journey to the Center of the Earth,* 1959); (3) non-orchestral groups derived from traditional ensembles such as jazz, rock, pop, folk, or non-Western (sometimes with singers); (4) synthesized scores—computer-generated music but may include the use of sampled acoustic sounds in MIDI technology; and finally (5) any combination of the above. To familiarize students with the standard symphonic studio orchestra, I assign them to listen to a recording of Miklos Rozsa's *Jungle Book,* a twenty-eight minute narration with music that uses the instruments of the orchestra for individual characterizations, much as Prokofiev did in *Peter and the Wolf.* Another effective piece is Musorgsky's *Pictures at an Exhibition,* where Ravel's instrumentation and orchestral color may be aligned with the images that they attempt to portray. Britten's *Young Person's Guide to the Orchestra* could, of course, serve a similar purpose but lacks the implicit narrativity of the other pieces.

15    These correspond to Gorbman's "connotative cueing." They function as semiotic "signifieds," possible meanings to which the signifiers or references point.

16    Bordwell and Thompson, *Film Art*, especially pp. 315–54; Hanns Eisler, *Composing for the Films* (1947; reprint with introductory essay by Graham McCann, London: The Athlone Press, 1994); Royal S. Brown, *Overtones and Undertones* (Berkeley and Los Angeles: University of California Press, 1994); James Buhler, Caryl Flinn, and David Neumeyer, eds., *Music and Cinema* (Hanover, NH: Wesleyan University Press, 2000); and Anahid Kassabian, *Hearing Film: Tracking Identifications in Contemporary Hollywood Film Music* (New York: Routledge, 2001). For additional writings on film music, two bibliographies are especially useful, although they are both dated. They are: Martin Marks, "Film Music: The Material, Literature, and Present State of Research," *Notes of the Music Library Association* 36 (1979): 282–325, and Steven D. Wescott, *A Comprehensive Bibliography of Music for Film and Television* (Detroit: Detroit Studies in Music Bibliography, No. 54, 1985). Jeff Smith's selected bibliography in *Sounds of Commerce*, pp. 271–76, includes many more recent items. Robynn Stilwell has recently prepared an extensive bibliography, but it is not yet published.

17    A useful supplement to a film music course is *The Hollywood Sound* (Sony Classical Film and Video, 1995), a documentary by Joshua Waletzky that examines Steiner's use of music in *Casablanca* and that of other composers working in the 1930s and 1940s.

18    An extraordinarily comprehensive and technically detailed overview of the process involved in film-score planning, composing, recording, and mixing can be found in Fred Karlin and Rayburn Wright, *On the Track: A Guide to Contemporary Film Scoring* (New York: Schirmer Books, 1990). This book also contains examples of spotting and breakdown notes. Older cue sheets are sometimes available by fax from individual studios.

19    I recall seeing this film in an art theater in New York around 1985. The music was no more audible under those conditions.

20    Though Mankiewicz and Rozsa experimented with stereophonic recording for the concluding battle scene of *Julius Caesar*, MGM did not begin recording consistently in stereophonic sound until 1954.

21    In 1995, *Alexander Nevsky* was re-released not only with remastered sound but with Prokofiev's music newly recorded by the St. Petersburg Orchestra and Chorus; the score was reconstructed by William D. Brohn and produced by Jay David Sacks, RCA Victor Red Seal, 09026-61926-2 (1995).

22    Film scholar Michael Matessino observed: "This is film scoring at its most triumphant—a cue unlike any other ever written for a movie, and so kinesthetically connected to the imagery that it is impossible to believe either existed before the other." Program notes to *Star Wars: A New Hope*, Original Motion Picture Soundtrack, Lucasfilm Ltd., 09026–68746–2 (1997).

23    Of these, in my view, Hitchcock's *Vertigo* and Spielberg's *Jaws* are two extremely satisfying films to teach in terms of consistent quality of music,

constant interplay of external and internal associations, original use of music, and depth of the music's psychological contribution to the narrative.

24    H. Stephen Wright, *Film Music Collections in the United States: A Guide* (Hollywood, CA: Society for the Preservation of Film Music [now called The Film Music Society], 1996). See the society's web site for a list of publications: <http: //www. filmmusicsociety.org/>.

**FIGURE 9.1**
**Functions of Music in Narrative Film**


I. MUSIC IDENTIFIES ATTRIBUTES OF CULTURE, TIME, PLACE, AND CHARACTER

1.  *Defines genre* (i.e., western, science-fiction, melodrama, epic, etc.)
2.  *Indexes musical style* (i.e., symphonic, jazz, country, ethnic)
3.  *Establishes time and place*
    a. using actual period music
    b. approximating period music
4.  *Indexes characterization:* [a]
    a. archetypal (groups or individuals)
    b. unique characterizations
    c. anthropomorphic treatment of animals and inanimate objects

II. MUSIC INCREASES THE SPECTATOR'S INVOLVEMENT AND RECEPTIVITY TO
THE FILM NARRATIVE

5.  *Creates a sense of spectacle—universalizes*
6.  *Creates a sense of identification with a character or group of characters—personalizes*
7.  *Establishes a pervasive mood (continuation of traditions from theater and silent film)* [b]
8.  *Illustrates, highlights points, or focuses attention on an object in the film space or on the action of a character*
9.  *Creates or builds suspense (lowers the threshold of belief)*

III. MUSIC ADDS PSYCHOLOGICAL COMPLEXITY TO THE SPECTATOR'S
UNDERSTANDING OF THE CHARACTERS AND DRAMATIC SITUATIONS

10. *Emphasizes a specific character's point of view*
11. *Interprets by adding a musical subtext to the images or dialogue similar to the commentary of a narrator*
12. *Seems to contradict the visual information* [c]

figure 9.1 (continued)

IV. MUSIC ASSISTS IN ORGANIZING AND SHAPING THE NARRATIVE ASPECTS
OF THE DRAMA

13. *Provides continuity and masks film editing (i.e., cuts, wipes, montage),
compensates for a change in location (outdoor/indoor) or time period
(day/night), or bridges an abrupt shift to a set of new characters or emotional
situations*
14. *Controls rhythmic pacing of a scene through fluctuation in tempo (or by
maintaining a steady tempo)*
    a. underscoring predominantly action sequences [d]
    b. underscoring predominantly dialogue sequences
15. *Creates emotional contour throughout an entire film sequence*
16. *Provides dramatic unity to the film as a whole*
    a. single theme or theme song predominates the entire film
    (monothematic)—other music (generally) non-thematic
    b. multiple themes and motives (leitmotivic)
    c. use of classical or traditional musical forms (developmental)
    d. compilation of songs by the same artist or group—or by different artists or
    groups
    e. use of connecting "pop hooks" or jazz riffs with an occasional pop song [e]
    f. combined use of pop or traditional songs with motivic underscoring

---

[a]  Subdivisions a and b from Burt, *Art of Film Music*, 18 and 39. Burt's "symbolic
meanings" include archetypal characterizations.
[b]  For the practice of adding live music to film before the sound era, see Martin Miller
Marks, *Music and the Silent Film: Contexts and Case Studies, 1895–1924* (Oxford:
Oxford University Press, 1997).
[c]  Michael Chion calls this "anempathetic music," music of indifference. Music boxes and
carousels, for example, often play indifferently to the action. The effect is the opposite
of "empathetic music" (number 6 above), where music participates emotionally in the
scene. See Michel Chion, *Audio-Vision*, 8.
[d]  Burt uses the term "pacing" in this context. See *Art of Film Music*, 115–42.
[e]  Types a, b, and c correspond closely to those of Prendergast, although I have described
them differently. See Prendergast, *Film Music*, 231–45. Type e is taken from Jeff Smith,
*Sounds of Commerce*, 8, 15–16, and passim.

## TABLE 9.1
### Film Sequence from *Star Wars: A New Hope* (Music by John Williams)

| Time | Tempo | Motives/Themes | Commentary | Film Sequence |
|---|---|---|---|---|
| **M32: BEN KENOBI'S DEATH** | | | | |
| 0:00 | ♩ ≈ 74 | Ben's theme (also "the Force") | French horn, *p*, minor mode, slow four-beat tempo strings tremolo, extremely softly, *ppp* | INTERIOR DEATH STAR—DOCKING BAY / Luke sees Ben in a lightsaber combat with Vader. / Ben stops fighting, smiles at Luke, then serenely raises his lightsaber in resignation... |
| 0:07 | ♩ ≈ 118 | | Sharp accented note (strings pizzicato) Suddenly tempo much faster strings enter, *f* | Vader cuts through Ben's cloak. Ben has vanished. Luke (yelling): "No!" |
| 0:11 | | Princess Leia's theme | Violins play first phrase of a surging, passionate melody major mode, fast four-beat, *f* | Stormtroopers begin firing on Luke, Leia, Han, and Chewbacca. They shoot back, defending themselves. |
| 0:17 | | | Second phrase of melody (sequences higher) | Leia tries to get them to stop fighting and make their escape. "Come on!" she shouts. |
| 0:23 | | | Third phrase of melody (sequences higher) cymbal crash, *ff*, secures a musical and emotional climax | Vader is briefly halted by closing doors. |
| 0:30 | | | Melody then seems to get lost, doesn't resolve (no clear cadence) French horns climb higher but seem directionless | Luke is transfixed with anger and awe. Voice of Ben: "Run Luke, Run!" Luke listens , then turns and races into the ship. |
| 0:37 | ♩ ≈ 126 | | New texture interrupts: timpani and strings, strong percussive rhythm, *f* | INT. MILLENNIUM FALCON Han powers the ship out of the docking bay |
| 0:40 | | Rebel fanfare | 3 trumpets in parallel motion, major mode - very assertive | |
| 0:47 | | | Changes mode (modulation) | |
| 0:49 | | Rebel fanfare | 3 trumpets now reinforced by 3 trombones, even more determined - followed by a upwards scale in the woodwinds and bells | The ship speeds away from the Death Star |

table 9.1 (continued)

| Time | Tempo | Theme | Music | Scene |
|---|---|---|---|---|
| 0:59 | | | Tempo slows down and becomes softer - modulates to... | |
| 1:01 | ♩ ≈ 84 | Ben's theme | Oboe plays a slow melancholy tune in a minor mode, this is answered by a flute that carries the melody to where it aligns with the harmony in a sweet resolution, but the resolution quickly turns bittersweet as a clarinet somewhat mournfully attempts a response | INTERIOR MILLENNIUM FALCON—CENTRAL HOLD AREA. Luke saddened by the loss of Ben stares off blankly as the robots look on. Leia puts a blanket around him protectively. Han and Chewbacca try to angle the reflector shield. Luke: "I can't believe he's gone" Leia: "There wasn't anything you could have done." |
| 1:16 | ♩ ≈ 74 | | French horn takes up the melody, now even more melancholic (violins play a gently consoling countermelody in the background) the oboe returns to complete the tune, but doesn't quite make it before... | |
| 1:32 | ♩ ≈ 124 | | Tension-filled oscillating theme in high strings and woodwinds - the rhythm is driving and persistent low strings play slower but accented pizzicatos | Han (to Luke): "Come on, buddy, we're not out of this yet!" Han and Luke take their positions at the laser cannons. |
| 1:50 | | | Bells and other percussion reinforce the oscillating theme, this grows louder and even more insistent. it crescendos to... | Han (to Luke): "O.K. Stay Sharp!" INT. MILLENNIUM FALCON—COCKPIT—GUNPORTS. Leia (into intercom): "Here they come!" |

M33: T.I.E. FIGHTER ATTACK (cont. from previous)

| Time | Tempo | Theme | Music | Scene |
|---|---|---|---|---|
| 2:04 | ♩ ≈ 142 | TIE Fighter Attack theme | Low brass, f, percussive, syncopated rhythm Strings, f, very percussive accompaniment | The 4 Imperial TIE fighters come swooping in towards the Millennium Falcon. |

table 9.1 (continued)

| Time | Theme | Music | Action/Dialogue |
|---|---|---|---|
| 2:12 | Rebel fanfare | Trumpets, alone at first, call out the fanfare timpani and strings manacingly hammer out a reply alternates again between the fanfare and the hammering timpani | Han and Luke fire but keep missing the speeding fighters. Fast cross-cutting between the two gunports and ext. space |
| 2:20 | TIE Fighter Attack theme | Low brass, *f*, percussive, syncopated rhythm Strings, *f*, very percussive accompaniment | Luke: "They're coming in too fast!" |
| 2:24 | Rebel fanfare | French horns, no accompaniment (four repetitions) + snare drum trumpets join in on the third repetition on the fourth repetition, the tune changes mode (modulates) | [After second fanfare] Leia: "We've lost lateral controls." Han: "Don't worry. She'll hold together. (Under his breath) You hear me baby? Hold together!" |
| 2:42 | TIE Fighter Attack theme | Low brass, *f*, percussive, syncopated rhythm Strings, *f*, very percussive accompaniment | |
| 2:50 | | Brass sequence upward, just at the high point... | Han's laser hits one fighter. It explodes. Luke scores a direct hit on the second. |
| 3:01 | (Rebel theme) | Big cadence, sense of relief, seems about to end (hint of rebel theme in the trumpets suggests triumph) | Luke: "Got him, I got him!" |
| 3:11 | | But suddenly the French horns spiral upward, false conclusion, continues... | Leia: "There's still two more of them out there!" |
| 3:14 | TIE Fighter Attack theme | Low brass again, *f*, percussive, syncopated rhythm; Strings, *f*, very percussive accompaniment with added snare drum | More cross-cutting of firing. Luke fires a blast on the third fighter. |
| 3:23 | | Texture change: strings in fast repeating notes, *f*, builds in strength, notes get higher and louder | Han, tasting success, is determined to get the last one. |
| 3:29 | Death Star motive | Climax, *ff*, full orchestra, rhythmic motion halts suddenly on an ominous minor-mode chord | Last TIE fighter heads straight for the Millennium Falcon. |
| 3:34 | | Gong crash (*ff*), timpani roll begins thunderously (*ff*), then slowly fades... (long slow diminuendo) | Han fires, scores a direct hit on last ship and it blows up. He breathes a sigh of relief. Luke: "That's it! We did it." |

Ends 3:50

*Source:* Film sequence derived from *Star Wars: The Annotated Screenplays*, ed. Laurent Bouzereau (New York: Ballantine Books, 1997), 80–86.

Chapter Ten

# Don't Fence Me In: The Pleasures of Teaching American Music

*Susan C. Cook*

I never intended to teach *American* music; I was not trained as an *Americanist*, after all. When I completed my Ph.D. in 1985, my allegiance was to twentieth-century music, which meant then—and often means today—the art music and/or concert repertories of Western Europe. My great love was the decade of the 1920s in Germany and France. While I had been shamed into a cursory appreciation of jazz and had a special fondness for Charles Ives, John Cage, and George Crumb, I felt little desire to know more about the particularities of music-making closer to home.

All that would change with my first full-time teaching job and an evolving research trajectory. In the fall of 1985 I joined the faculty of a small liberal arts college that boasted majors in the fields of American Studies and American Literature and had in its catalog a pre-existing American music course, orphaned by the untimely departure of its founding instructor. My department chair encouraged me to take the course on, to keep "our" hand in this popular and prestigious interdisciplinary program. Without tenure and seeking it, how could I refuse?

Around the same time and for similar careerist gain, I reached out to The Sonneck Society for American Music (now The Society for American Music [SAM]), with an abstract on the one topic from my dissertation that fit: an American composer who had worked in Germany during the 1920s. My paper was accepted, and the subsequent conference so welcoming in contrast to what I had previously experienced that I wanted to keep attending. Once I began to teach American music, my research increasingly brought me back to the U.S. as I began to explore feminist scholarship, the culture of ragtime social dance and, as a direct result of my teaching, Anglo-American balladry.[1] The many cultures of contemporary music still fascinate me, as does the decade of the 1920s, but now I consider myself an Americanist, not by training or credential but through on-the-job experience, a kind of scholarly sweat-equity.

My ever-evolving American courses—whether intended for music majors, non-majors, or both simultaneously; or for undergraduates or graduate students; during the regular semester or summer school; at a private liberal arts college or now within a School of Music at a state-supported research university—have brought unexpected pleasures and challenges: they have provided a kind of pedagogical *jouissance*. Teaching American music is serious fun and caused me to rethink both my teaching and my scholarship.

The reasons for this American *différence* are doubtless many, and I can only speak from my experience. I believe that a combination of factors global and local, extra-institutional and institutional, made and still make for the palpable change I experience in the classroom. Foremost among the factors is the perception and place of American music itself within the discipline of musicology and the "inter-discipline" of American Studies. Related are the perceptions of students regarding such a course, and certainly my initial self-perception as a kind of interloper played a role as well. And finally, the formalistic possibilities of organizing around a geographical "place" rather than a chronological "time" or, secondarily, a genre, cause this course to stand apart for me from the typical collection of "period" courses to which I also contribute.

At the global level, American music lacks academic prestige. While it has achieved scholarly legitimacy in the last two decades, thanks in large part to the growing number of loosely-defined academic programs in American and African American Studies, American music remains outside of the "canon." American repertories and their contexts are not central to what we do as musicologists and music historians or to the work of the cultivators of "high art." At best, American music is an add-on, a frill. Only in the rare place has it acquired the status of core.

The National Association of Schools of Music (NASM), for example, does not require American music courses for institutional accreditation. Many prestigious graduate-degree granting institutions get along quite nicely, thank you, without the expertise of an Americanist of whatever stripe, but would be loathe to run a program without a Baroque specialist. The American Musicological Society continues to belie its name as scholarship on American music-making remains underrepresented at national conferences and within the pages of its journal. Graduate students who pursue Americanist topics often find they must do double-duty preparing for comprehensive and preliminary examinations, learning repertory and scholarship for both Western Europe and North America, whereas their colleagues pursuing eighteenth-century studies would not be expected to hold forth on the current state of research on New England psalmody. It is no surprise then that Americanists, individually and collectively, often seek to prove their legitimacy with the same narrow measures that excluded them, arguing for "genius" status for particular male composers and creating counter canons of "great" works that largely embody preexisting norms of "excellence."

While this lack of prestige is deeply troubling for many reasons, not the least of which is the perceived lesser value of my own on going scholarship, it is also enormously liberating as a teacher. There is no formula for what an American course is supposed to do or be. The same cannot be said for my contemporary music course or even a non-major "appreciation" course, where faculty colleagues feel quite comfortable making claims about what I should be doing, what kinds of experiences students must have, what facts they must carry with them. Here, the syllabus is mine, all mine, to develop and teach well out of range of the canonical surveillance cameras.

What is more likely to be an issue is not the syllabus content but the presence of such a course at all within an individual department's or college's curriculum. While I inherited my first course, when I took my present position I had to add the course and justify its existence. Even though at least two other instructors with Americanist credentials had preceded me, no specific course had ever been created. Depending on the institution, instructors may have more success devising an American course for non-majors—as a cross-listed offering, or as a special topics writing-intensive offering for first-year students, or in a senior seminar—than as a more traditional required course or elective for music majors. While these extra-curricular options perpetuate American music's outsider status, they are worth pursuing and bring many benefits, as I will discuss below.

Most of us would rather teach students who are in our classrooms by choice. The students in my American courses are self-selecting; their personalities—individually and as a class—acknowledge and embrace the alternative nature of the course. They share a sense that something different is afoot and express delight in finding that sounds, experiences, and repertories they dearly, and often furtively, love—bluegrass, drum and bugle corps, rap, Broadway musicals—merit, if not legitimacy, at least being recognized and talked about within the classroom. And talk about them they will; discussion flourishes. It is as if we collectively respond to our marginality by finding our voices.

I learned early on that American music courses are powerfully popular with the non-music major. They attract students with competencies in American history or literature, who, if given the opportunity, have much contextual material to add to discussions of musical events and contexts and are hungry for the arts in all their variety. Students of American history or in American studies programs have often been introduced to sophisticated modes of analytic thought and critical interpretation, methodologies often foreign to the music major. While these non-majors may not read music or have had much exposure to musical practices *per se*, they know how to think. Such students can completely change the tenor of a classroom, providing pedagogical challenges and opportunities to teach across and among disciplines, of finding the connections between Langston Hughes's blues-based poetry, William Grant Still's blues-based *Afro-American Symphony*, and the multiple modernist meanings of "the blues" as commercially recorded in the 1920s and 1930s. Non-majors provide the subversive opportunity to reposition music and the arts in the general undergraduate curriculum. We can send these students back to their disciplinary courses with fresh outlooks and the materials to make further interdisciplinary connections that effectively make a case for the importance of musical cultures as active agents in human life and history.

I continue to advertise my American course outside my department as a course without prerequisites except for sophomore standing or above. This lack of prerequisites means that I cannot assume students read music, although I can still teach them how to find important contextual material through scores. While I decenter notation, listening remains foremost in the outside work for the class, and I teach active listening skills. Through individual written projects I ensure that students with music-reading skills can continue to hone them as well as provide a way for non-majors to explore their own interests and to foster interdisciplinary connections.

I came to that first American music course acknowledging that I was, in large measure, unprepared. (Of course, one could argue that we are rarely prepared for any course we teach, but that would be another essay.) In retrospect, I see that I gave myself a kind of permission to make up for in enthusiasm what I lacked in expertise. I admitted outright that I had inherited the course, and that the students and I would be traveling the road together. I see now that being in a liberal arts setting—one that offered small class size, bright students and at least some institutional commitment to experimental modes of teaching—made this first foray easier.

At the syllabus-creating level, a course in American music presents a historiographic challenge through the perspective of place over chronological period. While one can inscribe chronology onto this place, as most American music textbooks still do, in the classroom this chronology can be suspended in favor of other kinds of organizational constructs. How else can we present our materials and stories other than in a linear fashion? Doing away with presumptive chronology in the favor of topics has been one of the primary pleasures and great lessons of the course.

Acknowledging place over time provides the means to raise issues not only of historiographic presumptions but of categorization, of the politics of labeling. What do we mean, after all, by "American," an adjective I have been using from the beginning of this essay but have yet to define? Does it mean traditions within the confines of the political boundaries of the U.S. or the larger region of the North American continent? What are my obligations in this course to neighboring Mexico (Carlos Chávez and Aaron Copland were colleagues and shared many common concerns) or Canada? to Central and South America? On what grounds do we identify individuals and/or musical practices as representative of a place or of a nation? Do we dare, as Virgil Thomson did, to catalog specific musical gestures and traits as distinctly "American?"[2] How do we account for musical practices that transcend or blur national boundaries, such as balladry and now Tejano musics? No course can cover it all, so whose America, then, is this course about? Raising and trying to find answers to any of these questions provides an organizational point of departure and a challenging pleasure.

For my initial class, I drew on some of Richard Crawford's ideas, first expressed in *Studying American Music* (1985), of American music as underexplored terrain in need of mapping.[3] Crawford proposed five questions as part of a scholarly agenda that would lead to a fuller description and appreciation of American musical life. His first four questions—what music? by whom? where and under what circumstances? and how financially supported?—attempt to get at the choices people make and have made about the role of music in their lives, and especially how they support those choices with their time and money. The descriptive focus of these four queries neatly circumvent the value judgments that have long hampered American music through false comparisons with canonic European traditions. Instead, the many and often simultaneous processes, activities, and contexts of musical culture come to the fore. Only in his final question does Crawford raise the value-laden issue of importance.

Starting from the idea of a map allows for regional sensitivity and local specificity. The courses I taught in Vermont, where students had access to unique field recordings of Vermont traditional singers and their sung stories, are very different from the courses I teach now in Wisconsin, where active, if often invisible, tribal nations and communities afford the participatory experience of inter-tribal powwows. I require students to become participants in the many re-created and on going musical events in their region: sacred harp sings, gospel choirs, contradances, swing dances and the like. All afford the possibility for exploring local musical choices, multiple musical identities, traditional and evolving genres and styles, and kinds of financial support.

Through local and regional *foci*, students can explore the methodologies of oral history as well as archival documentation, balancing these different ways of understanding past and present events or experiences and people's investment in them.

A regional focus demands exploring the "regionalist," examining how certain parts of a landscape or nation acquire more worth and prestige. Within the context of the U.S., it is crucial to deal with the continuing perceptions of the American South and one of its most important exports, country music. I have only taught above the Mason-Dixon line, and when I ask students to rate their musical preferences and listening tastes, country music comes out on the bottom, below opera, even though country music is extraordinarily commercially successful throughout the U.S. In fifteen years of teaching, only one student has ever claimed country music as her preferred listening choice. *Somebody* is listening to it, and somebody is listening to it here in Wisconsin, as demonstrated by our local all-country music station and the number of major country artists who perform in our largest local venues. Country music continues to be a source of disdain and "southerners" along with it, even by the most theoretically enlightened students. The class prejudice at the heart of this regionalist bias can—and should—be explored as part of the intellectual landscape.[4]

I am well aware that the image of mapping an American musical landscape, one that appears in scholarship including Richard Crawford's own recent publication, is not without problems.[5] Mapping is rarely the innocent or objective descriptive process we might hope it to be. Like everything we do as teachers and scholars, mapping is, at some level, deeply implicated in ideological tensions over ownership and often uneasy relationships of power. As a way of demonstrating how mapping and the final product of maps emphasize or mute these relationships, I draw on the "Equal Area Presentation" world map created by German historian Arno Peters that decenters North America and colonial Europe by showing all countries and continents in proportion to their relative size.[6] Africa appears as a massive continent, truer visually to the many ways it has served the musical and cultural imaginations of the Euro-American West.

Similarly, mapping in any kind of American context plays too easily into a seductive national identity of "The Land." Borrowing from the well-known chorus in *Oklahoma!*: "we know we belong to the land, and the land we belong to is grand." This naive and simplistic formulation rarely asks about either the "we," the status of the land before "we" got there, and our subsequent claims to both belonging and ownership. Ironically, while the state name of Oklahoma was given to the former Indian Territory by its resettled native peoples,

*Oklahoma!* ignores those same people in its musical-theatrical celebration of pioneer domesticity and statehood. This blindness to the diverse Native American and Indian traditions is still perpetuated in some American music textbooks and much Americanist scholarship, and with it a troubling U.S. political history of genocidal acts done in the name of "The Land." I recommend consciously working against these unexamined notions of place and belonging, of colonization ("land of the free"), and expansion ("go west, young man"). Instead, uncover and track the riskier tensions over rural landscapes and urban cityscapes, the creation of suburbs, emigration (choosing to come to a place), and enslavement (brought without choice to a place), and resettlement (forcibly removed from a place), patterns of assimilation, neighborhoods and ghettos, regional dialects. These productive tensions reveal how musical culture becomes enmeshed in struggles over multiple and often competing representations of national- and self-identities.

More recently, I have used Christopher Small's understanding of music not as a thing but as an action, what he calls "musicking" in his 1998 book of the same name.[7] Small's anthropological and ethnomusicological emphasis on the social process of music-making—musicking—as a set of relationships can, like the process of mapping a particular place, help reconfigure music history as on going dynamic processes, as microcosms of larger cultural constructs and meanings. These perspectives work particularly well for students exploring local sites of musicking and to probe further their own individual musicking autobiographies or musical topographies.

How else might a non-linear topical organization work? As I have already suggested, if you are working in North America, you could begin from where you are. What is the musicking map of your institution, your city, your state, your place, and what does it reveal? Who makes music and where? How do performers understand what they do as American or not? Explore different kinds of song or kinds of singing and vocality. The rise of sheet music in the nineteenth century is tied up with the growth of mass-marketed periodicals and newspapers and an emerging urban middle class with an increasingly shared world view. Stephen Foster's songs, which can be easily sung by a class around a simulated parlor (classroom) piano, provide a compendium of images of shifting racial, class, and gender roles. The politicization of folk song and folk music from the 1940s onward and the creation and transmission of Freedom Songs as part of the organized struggle for Civil Rights provide other ways to look at issues of popularity, authenticity, and political musicking.

The many varieties of musical theatrical entertainments—minstrelsy, vaudeville, film, modern dance—provide a way to ask about what is entertaining and why. Explore how entertainers have and continue to draw on ethnic and racialized "others" as sources for both humor and pathos. (*West Side Story* and *Rent*, as well as any Marx Brothers movie, are good cases in point.) How does the music involved entertain and/or perpetuate musical codes of difference and through what particular musical means or contexts? Suspend the artificial distinctions between "opera" and "musical" or other genres. The aforementioned *Oklahoma!,* the collaborative product of Richard Rodgers, Oscar Hammerstein II, and Agnes de Mille, makes an apt comparison on many levels with the Martha Graham/Aaron Copland collaboration on *Appalachian Spring.*

Teaching American music is often perceived outside departmental confines as hip. Deans, faculty colleagues in other departments, and general consumers frequently express great enthusiasm for and interest in my American courses, often because they have their own beloved repertories that fall outside the narrow canon of presumed musical rectitude. While the interest can be patronizing ("that must be so much *fun* to teach"), it provides an important opportunity to talk about our concerns. These conversations become a place to argue for the importance of musical culture, for music-making and repertories as something other than a collection of "good music" or "great masterpieces" but a means to learn more about what it is to be human. If we can talk about music's power to entertain and to move us in personal and non-valuative ways, we begin to break down barriers in our musical institutions that continue to intimidate people and make them wary of academics who appear to be in the business of being smarter than everyone else. We might create new connections and, in a real sense, start to map territories we can only now imagine but would love to live in.

## Notes

1    For several years I had assigned written projects based on the materials in the Helen Hartness Flanders Ballad Collection at Middlebury College. One semester I finally heard these ballads and in response wrote, "'Cursed was she': Gender and Power in American Balladry," in *Cecilia Reclaimed: Feminist Perspectives on Gender and Music*, eds. Susan C. Cook and Judy S. Tsou (Urbana, IL: The University of Illinois Press, 1994), 202–24.

2    Virgil Thomson, *American Music Since 1910* (New York: Holt, Rinehart and Winston, 1971).

3    Richard Crawford, *Studying American Music*, I.S.A.M. Special Publications 3 (Brooklyn: Institute for Studies in American Music, 1985).

4    A good source for learning more about country music is *Classic Country Music: a Smithsonian Collection/selected and annotated by Bill Malone*, RD042

Smithsonian Institution (1990). This excellent collection helped foster my own growing fondness for the repertory, as did Bill Malone's regular country music show on our local alternative radio station, WORT-FM. The use of the term "classic," however, in the title suggests, I would argue, the need for legitimacy that continues to dog American music and especially American popular repertories.

5   Richard Crawford, *The American Musical Landscape* (Berkeley: University of California Press, 1993). See also Jean Ferris, *America's Musical Landscape*, third ed. (Boston: McGraw Hill, 1998).

6   *World Map in Equal Area Presentation: Peters Projection* (Oxford: Oxford Cartographers Ltd., [n.d.] and Cincinnati: Friendship Press, [n.d.]). See also *The New Cartography* (New York: Friendship Press, 1983).

7   Christopher Small, *Musicking: The Meanings of Performing and Listening* (Hanover: Wesleyan University Press, 1998).

# General Issues

## Chapter Eleven

# Teaching at a Liberal Arts College

*Mary Hunter*

Apart from a couple of semesters teaching freshman seminars as a graduate student, I have only taught at liberal arts colleges: Bates College, in Lewiston Maine, and more recently, Bowdoin College, only twenty miles from Bates. Thus, my sense of the particular pleasures and challenges of this teaching environment is not in any sense comparative, except to the extent that I have talked with colleagues who teach in other sorts of institutions and that my own undergraduate education (at the University of Sussex, in England) had quite different foundations and presuppositions.

Nevertheless, even with very little contrasting experience, it seems clear to me that perhaps, especially for music, the liberal arts college is a quite particular environment with quite specific opportunities and constraints. These give rise to comparably specific philosophical or historiographical questions—or at least to specific variants of the usual ones.

There are, of course, many liberal arts college characteristics that play into the way we address both our material and our students at Bates and Bowdoin: the small classes and modestly-sized overall community, a relatively un-diverse population of middle- and upper-class eighteen to twenty-two year olds (despite enormous efforts to diversify), the increasingly strong expectation of a nurturing teaching environment, and the particular feel or ambience of the specific college. These characteristics, however, affect the teaching of music history in rather intangible, and probably quite various ways, whereas the more or less universal logistics and mechanics of liberal arts college life have much more obvious and easily-discussed effects on the teaching of music history. These are the particulars on which I wish to focus. I should say that by "music history" I mean all courses that are not theory, composition, or performance. Music literature courses (Piano Music), genre courses (The Symphony), topics courses (Women and Music; The Beatles) and First Year Seminars all count here as music history, along with the obvious survey courses.

Five constants of the small liberal arts college seem to me particularly relevant to the way we teach music history. First, with some exceptions students typically do not come to a liberal arts college determined to major in music. It is more characteristic of our students either to find that something they simply thought they would continue for fun has turned out to be compellingly interesting, or to discover quite by surprise, in the course of taking general education courses, that the music department would be a happy home for them. Thus, such colleges need to offer a steady stream of non-technical courses on nifty subjects that will attract students who do not (initially) think of themselves as music major or minor material. Second, and related to the first, is the overall ethos in a liberal arts college (especially in the humanities and social sciences) that "out there in the real world" the words "liberal arts" describe a student's training as much as the name of the major. This has particular effects on music history teaching, since within music as a whole it is there (rather than in theory, composition, or performance) that the particular values of the liberal arts education—critical thinking, writing skills, a capacity to make connections across disciplines—manifest themselves. It is where we as teachers have the greatest obligation to reinforce the academic ethos of the institution as a whole. Third, liberal arts students must usually take between a sixth and a quarter of their courses in the general education curriculum or in distribution requirements, ensuring that they have been at least modestly exposed to the methods of a variety of disciplines. Students may also major in more than one subject and minor in one, and sometimes two. So, on the one hand, a major in music often takes up only a third (or even less) of a student's total number of courses, and on the other, music history courses can (and should) contribute to the curriculum available to general students. Fourth, especially in isolated or largely rural places like Maine, students increasingly take a semester or a year abroad, almost always in their junior year. More than half the juniors at Bates and Bowdoin take time away in this fashion. If students do not declare a major until the end of the sophomore year and then leave the country for a semester or a year, this inevitably affects what and how we teach. Finally, in most liberal arts colleges the human resources of the music department are both relatively limited and relatively inflexible. Usually there are rather small numbers of music majors to serve, and no floating nebula of graduate students and underemployed-but-qualified spouses to staff extra sections of required courses. Thus, courses required for the major can often only be offered once every two years, making the intersections between students' life-plans and a department's teaching capacities quite complicated.

These more or less ubiquitous "mechanical" characteristics of liberal arts colleges have several effects relevant to the teaching of music history. For example, the nature of our student body (always allowing for exceptions) generally means that while the students in our history or literature courses have often played one or several instruments, they typically have no strong or broadly-informed attachment to any significant portion of the repertory taught, whether that repertory is "classical," jazz, non-Western, or women's music. Our students have often not been longstanding or especially dedicated members of orchestras, chamber ensembles, jazz bands or combos that have played the music we study in history courses (though they spend many hours every day listening to music that is taught rarely, if at all). Thus, for the majority of our students, the music history course is as much (if not more) an exercise in getting to know pieces as in putting works they already know into some sort of context, either historical, social, or intellectual. I will return to this issue below.

In addition, a fully sequential music history education in which the teacher of a second-year course can presuppose knowledge of both the materials and the methods of the first year is often out of the question. Although there is really no choice about the order of at least the first three semesters of music theory (students cannot do chromatic harmony before they know their intervals), it is more difficult for the liberal arts music department to insist that students take "Baroque Music" before they take "Romantic," or even "Music from Antiquity until 1750" before "Music from 1750 until the Present Day." Half the relevant students might be in Australia or Scotland, or have schedule conflicts for either the first or the second of these periods. Thus, unless one teaches the entirety of Western music history in one semester, students are perhaps less likely to come away with the notion that chronology is the organizing principle of (Western classical) music history than are students who proceed in a more rigidly sequential fashion.

It is also difficult to insist that more than one theory course be accomplished before many history courses. Of course departments can (and most do) have upper-level music history courses that require at least a year of theory, most also offer a larger menu of middle-level history and literature or topics courses that require very little theoretical sophistication, but that can also count toward the major.[1] Thus, just as chronology is not strongly communicated as the primary (if also implicit) organizing principle of music history, so style history, with its expectation that all students can follow a modulation or identify a mode, cannot be the only (or even the primary) lens through which we communicate repertories, periods, genres, or topics in music.

The logistics of the liberal arts education also ensure that many, if not most, classes (with the possible exception of the senior seminar) have a pretty wide variety of students: first-years (though more often sophomores) with seniors; majors and minors with interested others; some with other disciplinary experience (history, a language other than English, women's studies, American studies) relevant to the course. Some have experience writing papers, some have none. Some can follow a score with no problem and others cannot; some can hear the theoretically weighted musical elements of form and harmony while others hear timbre, emotion, and words.

Finally, the combination of complicated student schedules and limited departmental resources requires that the vast majority of courses dealing with music history and literature be aimed simultaneously at majors and non-majors. A quick survey of liberal arts curricula shows that most colleges require of their music majors some sort of Western art-music survey—usually two semesters—but that the remainder of the history/literature curriculum is taken up with elective topics: courses that expand the students' horizons in terms of content-coverage and variety of approach, but which neither build on, nor explicitly react to, the survey. Music history in this educational environment has almost no verticality or institutionally reinforced sequence of skills or capacities.

Theoretical rather than historical competence is often the prerequisite for the senior seminar, for example. This breadth of audience and "looseness" of methodological expectation can be both liberating and frustrating, depending on the subject matter, the particular group of students one has to deal with, and one's own thinking at the moment. For myself, I found it marvelously liberating as I emerged from graduate school, partly because these courses seemed to me an opportunity to play in the field of big and unanswerable questions after working so hard at delimiting a dissertation arena in which I could become the reigning expert, however temporarily. More recently, although I still find the sense of open possibilities in teaching students of various backgrounds extremely stimulating, I find I have less patience for the vagueness of play and the journeys of self-discovery it should stimulate. I am now more interested in making sure that students have mastered materials and skills. Some teachers will move in the other direction over the years; others will stay teetering between the two possibilities. No liberal arts teacher of music history will escape the tension between wishing the curriculum could be more rigorously structured and being glad for the variety needed to appeal to non-vocational students.

While the survey course presents particular logistical challenges in the liberal arts environment, and those challenges certainly affect the way it is taught, its justification is probably not very different from that in any other institution of higher learning. Surveys are offered because exposure to the core repertory of the academic version of the discipline—whatever the core repertory might be—is thought to be indispensable for whichever students are required to take it. Similarly, the senior seminar, which requires conversance with at least chromatic harmony and which may introduce a select group of students to advanced analytic procedures or to some of the mysteries of musicology (i.e., source studies, bibliography, original research, methodological questions), is both easy to justify and probably not so different from one institution to another.

The "200-level" elective topics course, however, which can presuppose essentially no common knowledge among its students, seems to me especially characteristic of the liberal arts college, both logistically and philosophically. It is about this sort of course that my remarks below are concentrated.

I should say at the outset that I approach such courses with mixed feelings. On the one hand, as noted above, they offer quite wonderful opportunities to explore material that I would otherwise pay no attention to, and they allow me to experiment with everything from content to the dynamics of the classroom. Conversely, I have also consistently found this level of course the most difficult, both to teach and to get a sort of ontological grip on. I find myself continually asking what the course is really about, what I want the students to come out with, why I should teach this material from one perspective rather than another, and to whom the material is pertinent and why. (And while these questions naturally arise in other courses, they do not nag at me in the way they do with these mid-level courses.) Obviously the answers to these questions vary from course to course, as well as from institution to institution, as different students make different demands and shape the meaning of the experience in different ways. But over the years I have found myself repeatedly thinking some of the same thoughts about these courses, and some of the most recurring thoughts are both stimulating and comforting as I travel through the semesters with various groups of more and less excited students, and more and less tractable materials.

These thoughts fall into two broad categories: first, what is the reason or justification for teaching either this particular course or a course of this general sort? And second, what are the tensions, either of the enterprise in general or of this particular course? Some questions about justifying the course are pretty predictable in this context: does the content or method amplify material majors may already have been required to take? Does it connect in some way with things that students in other fields are likely to know about or be interested in? Does the course content interest me enough that I will be able to teach it with some enthusiasm?

The answers to these questions have led me in recent years toward topics courses that I think music majors need because either the subjects or the methods required by the subjects are typically not covered in other courses (and that other students may find appealing). These include: American music, women and music, and opera. More interesting sorts of justifications arise when thinking about what one hopes to communicate both about music itself (whatever that is) and about the act of responding to and writing about music. It seems to me that the liberal arts context requires music history teachers to demonstrate that music is as much a part of culture as any other form of artistic expression, and that it is as formed and permeated by social and economic pressures as many other aspects of life. The music major (who is often so excited by gaining some theoretical control over pieces that this comes to seem the only proper way to deal with music) should learn that there are ways of understanding music different from, but at least as important as, harmony and form (and subsidiarily chronology). The non-music major, on the other hand, should learn that music can fit into some of the cultural and epistemological frameworks that she or he has learned in other courses. These complementary ways of learning seem to me valuable in any context, but they are essential in the liberal arts environment for two related but contrasting reasons. The first is that if students are being taught—as they are—that (say) literature and art are formed in part to fill particular social needs, and that they interact with their circumstances of production and consumption in ways that affect many details of their internal or "inherent" elements, then it is crucial to assert that music works in society in many of the same ways as (though obviously not identically to) other media. This is crucial institutionally because it is all too easy for music departments to be seen as little enclaves of arcane and irrelevant ways of thinking; more importantly, it is crucial to the educational mission of this sort of college, which is, in part, to develop minds that can make connections and cross boundaries.

If we do not talk about music in ways that put it into the same category as literature or visual art, we risk reifying the notion that music, especially classical music, is disconnected from the "real" world of economic pressures and social contingencies. Connecting music with literature and visual art means something more than the standard music-appreciation gambit of showing the Fuseli painting of the nightmare in the same class as Berlioz's *Symphonie fantastique*. It means using a vocabulary of social location, and even, to some extent, of referentiality, comparable (though obviously not identical) to that used in discussions of literature and art. For example, if the novels of Samuel Richardson and the prints of Hogarth can usefully be said to have depended on both the disposable income of the (perpetually) emerging middle classes, and on new ideas about the relation between private and public in the consumption of art, do not the string quartets of Haydn (to take an obvious example) belong in that discussion too? And even (or perhaps especially) if students know nothing about Hogarth and Richardson, Haydn's quartets can be a wonderful way into the social dynamics of the late eighteenth century, as well as a satisfying aesthetic experience.

The second and related reason why it is important in this context to talk about music as a fully-embedded part of society and culture is that it often goes against the grain of why students (perhaps especially non-majors) take music classes. Students in liberal arts colleges are quite used to, and often very good at, discussions about politics and the environment, gender and sex, the reasons for World War I, and how advertising worms its way into such apparently personal domains as body image and choices about relationships. Music courses—especially courses in classical music—are often seen, I think, as something of a refuge from the rigors of perpetual relevance and argumentation, and thus, as places where discussion (as opposed to simply answering the teacher's questions) does not really have to happen. Or rather, where the notion of discussion as it plays out in the rest of their academic lives seems not useful. Students typically come into these courses with three fairly well ingrained, but largely unconscious, ways of thinking about music: as a matter of personal (and thus barely negotiable) taste, as explicable through technical vocabulary to which they have small access, and as the hook on which to hang historical and biographical "facts." These may contextualize the piece quite nicely, but in all likelihood do not affect the experience of hearing it, and are thus not really up for serious debate or discussion. If the mission of the liberal arts college is not only to help students cross boundaries, but also to push them into challenging received wisdom and into rethinking some of their assumptions, then surely it is our duty as music history teachers in this environment to challenge both ourselves and our students to find a mutually comprehensible language and a set of interesting questions, which both place music squarely in an intellectual, historical, or social context, *and* allow students to acknowledge and make use of the pleasure and nourishment they find in the purely aesthetic aspects of music.

For example, Gretchen Wheelock's argument that the end of Haydn's *Joke* quartet works as a joke only for an audience who could not actually see the score, and that this connects to the emergence of mass publication and consumption of chamber music, is exactly the sort of argument that I would want to push students toward.[2] It takes an utterly obvious element in the music, one that any student with ears can hear, and that most can enjoy, and uses the skills of critical thinking and cross-disciplinary expertise to illuminate that obvious and aesthetically pleasing element.

If finding ways to connect music to the broader culture is one justification for the typical liberal arts music history course, then helping students write coherently, eloquently, and truthfully about it is another. Writing is a central part of the liberal arts curriculum, as the most superficial glance at the myriads of writing workshops, freshman seminars, writing-across-the-curriculum programs, and senior thesis requirements at most places will show. With most classes being relatively small, papers are the normal mode through which students demonstrate their understanding of the course materials and concepts, and competent writing is one of the things that is supposed to distinguish the liberal arts graduate from a student who has gone in a more vocational direction. Again, music history is (or should be) consistent with, and connected to, college-wide values about writing. At the same time, however, it seems to me that one of the real values of the music history course is that the students have to write about music in terms that simultaneously call on the shared theoretical or conceptual vocabulary of the class, and honestly and sensitively draw upon their own responses to that music, responses that inevitably include, but are not limited to, whether and how they like or dislike it. Perhaps this is especially true of the "200-level" course, which is unmoored from the chronological framework of the survey, and which cannot—or perhaps in a liberal arts environment, should not—always rely on the comforting technicalities of roman-numeral analysis and formal designations.

Liking and disliking individual pieces are often the key to whether a course of this sort works or falls flat on its face—and not only because liking and disliking are part of the ethos of consumer-satisfaction endemic to most educational institutions these days. I have almost always found it difficult or impossible to get students to care about the history or other social context of a body of music if they have not developed some sort of authentic-feeling (and preferably positive) relationship to at least some of the works in the course. I have found that the courses work best when the students feel that there is room for their responses, however nudged (or bludgeoned) by me into a form that goes beyond the purely personal association or sensation. It must be admitted that it is hard work (and I have often failed) to come up with assignments that will push the students both to demonstrate mastery of the factual material of the course and to take a position about a piece based on a more or less personal response. Not to ask students to make this effort, however, seems to me to lose the opportunity to connect the music history experience with the best of the rest of the liberal arts education. To write well about music is often (though not always) to reach for truth without any real chance of fully getting there, partly because of the inaccessibility of certain historical or contextual circumstances, but more peculiarly and importantly because of the complexity, fleetingness, and inarticulateness of our responses to music. Because of the time one can spend on writing, and because of the students' general expectation that writing will be taken seriously, music history and literature classes in the liberal arts context provide a unique opportunity to work with ambiguity and transience, to capture something while at the same time acknowledging that it got away, and to weigh often heartfelt reactions in the balance with colder, but more graspable, contextual information. In other words, writing about music in the liberal arts context should be not simply the most convenient or gradeable way to assess knowledge of the material, but an opportunity to engage memory, heart, and imagination in the pursuit of some version of the truth. As everyone reading this essay will know, this is difficult; but for me, at least, it is the most worthwhile effort I make in teaching.

If the justifications for these mid-level courses in music history are basically that they are the place where the study of music and the core values of the liberal arts curriculum come together most strikingly, those very justifications, and the efforts they provoke, produce tensions perhaps not unique to music history, but certainly characteristic of it. For instructors, these tensions may be most acute as they move from the extreme specialization of graduate school to the very different demands of the teaching environment. One logistical tension in these courses is how to keep the music major interested and engaged while not overwhelming or losing the non-major. As a teacher in such courses one always hopes that the questions one asks are interesting to everyone and can be answered with varying sorts of expertise. And sometimes one's hopes are fulfilled. One solution is to teach courses that put everyone on more or less the same footing, since they do not deal in any detail with the music *qua* music. I have, for example, taught a course on film biographies of musicians—classical and popular—that fits this description, and which did, in fact, elicit equally intelligent and engaged responses from students at various levels of musical sophistication. It also (quite unusually in my experience) stimulated students to contribute knowledge from perspectives developed in quite different courses. In the normal course of events, however, the curriculum demands some number of mid-level history courses that do engage with the notes and sounds of the music. In these courses, I have generally found that broad questions about the nature of individuality, of gender or sexuality, or about the conditions of production and consumption provide access for everyone. If, however, the material does not easily lend itself to these broad historical or social questions, or if the teacher wants to stress the content of the music, then alternative paper topics, some of which require technical knowledge and some of which require a different sort of research, are another way around the students' differences in knowledge and experience. And sometimes, of course, the divide between those theoretically competent and those with other backgrounds simply makes the course difficult to teach.

More interesting than the tensions between musically advanced and beginning students, however, are the questions about how a liberal arts context for teaching music history produces conceptual tensions. The most striking of these tensions is that between pulling the rug out from under the students and putting it there in the first place. My colleagues in such disciplines as anthropology, American studies, women's studies, and literature, talk regularly about the importance of encouraging students to see that the world they may think is natural and (perhaps) God-given is, in fact, culturally constructed, and that the distributions and uses of money, power, and cultural and spiritual capital in any given society radically affect the ways individuals understand themselves both as individuals and in relation to each other. These topics typically make students uncomfortable, but the public rhetoric of both institutions where I have worked asserts that this sort of discomfort is good—even at the core of the college's mission—and that getting young people to question the social structures that put them where they are can lead to a general bettering both of those students individually and of society at large. I fully agree with that rhetoric. It presupposes, however, that students come with fairly well-developed ways of dealing with the world and with texts, which then need to be shaken loose and put up for inspection. In music, though, while students do come with certain suppositions about the social location of music (it is the result of the individual inspiration of geniuses, it is about "self expression," it is there primarily to manipulate mood, it has in some way to do with individual or cultural authenticity), they normally come unencumbered by any preconceptions about how to hear or make sense either of individual pieces or of whole repertories. They have, by and large, had no music theory in high school, their instrumental or vocal lessons were innocent of any theoretical or contextual information, and music has not been a standard element in their American, European, or World history courses. In other words, for many students there is no factual rug to pull out, particularly with respect to the classical repertory.

Within the overall sequence of the music major (however un-sequentially taken), we can reasonably expect our senior majors to be able to cope with questioning the assumptions of the discipline: is the canon made up of obviously great music? What do we do with the idea that Beethoven's genius was not a simple bolt of lightning but a complex negotiation with the needs of his patrons? Why do we learn more about harmony than about rhythm? What difference does it make to our understanding of Western music that we take the score to be more important than the performance? What happens to our analysis of Schubert's music if we take sexuality into account? Can you tell anything about gender from just listening to a piece? Is that even a smart question? And so on. These are questions that have exercised music historians in recent years, and they raise important issues. I cannot imagine sending students to graduate school without having had them at least begin to wrestle seriously with some of them. But all of these questions require students to know some pieces, to have developed a relationship to a repertory, and to be conversant not only with the material of the field, but also with some more or less positivistic ways of dealing with it. Despite years of trying, I am finally convinced that you cannot deconstruct before you have constructed. At the same time, as I suggested above, we are not taking the liberal arts charge seriously (especially for non-majors) if we do not ask them to work in ways that may seem to go against the grain. In the "200-level" courses I have chiefly been talking about here, the balance between laying the rug and whisking it out is usually, perforce, weighted in favor of the former, but it is almost always possible at some points (in even the most doggedly informative course) to suggest that there are other ways of looking at the material, that the gap between what they really hear and what they have analyzed may be worth taking seriously, and that there is an essay they should read that stands the assumptions of the course on their heads—or something (anything) that may jolt some of the students into problematizing what they have learned.

Finally, it is important to mention that partly because of small numbers, and partly because of the ethos of the liberal arts college, teaching at such an institution is (or can be) extremely personal. Not only do we get to know our students quite well, but they also get to know us. This means, in addition to all the obvious stuff about nurturing and guidance and quality time, that it is very hard to teach dishonestly. I do not mean that it is impossible to teach things you know rather little about, which, in fact, is one of the standard delights and terrors of this sort of place. Rather, I mean that it is very hard to carry off a course based on assumptions that you yourself cannot endorse. Thus, the balance between laying foundations and questioning them, between pushing students to work with their own responses and insisting that the facts be in place, between presenting music as an integral part of the liberal arts curriculum and presenting it as special, will vary from teacher to teacher, and with any given teacher, probably from course to course. Rather than being a series of "tips for the successful teacher," the present essay is intended to indicate the questions that this environment forcefully raises, and to suggest that struggling with those questions is both necessary and stimulating.

*Thanks to Jim McCalla, Jim Parakilas, and Sanna Pederson for comments on this essay.*

**Notes**

1    One might counter that science departments often seem to run more rigorous sequences of courses than music departments seem to manage. This is true, but students come to liberal arts colleges already preselected as science majors; they take the introductory courses as freshmen, and the culture of science in liberal arts colleges is distinct from the more "fuzzy" exploratory culture of humanities and social sciences.

2    Gretchen A. Wheelock, *Haydn's Ingenious Jesting with Art: Contexts of Musical Wit and Humor* (New York: Schirmer Books, 1992), 9–15 and 97–110.

Chapter Twelve

# Teaching in the Centrifugal Classroom

*Pamela Starr*

*To the memories of Michael Starr, Philip A. Friedheim, and William B. Kimmel, who taught me how to teach.*

One day in the middle of my musicological career, I awoke to the fact that I was a postmodern feminist—not, I hasten to add, with respect to my scholarship, where notwithstanding the excellent examples of many in our discipline, my research has, until very recently, remained firmly grounded in the investigation of the doings of very dead white male musicians of the fifteenth century. But somehow, and almost without my having noticed, the refreshing breeze of new ways of understanding our discipline and of communicating it to students entered my teaching. This fact was brought sharply into focus while reading an essay by a prominent literary scholar, Linda Woodbridge. In "The Centrifugal Classroom," Woodbridge describes

> The postmodern: a decentered world where hierarchical, central authority yields to the power of the people, where the official feast succumbs to the anarchic, centrifugal forces of carnival—the decentering, antihierarchical perspective of feminism has contributed a good deal to the construction of that world. The modern city with its centralized skyscrapers and its Central Park is dissolving into the unfocalized postmodern landscape whose democratic suburbs and shopping malls refract each city's center into many centers.[1]

She goes on to demonstrate vividly the ways that postmodern and feminist approaches can inform the teaching of any subject. This article resonated strongly with pedagogical ideas and practical teaching strategies of my own. For some years I had recognized that the music history being taught to today's students had changed in important ways from that taught to me and to most of my colleagues, and with this, the role of the instructor had changed as well. We have moved, I believe, from a discipline in which the instructor delivers prepackaged information to one where the instructor sets in motion the structures and processes that enable students to develop (through readings, practice in analyzing musical repertoire, and discussion) their own understanding of the evolution of musical style and to use this understanding to enrich their careers as performing musicians and teachers.[2] For some years, I have worked to develop strategies that would fulfill the new requirements of music history as taught both to undergraduates and graduate students in performance. I shall explore two of these: first, a new curricular structure to replace the traditional lecture format, and second, the use of a research journal to replace the traditional undergraduate writing assignment, the research paper. Both of these strategies work toward de-centralizing and deprivileging the authority of the instructor to the important and practical end of fostering the skills of music history necessary for the development of every performing musician.

## The learning circle

Who has not had the experience of standing at the front of a music history classroom, delivering a carefully prepared and insightful lecture, replete with gentle humor and compelling detail, only to sense an ever-widening ripple of disengagement as the hour wore on; or, of reading in the final exams the inevitable, tired repackaging of your ideas, the sparkling humor gone utterly flat with repetition? For the first few years of teaching, I had this experience often, and eventually it began to urge me to find another way to teach my history courses. The process of discovery was helped along by encounters in various pedagogical essays with quotations like this one by Janet Emig: "A silent classroom, or one filled with only the teacher's voice is anathema to learning;"[3] or this by Page Smith,

> There is, I think, much truth in [Patricia Nelson Limerick's] observation that "lecturing is an unnatural act, an act for which providence did not design humans. It is perfectly all right, now and then, for a human being to be possessed by the urge to speak, and to speak while others remain silent. But to do this regularly, one hour and fifteen minutes at a time ... for one person to drone on while others sit in silence? ... I do not believe that this is what the Creator ... designed humans to do."[4]

More systematic reading in the literature on teaching and learning only served to confirm my intuition that various disciplines were moving toward teaching strategies that employed active learning.[5] My own discipline, however, seemed silent on the subject, at least in print.

I finally found the key to a new teaching strategy, or rather, it was generously given to me by my colleague, Dr. Quentin Faulkner, professor of organ and music history, who had taught one of the upper division period courses that was now to be assigned to me. He not only offered to share his innovative course structure, but even agreed to "show me the ropes" by team teaching the course before he handed it over to me as a permanently solo assignment.[6] As I watched (and helped) this course unfold, it became clear that its special design facilitated the active approach to learning I had been searching for. It worked marvelously—so well that I developed a version of it for each of the four upper division period courses I teach, with significant modifications depending on class size (anywhere from seven to twenty-five) and historical period (Renaissance, Baroque, Classical, and Romantic).

The transformation of the course begins, as Woodbridge suggests, with a rethinking of the physical geography of the classroom, an act that inevitably alters the mental geography of the course as well. I start the process of decentralizing the class by arranging the seats in a circle, in which students and instructor intermingle. I work hard each semester to overcome students' tendency to leave a safety zone of vacant chairs flanking the instructor; by the end of the semester, students have accepted that there is no central focal point (i.e., the position of the professor) but a continually shifting point, as class discussion flows among students and teacher. The new seating arrangement serves also to discourage any tendency I might have to launch into anything more prolonged than a casual couple of minutes expanding on an issue raised in discussion.

The point of the circular seating is to emphasize the new role of the students. By the end of the course, they will have taken ownership of a number of musical works from the historical period through the device of teaching themselves and the rest of the class how to understand and to discourse on the musical style of these works. Each student is asked to present a short report (about five minutes) on a particular work; or, in the case of larger or more complex works, to formulate questions and lead a discussion of the work. Responsibility for either reporting on or leading a discussion of a musical work prods a student to become very familiar indeed with its stylistic characteristics. The relatively brief format of the report ensures that students will determine and select the most important characteristics to be discussed. Often, two students will work collaboratively: one to create a report on a work, the other to use that information as a springboard for a comparison with another work in the same genre or by the same composer.

Although it might appear that with this approach I have surrendered the teacher's authority, it is not, in fact, the case. Rather, I have transmuted that authority to a more subtle and less overtly controlling mode, one that establishes the structure for student learning and facilitates that experience. I am there to guide class discussion after the reports are delivered, to make sure that points left out are considered, and to make sure that all students have a chance to comment or to question the reporter. One does have to exercise a certain amount of tact when correcting inaccuracies. On the whole, though, students are willing to take criticism or correction if considerately offered, and are eventually even able and willing to critique their colleagues' reports. I also ask them to summarize their findings in a brief (two to three pages) written report, which sharpens their skills in written discourse. As the semester proceeds, I am always amazed at the growth of sophistication, insight, and (most important) self-confidence in the reports and comments of even the most initially self-effacing students.

So that the course does not become merely a loosely connected mosaic of literature, I also ask students to read, annotate, and discuss in class carefully chosen material in an appropriate historical textbook or related group of readings. These readings help to focus students' attention not only on musical style, but on the historical processes that lead to changes in style. We consider together not only the biographical careers of musicians, but the socioeconomic milieu of composers, performers, patrons, and audiences. We explore the purposes for which music of the period was composed. And we consider the effects of historical events on developments in music and musical style.

There will always be students who long for the less challenging road of a traditional, lecture-based course. But for each one of these there are dozens who express, in evaluations and personal conversation, their pleasure at being given the tools to teach themselves. This, after all, is why performers study music history.

## The research journal

An even more discouraging sight, if possible, than the expanse of somnolent students during a lecture is the stack of undergraduate "research" papers awaiting our attention during the final days of a semester. We know what to expect from these papers: the clumsy parody of historical material drawn from the least appropriate authors; the mind-numbing, bar-by-bar musical description that passes for stylistic analysis; the stilted and pretentious language; the naive interpretive conclusions. The truth is that our undergraduates enrolled in the introductory survey of music history are not yet ready for the extended and sophisticated discourse of a research paper on music. After several years of facing that stack of papers, I began to search for a better way to introduce undergraduates to the written art of extended musical discussion.

In this case, help came from outside my department and discipline. I had the privilege of participating in the 1990 Nebraska Writing Project, a seminar for faculty chosen from departments in colleges as diverse as Arts and Sciences, Engineering, Agriculture and Life Sciences, and Architecture. Together we explored the ways that writing and learning support each other; we were introduced to a veritable blizzard of theoretical and practical writings on this subject. From these, and from the articles I encountered subsequently, the notion of the journal emerged as a strong resource for developing student writing and learning.[7]

The power of the journal lies first of all in its informality and in the personal nature of its diction. Bryant Fillion, quoting a study from 1976 of the National Association for the Teaching of English, remarks that "theory and practice suggest that if a learner at any level is able to make his own formulations of what he is learning, this is more valuable than taking over someone else's preformulated language." "Students need," he says, "to say or write things in their own ways, their own styles ... ."[8] Peter Elbow and Jennifer Clarke speak to the restricting influence of audience on a student's writing style in formal papers. "Writing for an audience of one (the writer) can unblock prose, making it clearer, if not absolutely elegant."[9] The journal also allows for a gradual development of ideas and of engagement with a subject. It reveals the process of learning, as well as the final products of an extended encounter with a historical problem or a work of literature or art.[10] And, not least important for the beleaguered instructor, the journal provides the opportunity for and the joy of responding directly to students in a manner that guarantees their attention; it ameliorates "the isolation, the loneliness of teaching," through dialogue with students one on one.

Armed with examples and encouragement from the literature on teaching and writing, I set up a research journal project for my second-semester music history students—a project that, with small revisions, I continue to use. There are two goals for the project: first, to enable students to encounter a work of substance from the twentieth century;[11] and second, to give students practice in chronicling all stages of the process of learning about a new piece of music. In this project, they record informally the information and insights they have gleaned—information that could form (and on some occasions *does* form) the basis for a traditional research paper on the chosen work. Students are expected to keep a record of every stage of the process, from the initial choice of a musical work and the reasons for that choice, to the answering of several final questions intended to summarize what they have learned about the work, its composer, and about the research process itself.

I provide the students with a list of possible choices but also encourage them to consider choosing a work not on the list, one that might relate closely to their applied studio lessons or ensemble experience. Once the choices are made, I compile and distribute a list of them, so that students working on the same piece can consult with each other (another departure from the traditional research project, where independent and usually isolated research is emphasized). In keeping with the notion of "centrifugality," I encourage collaborative work, the sharing of both ideas and library resources in the journal project.

The project begins with a series of "questions" appropriate to each phase of the project that serve to jump-start the students' research.[12] The journals are collected biweekly, my graduate assistant and I sharing the responsibility of reading and commenting on the entries in detail.[13] We try gently to guide the students' thinking and research, making suggestions about additional research resources or analytical strategies as needed. But the students are usually able and willing to run with the project on their own. They manage to find the appropriate research materials with only the minimum steering from the instructor, and often emerge with remarkably sophisticated analytical insights.

Our comments are couched in the form of dialogue with the student, asking questions and expressing enthusiasm for particularly good observations or research strategies. For example, with a student working on Prokofiev's *Classical Symphony*, I read her preliminary plan of action and wrote: "I like the idea of posing logical questions as they occur to you and trying to answer them. Other things you might think about: the role of orchestration; how form plays out here (as compared with, for example, Haydn); and Prokofiev's career—why did he decide to write a 'classical symphony' at that time?" The student integrated these questions into her own research agenda for the piece, with excellent results for her overall grasp of its style and significance. When the student identified the second movement as a "gavotte," I prompted her to listen to and compare it with one from an eighteenth-century dance suite. To her penetrating observation that "it would be interesting to examine the whole symphony for any 'pointing fun' characteristics and how you tell the difference between his respect for the Classical style and his disrespect for it," I responded by encouraging her to consider the difference between imitation and (gentle) stylistic parody, which she did with exceptional insight.

I often discover comments in the journals that reveal elements about a work that I had not before contemplated myself, a fact I am delighted to share with the student. Only very occasionally must we include remarks designed to rouse the student from apparent apathy. We rarely address specifics of writing style, as I want the students to feel unencumbered and as little observed as possible while they explore their adopted musical work. Most students develop a spontaneous and refreshingly informal style for their journal entries, one that reveals a personal voice not always evident in classroom interactions or in more formal writing assignments. And, contrary to my own initial expectation, and probably that of my readers, students tend to write clearly and correctly (on the whole) when they do not feel they must write to impress.

Evaluating a process like the journal project, as compared with the finished product of a research paper, requires a different set of criteria, one that charts growth in various related skills of learning and processing information, as articulated in the journal project assignment: (1) regular and steady work with the music, demonstrated by consistent and regular journal entries; (2) a growing sophistication in the analysis of features of musical style, through use of score and recording; (3) a carefully thought out program of research into the music and the background of the music and of its composer; (4) signs of an attempt to organize and prioritize the features of the music believed to be most important to the understanding of the work; and (5) evidence that the student has reached some insight or understanding about the nature of the music, of its composer, and of its place in the history of twentieth-century music. Each time the journals are collected and read students receive, in addition to our comments, an interim grade ("satisfactory," "excellent," "outstanding," or "needs to work harder"), one that takes into consideration signs of improvement and growth from preceding weeks (or, rarely, the reverse). The final letter grade for the project will similarly reflect both the interim grades and the evidence of a student's success in negotiating the hurdles of a research project.

Manifestly, the research journal represents a significant investment of time and energy, both from students and from the instructor. Is it worth it? I suspect that the pedagogical advantages of the research journal over the traditional research paper will be obvious to anyone reading this essay. What has startled me is the degree to which students, in their own critiques of their journals and in their course evaluations, are aware of these advantages. Students acknowledge the time-consuming, sometimes frustrating demands of the assignment, one that requires them to find time for the journal while still preparing daily class assignments throughout the semester (instead of in the two intense final weeks with the traditional research paper). But most students also identify some aspect of the project that enhanced their learning or their enjoyment of the musical work they had chosen to study. A recent examination of student responses to the journal project emphasized several areas of new learning or intellectual maturity, exemplified by the experiences of individual students, whose names I have changed for reasons of confidentiality.

John, among others, was pleased with his new knowledge of the ways to tackle an unfamiliar musical work. "I have to admit," he wrote, "that I went through phases of liking and disliking the piece, but this was through frustration and discoveries that I made during the time. Thanks for making us do this, because I honestly would have never done it on my own. Now because of this experience I'm more adventurous at discovering new music." Annie was a student with, as she thought, a learning disability. After having competently tackled Messiaen's *Quatuor pour le fin du temps,* she observed that "at the start of the semester I was a little worried if I could handle a project of analyzing a peice [sic] all alone! But this journal helped me to realize that it is a step by step process which does not need to be so overwhelming. Over the course of this semester I have found myself feeling more confident in analyzing the compositions assigned to us." With a newly gained confidence in her learning and reasoning powers, Annie stopped classifying herself as learning-disabled. Karen, an honors student used to "toughing out" intellectual problems on her own, enjoyed the opportunity to consult with, and share ideas with, her colleagues who were working on the same piece. Greg discovered the importance of healthy skepticism in research: "I learned that even though you might find ideas in books and such, *they are not always right!*" [emphasis his]. Elena, a bright but buttoned-down student, learned a crucial lesson about the use of imagination and creativity in research—the freedom, as she put it, "to follow any crazy instinct, or just to browse." Several students chose to study repertory for their instrument that was beyond their present performing abilities. Some, like Sarah, found through their new understanding and appreciation the motivation to take on the technical challenges as well. I had the pleasure of hearing Sarah's excellent performance of Bernstein's Clarinet Sonata just one year after she had proclaimed the work "far too difficult for me, but probably worth getting to know." In the program of her senior recital she acknowledged the journal project as the gateway to both understanding and performing Bernstein's fine work. Occasionally students will register in their journals an epiphany of emotional response to a masterpiece, as did three voice majors studying Britten's *War Requiem* who were stunned by its power when they heard a live performance of that great work at the national meeting of the American Choral Directors Association. In the traditional term paper format, there would have been no opportunity to record the impact of that performance on their grasp of the work's meaning.

Let me conclude this essay with a personal observation, one unlikely to be raised in any student's evaluation. As worthy as the advantages mentioned above may be, the greatest benefit for me of the journal project is the opportunity to talk to the students, one at a time, about their work, their ideas, and their discoveries. As with the "learning circle" in my upper level history classes, the journal project affords me the luxury of becoming one of many voices in a colloquy of learning, as the "centrifugal classroom" is widened to include the entire intellectual and musical life of the students.

*This essay owes much to the advice, insights, and assistance of colleagues and friends, including Quentin Faulkner, George Ritchie, and Deborah Reinhardt in my own department; Joy Ritchie and Jim McShane of the English department; my colleagues in the 1990 Nebraska Writing Project (where I first encountered the word "journal" as an intransitive verb); and in the AAHE Peer Review of Teaching project. Most of all, thanks are due my students, who patiently endured while I developed as a teacher.*

## Notes

1   Linda Woodbridge, "The Centrifugal Classroom," in *Gender and Academe,* Sara Munson Deats and Lagretta Tallent Lenker, eds. (Lanham, MD: Rowman and Littlefield, 1994), 133–51, at 133.

2   See, for example, the forum on "Musicology and Undergraduate Teaching," in *College Music Symposium* 28 (1988): 10–23, and especially the contribution by James A. Hepokoski, "'Music History' as a Set of Problems: 'Musicology' for Undergraduate Music Majors," pp. 12–15; and see Anne Hallmark's excellent overview, "Teaching Music History in Different Environments," in *Musicology in the 1980s: Methods, Goals, Opportunities,* D. Kern Holoman and Claude V. Palisca, eds. (New York: Da Capo Press, 1982), 131–44.

3   Janet Emig, "Writing as a Mode of Learning," in *Cross-Talk in Comp Theory, a Reader,* ed. Victor Villanueva, Jr. (Urbana, IL: National Council of Teachers of English, 1997), 7–16.

4   Patricia Nelson Limerick as quoted in: Page Smith, *Killing the Spirit: Higher Education in America* (New York: Viking, 1990), 210.

5   See, among many useful examples, Kenneth A. Bruffee, "Collaborative Learning and the Conversation of Mankind," in *Cross-Talk in Comp Theory,* 393–414; Paul L. Dressel and Dora Marcus, *On Teaching and Learning in College* (San Francisco: Jossey-Bass, 1982); and Charles C. Bonwell and James A. Eison, *Active Learning: Creating Excitement in the Classroom,* ASHE-Eric Higher Education Report No.1 (Washington, D.C.: George Washington University, 1991). A recent formulation of the opposing point of view testifies to the persistence of the traditional lecture-based mode of teaching. See

Kenneth R. Stunkel, "The Lecture: a Powerful Tool for Intellectual Liberation," *The Chronicle of Higher Education* (26 June 1998): A52.

6    I would like here to thank Dr. Kerry Grant, former Director of the School of Music at the University of Nebraska, for his enlightened willingness to cut the Gordian knot of credit-hour production in order to allow this tyro teacher the opportunity to work with, and learn from, an experienced colleague.

7    Space would not permit a complete array of citations from the vast literature on the journal as a writing and learning tool. I will, however, mention here the remarkably useful volume edited by Toby Fulwiler, *The Journal Book* (Portsmouth, NH: Boynton/Cook, 1987), a collection of essays from teachers and scholars in a variety of disciplines. There are even two essays that deal with the use of journals in music courses, although neither touches specifically on the research journal for music history. See Catherine M. Larsen and Margaret Merrion, "Documenting the Aesthetic Experience: The Music Journal," 254–60; and Jane Ambrose, "Music Journals," 261–68.

8    Bryant Fillion, "Language Across the Curriculum," in *To Compose: Teaching Writing in High School and College*, ed. Thomas Newkirk, second ed. (Portsmouth NH: Heinemann, 1990), 235–50. Fillion quotes from *Language Across the Curriculum,* a Report of the National Association for the Teaching of English (London: Ward Lock Educational, 1976), 8.

9    Peter Elbow and Jennifer Clarke, "Desert Island Discourse: The Benefits of Ignoring Audience," in Fulwiler, *The Journal Book,* 19–32.

10   O.T. Kent, "Student Journals and the Goals of Philosophy," ibid., 269–77.

11   I decided to focus on a twentieth-century work because, despite our entry into the next century, the twentieth century remains largely *terra incognita* for undergraduate music students. I insist on a complete and substantial work, and one not included in undergraduate historical anthologies. Students may choose among recommended works such as Bartók's Fifth String Quartet, Berg's Violin Concerto, Boulez's *Le Marteau sans Maître,* Britten's *War Requiem,* Crawford Seeger's String Quartet, and a selection of important works by Ives, Carter, Messiaen, and Stravinsky: all mainstream "classics" of the century that one would like students to know. If they decide to study a work not on this list, it must be at least a half hour in length and by a composer recognized as important to twentieth-century music history.

12   See Appendix 12.1 for excerpts from the journal project assignment that include questions and suggested strategies for studying the new piece.

13   In the nine years since I implemented the journal project, I have relied with gratitude upon the assistance of a number of able graduate students—among whom particular recognition goes to Peggy Holloway, Hannah Jo Smith, and Tim Howe—whose enthusiasm for the project matched my own. Without them, I am sure I could not have sustained this time-consuming pedagogical approach, especially in recent semesters, with a class size approaching fifty students.

**APPENDIX 12.1**
**Excerpts from the Journal Project Assignment**

What are some questions to ask (and answer) at various times in the journal?

Different questions will be appropriate to ask at different stages in the journal project. Some questions will be suitable for all the pieces on the list; other questions will be specific to a particular piece at a particular stage in your acquaintance with it. One of the goals for this project is to develop a sense of what questions *should* be asked for a particular kind of piece and when to ask them. But here are some general suggestions to spark your own imaginations:

1. When deciding what piece to choose

Do I already have a slight familiarity with any of them? Should I go with that or opt for a completely new experience? Should I go with a piece for my instrument, or look at one in a completely different medium. Have I heard anything else by these composers? Are there titles that intrigue me? Should I quickly listen to a few before making my final choice? Are there any pieces that inspire an allergic reaction at first sight or sound? Should I explore why, or turn to another choice?

2. When first encountering seriously your chosen pieces

Should I first listen to the piece with or without score (to get a sense of the whole piece)? If there are words, should I first read a translation of the text? If it is a dramatic work, should I first encounter it on video? (The library has many opera videos, plus a VCR to watch the videos on.) How will I locate a recording to go along with the score on reserve? Should I be discriminating about which recording I listen to? etc.

3. Strategies and questions when studying your chosen pieces

What are the analytical strategies I will have to employ to begin to make sense of the piece? (These will differ according to the type of piece. For example, text/music relationships will be very important for a vocal work; formal analysis may be more important for an instrumental work.) In what order should I tackle the analysis? (For example, do I figure out the formal design before looking at the harmonic structure?) Should I get a general sense of all the musical elements—structure, harmony, melody, rhythm.

Appendix 12.1 (continued)

text, texture, etc.—before studying each of them in detail? Should I be asking larger questions such as "what is this piece about?" or "how does this piece fit into the composer's musical output?—into the prevailing cultural and philosophical mind-set of the time?—into the composer's national background?" If the piece relates to a non-musical art work (such as a play or a novel), should I read that work and consider how it relates to the musical piece? What can additional research tell me about this piece? (This should come well after you have entered a substantial number of personal observations about the piece, drawn from your own analysis.) Does the library own reference books (such as the *New Grove Dictionary of Music* or the *New Harvard Dictionary*), circulating books, even periodical articles that might add to my own insights? What do my colleagues think about this piece? Do I agree with their analytical approaches? Do I agree with the interpretations of the piece on recordings? Would I do things differently? How does this piece fit into my understanding of the period it comes from (as gained from textbook readings and class work)? Did I like this piece at the beginning? Do I like it more now that I know it better, or less? Do I want to hear and study more works by this composer? etc.

What material should be included in the journal?

Include everything that seems relevant to your encounter with these pieces: false leads; fairly naive initial impressions; ideas that do not pan out—all are equally valid alongside more informed opinions based on growing understanding of the pieces you have chosen. There are no wrong answers! The journals will ultimately be evaluated on the quality, perceptiveness, effort, and imaginativeness of your strategies in coming to know a composition from the twentieth century. By the end of the semester, you will have developed the skills to deal responsibly with any musical work that might come your way as a teacher or as a performer. You may also enjoy yourselves in the process!

Chapter Thirteen

# The Myths of Music History

*Vincent Corrigan*

Teachers of music history often use instructional devices to simplify complicated information for our students or to provide them with mnemonic devices. Equally often we use these tools when our knowledge of a particular topic is not great, and we are forced to transmit to our students the abbreviated information that was passed down to us. These tools are shortcuts that communicate basic information in an easily digestible format. Unfortunately, they also engender myths or fallacies in the minds of our students.

These myths can take several forms. First, there is the "Great Person" theory of history, in which we describe the course of music history in terms of the prominent composers of each era. We use this tool of personification whenever we describe an individual as the "Father" or "Inventor" of a general phenomenon or style, or when we associate a standard stylistic feature with an individual (the Rossini crescendo, the Corelli clash). There is the tool of terminology *ad antiquitam*, which, by using a Latin or Greek term, gives the topic a fictional ancient lineage. Finally, there is the technique of overgeneralization, in which we exaggerate a particular situation for rhetorical effect, and our students, who read our statements as truth, add their own exaggerations on top of that. In all these cases, albeit for the best of intentions, we have falsified the subject matter and substituted myth for a more accurate understanding of the topic.

Here are some of the most frequently encountered myths and fallacies. I expose them not to discourage their use, but to provide something of the deeper significance each one of them carries.

## Personification

This type of fallacy goes by the wonderful name *prosopopoiea*, and we fall into it when we use a particular individual to represent a general and widespread musical phenomenon. "Gregorian chant," "Wagnerian music drama," "Guidonian gamut," "Mozartean grace," and "Franconian notation," perhaps even "Schoenberg's 12-tone system" are familiar examples of *prosopopoiea*. The problem with this tool is that our students come to believe that these individuals created the phenomena complete and with no outside influence. Yet this is hardly the case. Gregory the Great certainly did not compose the entire body of chant that bears his name. The phrase "Mozartean grace" is a fine memory aid, provided we stress how much of that grace is owed to J. C. Bach; and in our enthusiasm to attribute serialism to Schoenberg, we may entirely forget the nearly contemporaneous work of Josef Hauer.

*Leonin and Perotin*

The case of Leonin and Perotin can provide a detailed example of *prosopopoeia*. For over 500 years, Anonymous IV was our only source of information for these individuals:[1]

> Having understood the formation of melodies according to the system of eight modes and according to the use and custom of the Catholic faith, we must now deal with their measurement according to length and brevity, as the ancients discussed them, and as master Leo and very many others advanced and regulated them according to *ordines* and *colores*.

> And note, that master Leonin, it is said, was the best composer of organa, who made a large book [or *Magnus Liber*, literally] of polyphony for the gradual and antiphonary to elaborate the divine service. And it was in use to the time of Perotin the Great, who edited it [shortened it? wrote it down?][2] and made many better clausulae or points, because he was the best composer of discant, and better than Leonin was. But this cannot be said about the subtlety of organum, and so forth.

But this meager source material in no way limited the writers of music history texts, because there is always a tendency to invent biography in the absence of factual information, and this results in the creation of myth. John Hawkins, who wrote one of the first histories of music in English (1776), and who had read Anonymous IV, has this on Leonin:

> The tract now ... goes on to say of Leoninus, before-mentioned, that he was a most excellent organist, and that he made a great book of the Organum for the Gradual and the Antiphonam, in order to improve the divine service; and that it was in use till the time of Perotinus; but that the latter, who was an excellent descanter, indeed a better [one] than Leoninus himself, abbreviated it, and made better points or subjects for descant or fugue, and made also many excellent quadruples and triples.[3]

Reputable nineteenth-century sources such as Baltzell's *Complete History of Music* often invented a student-teacher relationship between the two:

> Leonin (about 1140) and Perotin (his pupil) were organists at Notre Dame in Paris. The former was noteworthy in the reform of notation, while the latter is known principally for his use of crude Imitation, and a tendency not to use consecutive fourths and fifths, though he never entirely succeeded in eradicating them.[4]

Emil Naumann's *History of Music* has the most remarkable statement, attributing to Leonin:

> ... a treatise on organ playing, especially with manner of performing graduals and antiphonals, noting his compositions according to a method invented by himself. This book contains ... harmonic accompaniments set to original and traditional sacred melodies.[5]

These may strike us as humorous now, but we should try to sympathize with the efforts of these early authors. Historians of this time were trying to communicate to their readers unfamiliar information in a recognizable form. (Are we so different?) Unfortunately this entailed mistranslation (organist for *organista*) or fanciful relationships that were familiar to nineteenth-century readers (the master/pupil relationship) but not applicable to the twelfth and thirteenth centuries, and certainly not substantiated in the case of Leonin and Perotin.

Myth becomes hagiography when the actions of the individual become superhuman. This is what happens in William Waite's *The Rhythm of Twelfth-Century Polyphony*:

> [On his compositions and significance as a composer] When Leonin undertook the composition of his great cycle of polyphonic music for the major feasts of the church year some time around 1160, polyphony had already lived through three hundred years of recorded history.[6] ... To Leonin must be ascribed a position equivalent to that of Monteverdi and Haydn, men who almost singlehandedly created out of existing musical categories new styles and new forms that were to become the dominant characteristics of a new age. ... Systematically Leonin set about to embellish the great feast days of the church year with elaborate polyphonic settings of the responsorial forms. Before his death he had accomplished a great cycle of liturgical organa, providing a uniform repertory for the major

days of the church year. ... The relatively limited melismata of the St. Martial organum became in his hands vast melodic sweeps moving over greatly extended sustained tones in the tenor part.[7]

[On his contributions to music theory] It was Leonin's incomparable achievement to introduce a rational system of rhythm into polyphonic music for the first time and, equally important, to create a method of notation expressive of this rhythm. ... In his search for a rhythmic basis for his music Leonin turned directly or indirectly to the treatise on rhythm by St. Augustine, *De musica libri sex*. From this work he derived, with but slight modifications, the fundamental doctrines of rhythm that came to be known as the rhythmic modes, i.e., rhythmic patterns derived from metrical feet. ... In the melismatic sections of his organum Leonin utilizes the first mode with the greatest freedom, the long and short values frequently being broken up into still smaller values so that the rhythm becomes extremely pliant, although the underlying modal pattern is still discernible. In the sections of the organum where the tenor itself has a melisma, Leonin speeds up the rhythmic progression of the tenor so that the duplum has only one or two statements of the modal pattern to each note of the tenor. In these clausulae, which are equivalent to the sections of St. Martial organum written *nota contra notam*, Leonin adheres much more strictly to the simple values of the modal pattern.[8]

Shorn of exaggeration, Waite credits Leonin with the following:

1. The composition of the *Magnus liber organi de Graduali et Antiphonario*,[9] polyphonic settings of chants for the entire church year.

2. The application of rhythm to polyphonic music, derived from a study of Augustine.

3. The invention of the rhythm and its categorization into six rhythmic modes, based on poetic meters.

4. The invention of a notation to express these rhythmic patterns, modal notation.

5. The creation of a new type of setting, the clausula, derived from earlier polyphonic practice.

At some point, the cautious person needs to say: "Hold the phone! This is too much for a single individual to accomplish."[10] Perhaps Anonymous IV was using Leonin to personify a series of advances that were really the result of many people working for a long time? Hendrik van der Werf has advanced this idea, calling Anonymous IV a chronicler, not an historian.

> ... it would not have been unusual for a medieval teacher to make up a story about the origin of a phenomenon in order to clarify its goal or explain its features. Similarly, it would not have been contrary to medieval traditions to lend authority to a given practice by claiming that it had been first proposed by a famous person in a highly respected locality.[11]

To replace fantasy with fact, Hans Tischler, Ernest Sanders, and others scoured the Notre Dame archives for mention of Leonin and Perotin. Perotin was the first success. Depending on whom you believe, he was active in the late twelfth and early thirteenth centuries, and his four-part organa were late works of "a mature master," or he was active in the early thirteenth century, and those same organa are early works. The evidence can support either contention. Recently, Craig Wright has uncovered a wealth of biographical information on Leonin, and his ideas have now been incorporated into music history texts. Yet caution is still necessary. None of the documents Wright cites associates Leonin with any musical activity at all, and so Wright, to maintain the myth, is forced to mention music at every turn.[12]

Why is the existence of Leonin the musician such an important thing, and why do we continue to harbor the hope, in the face of disappointment, that documentation will show him to us? It is because the discovery of his identity would extend the most significant feature of our musical heritage back by nearly two centuries. Western European music is distinguished by its concentration on polyphonic composition, carried out through the creative activity of single individuals. We have all but given up monophonic writing, and group composition is completely foreign to our way of thinking. Our search for Leonin is really a search for the beginning of our musical culture. It is a search for the first "Western" composer, the first person to devote a great deal of time to *polyphonic* composition. Right now Machaut holds that laurel, with collections that date from the mid-fourteenth century. But even Machaut's prominence may be based more on the fact that his collections still exist, rather than on any real claim as the "first polyphonic composer."

## The Landini cadence

Another example of *prosopopoiea* is the so-called Landini cadence.[13] Students encounter this term in a wide variety of reliable secondary sources, and they come away with the idea that Landini invented the cadence.[14] I know this because they tell me so on tests, in papers, and in discussions.

But the true situation is much more complicated. Study of Landini's music begins in March 1827, when François Fétis announced the discovery of a manuscript containing music of trecento composers, one of whom was Francesco Landini.[15] As an example of the music in this manuscript, Fétis published the first section of *Non avrà ma' pietà*, the ballata which has become the canonic example of Landini's music.

Later in the century, August Wilhelm Ambros included what we now call the Landini cadence, with examples from Dufay and others, in his *Geschichte der Musik*. He referred to it as a "peculiar idiom," and emphasized how widespread it was. August Gottfried Ritter, in his survey of organists, is the first author I know to associate the cadence, "a conspicuous closing phrase," with Landini in particular.[16] For all of these authors, the cadence was significant because it represented a step in the "evolution" of nineteenth-century harmonic language. This idea occupied the attention of the finest scholarly minds of the day. Over the course of the late nineteenth and early twentieth centuries, the idea went out of favor, perhaps as changing musical language brought on the realization that the harmonic language does not evolve, but only changes.

Who first coined the term? I find the term *Landinosche Sext* first mentioned in the tenth edition of Hugo Riemann's *Musiklexikon* (1922), the first edition edited by Alfred Einstein after Riemann's death. Because this dictionary was so influential, the term rapidly achieved currency, but the role in harmonic development was never mentioned again.

Other examples of *prosopopoiea* are easy to come by. A very popular story falsely relates that the Council of Trent very nearly banished polyphony from the Catholic service, and that only a performance of Palestrina's *Missa Papae Marcelli* prevented this from happening. This story, now nearly four hundred years old, can be traced to Agostino Agazzari's *Del sonare sopra il basso* (1607):

> And on this account music would have come very near to being banished from Holy Church by a sovereign pontiff had not Giovanni Palestrina found the remedy, showing that the fault and error lay, not with music, but with the composers, and composing in confirmation of this the mass entitled *Missa Papae Marcelli*.[17]

The story was further promoted in Hans Pfitzner's opera *Palestrina* (1917), where the title character sees himself as a defender of the tradition of serious composition. It is now common to describe this story as a legend and to say that the council was not really about to banish polyphonic music, and that other composers probably influenced the Council too (principally Jacobus de Kerle). But students still carry the legend with them, and hold it more firmly in mind than they do any qualifications.

## Terminology *ad antiquitam*

We have already seen how a Latin title provides a measure of authority to an attribution. It was often popular in certain texts to introduce indeterminacy with a reference to the Latin word for dice (*aleae*), hence aleatoric music. A Latin name can also make something appear to have an ancient lineage, when in fact it does not. The term I have in mind is the *diabolus in musica* (devil in music), which, one often reads, was used by medieval theorists to denote the tritone.[18] Perhaps it is a shortened form of an adage, *Mi contra fa/est Diabolus in musica* found in some eighteenth-century sources. Or it may simply have been a memory aid for those more familiar with theology than music.

The difficulty with this fallacy is twofold. In the first place, an interval composed of three equal parts may just as well have been called *trinitas in musica*, with completely different, although counterintuitive, theological associations. Secondly, *no one who has investigated the term has found a medieval source for it*, including those who have written articles on the subject.[19] Medieval theorists concerned with intervals include the two forms of the tritone among the dissonances, but do not accord it any special significance or give it any special name. In 1980 Andrew Hughes mentioned that he could find no medieval writer who used the term, and the passage of time has not changed that situation.[20] It does not appear in the *Thesaurus musicarum latinarum*, and the earliest mention one writer found (Moser) comes from early eighteenth-century German writers.

I confess I have no idea why this term continues to live on so persistently. Perhaps it is because it is mentioned by so many other sources, and our students need to know what it means. Although it may be the most firmly ingrained myth of music history and theory (among students *and* professionals) it certainly seems to be a saying that should be erased from our collective memories.

## Overgeneralization

It is sometimes believed—although one will never read such a flat statement—that women did not sing in the Middle Ages. This notion is derived from an overgeneralization of Paul's epistles.

> 1 Corinthians: 14: 34–35. Women should keep silent in the churches: for it is not permitted for them to speak, but to be subordinate, just as the law says ... . It is shameful for a woman to speak in church.

> 1 Timothy: 2: 11–12. Let a woman learn in silence, with all subjection. I do not permit a woman to teach, or to be dominant over a man, but to be in silence.

This was reinforced in the first three editions of Grout's *History*:

> Gregorian chant ... consists of single-line melody sung to Latin words by unaccompanied men's voices ... .[21]

But *of course* women sang in the middle ages. The trobairitz existed and created their song/poems just as the troubadours did. Hildegard of Bingen existed. Convents existed, and services had to be performed in them. I recently found an example of this in the manuscript Brussels, Bibliothèque royale, 139. This is a Dominican *cantatorium*, which means it contains only the portions of responsorial chants that the soloist, the cantor, would have sung. At the end of this manuscript is the following statement: "Prioress sister Yoles (Yolanda) of Vienna had this book made for the sisters in Marienthal in the year 1269 to be held there in her memory." In other words, the manuscript was to be used by the Dominican nuns of Marienthal in their performances of the mass and office, and this is by no means the only instance of such a manuscript.[22]

A more limited version of this myth maintains that women were forbidden to perform on the operatic stage, and this situation, in some vague way, is related to the rise of the castrato. While it is never so baldly stated, it arises from brief statements in reputable texts. Take, for instance, Tim Carter's essay on seventeenth-century opera in *The Oxford Illustrated History of Opera*:

> However, Rome remained ambivalent about opera—still more about the use of female singers therein (women's roles were often left to castrati)—and the genre remained subject to the whims of individual patrons.[23]

Virtually nothing of this myth is true. Women were forbidden to perform on the Elizabethan stage and in the Papal States, but not elsewhere.[24] We have cast lists from a variety of early operas that show women to have been active performers. The castrati arose much earlier and for a completely different reason—the performance of treble parts in sacred polyphony, where women were indeed banned from participation because of St. Paul's dicta.[25]

## Conclusion

It is not possible for teachers of music history to know everything about the subject, and so these shortcuts will continue to be important, though still rather misleading, teaching tools. It is even less possible for our students to learn everything about the subject, and so these shortcuts are even more important to them, especially in their first exposure to the material. But, as responsible instructors of music history, we at least need to be aware of the truth behind such shortcuts, not simply relying on what we read or were told in our own (perhaps dated, or unreliable) undergraduate surveys. When time permits, we should show our students the deeper side to these mythologies, and so communicate to them the excitement of the discipline, the detective-story quality to so much of history, and the ever-changing context of historical inquiry.

## Notes

1    The name Anonymous IV derives from the series of theoretical treatises that Charles-Edmond-Henri de Coussemaker published between 1864 and 1876, in which this treatise is the fourth anonymous work in Volume I. A more reliable Latin text can be found in Fritz Reckow, *Der Musiktraktat des Anonymus IV*, Beihefte zum Archiv für Musikwissenschaft IV (Wiesbaden: Franz Steiner Verlag, 1967). An English translation was published by Jeremy Yudkin, *The Music Treatise of Anonymous IV: A New Translation*, Musicological Studies and Documents 41 (Stuttgart: American Institute of Musicology, Hänssler-Verlag, 1985), from which these translations derive.

2    This word has always posed a problem for translators because it was used, at one time or another, to indicate any of the meanings given in the text above.

3    John Hawkins, *A General History of the Science of and Practice of Music*, reprint of the 1853 ed. with introduction by Charles Cudworth (New York: Dover Publications, 1968), I: 238.

4    W. J. Baltzell, *A Complete History of Music for Schools, Clubs, and Private Reading* (Philadelphia: Theodore Presser Co., 1905), 104.

5    Emil Naumann, *History of Music*, trans. F. A. Gore Ouseley (London: Cassell and Co., Ltd. [n.d., 1880–85?]), I: 290–91.

6    William Waite, *The Rhythm of Twelfth-Century Polyphony* (New Haven, CT: Yale University Press, 1954), 2.

7    Ibid., 7.

8    Ibid., 8–9.

9    So-called in Waite and elsewhere, but compare with Anonymous IV's passage and note how retaining the Latin and capitalizing some of the words changes the significance of the statement. Here is a case of terminology *ad antiquitam*.

10   Someone seems to have realized this, either Waite or his advisor Leo Schrade, because a cautionary sentence is interjected at the beginning of the second quotation: "These advances in musical art are so revolutionary that one hesitates to ascribe them to one man alone."

11   Hendrik van der Werf, "Anonymous IV as Chronicler," *Musicology Australia* 15 (1992): 11.

12   See Craig Wright, "Leoninus, Poet and Musician," *Journal of the American Musicological Society* 39 (1986): 1–35, especially pp. 6, 11, 13, and 14. See also Wright's *Music and Ceremony at Notre Dame of Paris, 500–1500* (New York: Cambridge University Press, 1989), 281: "Adam and Albertus [Leonin's two immediate predecessors at Notre Dame] were the last cantors at Notre Dame to leave evidence of musical skills beyond those necessary to execute merely the ceremonial duties of that dignity."

13   A readily available example can be found in mm. 28–29 of Landini's ballata *Non avrà ma' pietà*. See *Norton Anthology of Western Music*, ed. Claude Palisca (New York: W. W. Norton, 1998), I: 93.

14   See Donald J. Grout, *A History of Western Music* (New York: W. W. Norton 1960); hereafter, "Grout I." During a discussion of Machaut, but not of Landini, Grout writes: "This figure is sometimes called the Landini cadence after its supposed inventor, the fourteenth-century Italian composer Francesco Landini" (p. 114). In the fifth edition (1996), the term has been moved to the section on Landini and the attribution of "inventor" removed, but references to it still occur: "... of the type that has become known as the 'Landini' cadence" (p. 115).

15   François-Joseph Fétis, "Découverte de manuscrits intérressans pour l'Histoire de la Musique," *Revue musicale* 2 (March 1827): 106–13.

16   August Gottfried Ritter, *Zur Geschichte der Orgelspiels* (Leipzig, 1884; reprint, Hildesheim: Georg Olms Verlag, 1969), 5.

17   Oliver Strunk, *Source Readings in Music History* (New York: W. W. Norton, 1950), 430.

18   E.g., *The Harvard Dictionary of Music*, ed. Don Randall, s.v. Diabolus in musica: [Lat., the devil in music]. "In the late Middle Ages, the tritone, the use of which was prohibited by various theorists."

19   See Hans Joachim Moser, *Musik in Zeit und Raum* (Berlin: Verlag Merseburger, 1960), 262–79 (this is an article titled "Diabolus in Musica") and Leo Schrade, "Diabolus in Musica," *Melos* 29 (December 1959): 361–73. Moser admits (p. 268) that he can find no source for the *diabolus* reference earlier than the eighteenth century and guesses that it was transmitted by word of mouth from singer to singer before being committed to print.

20   Andrew Hughes, *Medieval Music: The Sixth Liberal Art*, revised ed. (Toronto: University of Toronto Press, 1980), S.v. "Diabolus in musica."

21   Grout I, 34. This sentence was retained in the revised edition of 1973 and the third edition of 1980. It was removed only with the fourth edition in 1988, but by then it had had twenty-eight years of influence.

22   See Anne Bagnall Yardley, "'Full weel she soong the service dyvyne': The Cloistered Musician in the Middle Ages," in *Women Making Music: The Western Art Tradition, 1150–1950*, ed. Jane Bowers and Judith Tick (Urbana IL: University of Illinois Press, 1986), 15–38.

23   *The Oxford Illustrated History of Opera*, ed. Roger Parker (Oxford: Oxford University Press, 1994), 20.

24   Under decrees by Sixtus V (1585–90) and especially Innocent XI (1676–89), whose ban lasted, on and off, from 1676 to 1798.

25   For a brief history of the castrato voice, as well as biographies of the most famous operatic castrati, see Angus Heriot, *The Castrati in Opera* (London: Secker and Warburg, 1956).

Chapter Fourteen

# Score and Word:
# Writing about Music

*Carol A. Hess*

Why can't college students write? Throughout the United States, this question puzzles and exasperates instructors, administrators, parents, and the media.[1] These groups have targeted the most likely culprits: insufficient rigor at the primary and secondary levels, limited exposure to the printed word, the shrinking American vocabulary ("So I'm like, whatever"), and lack of empathy in our culture for intellectual values.[2] As instructors of music history, many of us regularly confront this gloomy landscape while acknowledging our limitations in ameliorating it. For despite some training in writing, editing, or rhetoric, we are not primarily writing teachers. Perhaps we have never diagramed a sentence or can only haltingly identify a participial phrase or object pronoun. Further, we may have acquired a smattering of rules we believe to be "correct" but have swallowed largely on faith. Why is beginning a sentence with "however" to be avoided? Why is "hopefully Yo-Yo Ma will come to town this year" taboo while "unfortunately Schubert died young" acceptable? When students ask such questions we may find ourselves hard-pressed to rationally defend (note split infinitive) these and other largely arbitrary conventions.[3]

Yet a music history survey course is as good a place as any to instill an idea of what coherent, even elegant, writing involves. Some of the writing problems encountered are general, others discipline-specific. The more significant include: students' inexperience in synthesizing information, in organizing an argument, in manipulating analytical language, and in self-editing, all coupled with insensitivity to historical place and circumstance.[4] Further, many students' lack of personal involvement with the material inhibits them from reconciling their own day-to-day experience—and way of talking about it—with the often alien world of "classical" music. This essay's modest intention is to describe strategies I have tested, some in classes of ninety or more, at Bowling Green State University (Ohio), where students are often from working class or rural backgrounds and may be the first in their families to attend college. The strategies encompass informal in-class writing, short essays, analysis, writing for exams, editing, and term papers, each requiring a different level of refinement and intensity of professorial intervention. Besides addressing the problems mentioned above, my goal in insisting on writing as a necessary component of music history study is to persuade students to draw parallels between the process of writing and the process of making music. By cultivating an ear for rhythm, balance, and "phrasing" in writing, many music students, accustomed as they are to repeating, persisting, and polishing, become more motivated writers than we—and they—might have imagined.

## Warming-up: in-class writing

To learn writing, students must write. Instructors who have taught a large lecture class are keenly aware that many will sit through the hour without taking a single note. To encourage students thus unengaged, I ask them five minutes before the end of the hour to summarize the main points of that day's class in an informal essay no longer than one page. In the best-case scenario, abstainers suddenly find themselves writing, while the more involved produce a cogent précis of recently formed thoughts, one that may save thirty minutes of mental backtracking the night before the midterm. One might ask if the instructor who makes such an assignment to that many students will have the stomach to read it. My answer is: "yes, but not slavishly." As I shall argue later, intensive and detailed editing is a must for addressing students' writing problems. But that level of polishing I save for other occasions. Skimming one hundred such assignments, circling inconsistencies or errors of fact without offering a written explanation of them, takes around ninety minutes. An added benefit is my own feedback: well before the end of the semester and without the apparatus of a formal departmental evaluation, I get a sense of how my lecture came off and what to do differently next time.

Another in-class assignment asks that students put themselves in the position of some historical figure we study. Although we can address only so much general history in our classes, we can still make students aware of history's human dimension, mainly via the composer. In survey courses, I ask students to prepare a résumé for each of the main composers studied. It should address the usual career-related categories (education, special training, work experience, publications and compositions, awards and honors, with optional categories for health and marital status). Since many undergraduates are unfamiliar with résumé-writing, the assignment has practical benefits as well. Unlike a real résumé, a category for "historical significance" (as well as a death date!) may be included. With the résumé as a point of departure, composers are seen more empathetically as actors against the backdrop of history, which itself can become increasingly "real."

In highlighting this human dimension, I have discovered that the psychological aspects of music history make a vivid impression on students. Probably many, in declaring their major, were responding on some level to music's affective power. At the same time, their college years may be the setting for intensely emotional inner lives, when they grapple with the throes of first love, sexuality, separation from home, and other issues. This vast reservoir can be tapped so as to shed light upon important works of art. For example, after we have studied the gestation of Brahms's First Symphony, I announce (five minutes before the end of class): "You are Brahms. It is 1855. Write a letter to Clara Schumann describing some of the difficulties you encounter as you contemplate composing a symphony." To adequately address Brahms's circumstances, students must know the tortured history of the First Symphony, the "germ" of which may have originated in the mid-1850s, when his love for Clara Schumann had deepened. Students would be aware of Robert Schumann's suicide attempt the previous year, the untenable situation Brahms confronted with Clara, and possibly even the argument that certain motives directly refer to his personal turmoil.[5] While I cannot verify that students will hear the First Symphony differently after performing this exercise, to judge from their impassioned letters the work takes on new meaning for them.

Another in-class assignment takes the familiar as a point of departure. Like it or not, the speech for which students have developed an unusually acute ear hails from Madison Avenue, the scooping intonation, staccato diction, and hammering rhythm of which ceaselessly emanate from hard-sell ads on AM radio. Once we have studied grand opera I announce (five minutes before the end of class): "You are Louis Véron's secretary. Write a one-page radio spot on the forthcoming premiere of *Les Huguenots*." Students must select the most compelling details of the opera's plot (usually they focus on Valentine's conflict between her Catholic faith and Protestant lover) while taking into account the extent to which sixteenth-century wars of religion resonated with Meyerbeer's public.[6] They must also understand the importance of spectacle in grand opera, and why the Parisian bourgeoisie paid hefty prices to see it. Perhaps closest to the experience of the American undergraduate is grand opera's commercial potential as manifested in Véron's unerring eye for profit, which ranged from organizing fund-raising balls to selecting claque leaders. That students are given permission to synthesize these elements in a language they normally associate with the sale of running shoes and stereo equipment helps connect their world to Meyerbeer's.

At this juncture, it may be argued that such assignments denigrate the purpose of music history classes, which, after all, is not playing games of make-believe. Some might find offensive the idea of using the language of

Madison Avenue to describe works of art, or hold that such an approach can degenerate into gimmicks (make up a skit called "The *Wachet auf* Pajama Party"?) unrelated to music history. These assignments, however, are only one activity, usually three percent of the final grade, in the conventional package of lecturing, quizzes and exams, and directed listening. Students, moreover, must respect the material. They may not commit errors of fact and must make a discernible good-faith effort to recreate historical situations with honesty and sensitivity. Admittedly these in-class assignments require neither venturing beyond a familiar language nor sustaining an argument. For a slightly higher level of writing, other strategies can be tried.

**The short essay**

In one of his pleas for "serious music criticism—academic music criticism, if you prefer," Joseph Kerman has commented on the historical links between the musicologist and the music critic, citing Virgil Thomson, Andrew Porter, and others as examples of this affinity.[7] Although the concert report is a staple of large-lecture music appreciation classes, its value is limited in that setting; indeed, given non-majors' less-than-secure grasp of musical terminology it would seem to be a prime example of the traditional limitations of musical journalism Kerman describes ("lack of space and [unsophisticated] level of technical discourse").[8] Yet awareness of journalism's role in music history is both valuable and relevant, and most music majors will benefit from writing concert reviews (preferably not performances by peers or faculty). They should address the music—ideally repertory they are studying themselves—as well as the performance and, like the professional critic, be constrained by prearranged space limitations, say, 750 words. In communities without access to non-school performances, a form of musical journalism can be practiced via an imaginary letter to the editor. For example, having learned about program music and the polemics it aroused in the late nineteenth century, students study Strauss's *Death and Transfiguration*. Next, they read Eduard Hanslick's 1893 critique of the work and write a letter to the editor of the *Neuefreie Presse* supporting or rebutting Hanslick.[9] My experience is that while students may take an excessively opinionated tone (in this differing little from Hanslick himself) they engage with the material to a far greater degree than if asked merely to "write an essay on program music."

Other assignments introduce problems of historiography. Suppose students are told to recreate the evening of 29 May 1913, when the *Ballets Russes* premiered *The Rite of Spring* at the Théâtre des Champs-Élysées. They must weigh different accounts of that infamous event, attempt to assess each plausibility, and comment on any inconsistencies among them. Given that Stravinsky's account will be included, studying the premiere of this work can also invite consideration of Stravinsky's exploitation of the burgeoning mass media through interviews and open letters to musical journals, certainly a matter of interest to aspiring composers.[10] Related issues affected the reception of *Pelléas et Mélisande,* which Jann Pasler has treated in a highly readable article that my upper-division students have greatly enjoyed.[11] In recognizing the presence of bias in some aesthetic discourse, students are more inclined to think critically about what they read, about the perspective of the writer, and how such biases may have affected beliefs about music we hold today.[12]

Similarly, writing about oneself involves problems of perspective and selection. An assignment that works well in smaller classes, such as Symphonic Literature, asks students to pretend they have been engaged as soloist with an orchestra, and that part of their contract is providing a short biographical statement and program notes (two symphonic works and a concerto in their repertories, present or future). Since many students have not taken stock of their accomplishments since applying to college, the assignment has practical benefits in that it motivates them towards self-assessment; further, portions of their biographies may be funneled into future cover letters for employment, grant proposals, and the like. I edit the assignment with great care, allowing students to submit more than one draft (more on multiple drafts later). My goal is that students recognize how weak writing can diminish their accomplishments, while strong writing can truthfully enhance them. I am often surprised at what seems to be students' failure to offer relevant information, as if unwilling to dig into their own historical pasts. But after a bit of prodding on my part (How many years did you play principal flute in the All-County Orchestra? What exactly were your duties as Bell Choir director?), even students with relatively modest accomplishments are pleasantly surprised at how professional they have managed to make themselves look on paper—and without "padding."

## Analysis

More the domain of the theory instructor, analytical terminology is nonetheless an indispensable tool for writing on music history. Probably the most direct way to incorporate it into our students' work is via the "mystery" listening question on the quiz or exam. Here students identify an unfamiliar selection based on their aural cataloging of its more salient style characteristics. To do this, they must show their reasoning process by describing a variety of factors (harmony, harmonic rhythm, melody, metric structure, phrase structure, form, instrumentation, texture, orchestration, treatment of dissonance, etc.) in precise language most likely to be understood by professional musicians. Texture, for example, may be described as monophonic, polyphonic, or homophonic, but not "thin." Questions are formulated so as to avoid blurring of categories: among possible descriptors for harmony we might find "diatonic" or "chromatic" but not "fast," "slow," or "full." After wrestling with several such categories, which will differ from example to example, students are far likelier to successfully identify a possible time frame (broad or narrow, depending on our expectations) and probable composer.

**Writing for exams**

Another simple but useful writing exercise is the short-answer question on the quiz or exam. When I first began teaching at the university level I was surprised at how many students struggled with (or gave up on) clearly explaining musical terms, style characteristics, or historical phenomena. I almost got the impression that if some students were asked to define a shoe, they might say something to the effect that "it's like on a foot." Giving credit for sound bites like these, even if we know what students really mean, will only jeopardize their progress. Those aspiring to be teachers will someday be expected to communicate difficult concepts to young or inexperienced musicians (with some musical explanations of course, such as the shaping of a phrase, or inflection of a lyric, rightly taking place in the non-verbal realm). By opening undergraduates' minds to the importance of precision in word and thought, we offer them one more professional advantage.

To this end, I distribute weekly lists of terms, concepts, historical events—perhaps twenty-five to thirty—from which quizzes and exams are drawn. As a "rehearsal" for the short-answer portion of the test, students are expected to verbally explain these musical terms, the building blocks of their professional vocabulary. On the test, they need not use full sentences, provided the essential points are clear. In short, the lowly short-answer question, when well conceived and thoughtfully corrected, can crystallize a student's powers of reasoning while developing a predilection for brevity.

Like short-answer and "mystery" questions, the essay portion of the test can be designed to encourage maximum success while challenging students. The week before midterms and finals I distribute five essay questions, one or two of which will appear on the exam (although all are related to it).

Depending on the level of the class, the question may include a built-in organizational strategy. For example:

1. Describe Beethoven's Middle and Late style periods. Give their time frames and link both periods to the more significant events in his biography. For the characteristics you cite from each style period, give detailed examples from specific works; or

2. Summarize the achievements of Wagner in two ways: (a) discuss his contribution to opera and (b) explain the historical importance of his use of chromatic harmony. For (a) be sure to discuss representative works from various stages of his career. You should also define several terms related to Wagnerian opera. For (b) you should discuss the specifics of Wagner's chromaticism and its subsequent effect on his music, making sure to cite the accomplishments of his followers.

Students may consult me before the exam to find out if they are on the right track. They understand that with this amount of lead-time their essays must not only be grammatically coherent but reflect thoughtful command of factual information. Consequently they may not practice a technique prevalent in many high schools in which students are told to "write everything they know on X," are not marked off for wrong information, but are given points when they happen to get something right, no matter how disheveled their way of writing about it. Why assume that today's students are incapable of crafting clear, well-conceived essays by encouraging them to indiscriminately discharge uncontextualized facts?

## Editing

David Lodge, who captured the vicissitudes of academic life in novels such as *Changing Places* (1975), *Small World* (1984), and *Nice Work* (1988), has elsewhere addressed the necessity of uniting writer and critic in the same person (much the same way that Sviatoslav Richter's teacher, Heinrich Neuhaus, in discussing the importance of critical self-listening during rehearsal, aptly described the musical incarnation of this phenomenon as "both servant and master"). Lodge also refers to cultivating "a craftsmanlike approach to writing, a willingness to take pains, a commitment to making the work as good as you can possibly make it."[13] These "pains," by means of which the writer comes to read his or her work as someone else would, are equivalent to the daily toil of practicing. How can we help students accomplish on paper the equivalent of listening objectively to themselves, of "sitting in the back row," while playing or singing? As time and enrollment permit, I bring writing samples to class for students to edit. Problems therein may relate to grammar, organization, vocabulary, spelling, lack of concision, or other matters; also enlightening are longer samples in which more than one organizational scheme can be defended.[14] I concoct the two-to-three-paragraph samples myself, sometimes drawing on problems I have seen in recent student work, although these, of course, must be thoroughly disguised. The student critique, done in informal class discussion, operates on the assumption that timid or uncertain students will be goaded by their more verbally agile peers. Although it is rarely possible to devote more than thirty minutes or so a semester to this exercise, it never fails to provide me with clues as to how students think about writing. Most seem downright surprised when they learn that grammatical correctness is not our ultimate goal as writers, even though we expect it as we would the right notes in a performance. To go beyond "the notes" we explore a staple of undergraduate education (one with all-too-familiar limitations), the term paper.[15]

## The term paper

The strategy I use for the term paper arose from the admittedly primitive desire to deter students from beginning their papers the night before the due date.[16] This normally calamitous procedure may work well for the one individual out of thousands who, like Schubert or Wolf, really does work best at white heat. Most of us, however, are condemned to a more pedestrian formula, one that can be divided into three approximately equal parts: research, writing, and editing. The last component, often uncharted territory for students, is the most labor intensive for the instructor. I divide the assignment into three steps, all required for the final grade. These include:

> Step 1. Detailed, thoughtful outline and annotated bibliography. The outline need not be arranged with Roman numerals nor appear in any formal structure. It should, however, show that the student has carefully thought through the various angles of the topic or problem and conceived of some logical order in which to address them. Given that thought happens differently on paper, the outline is not binding. Bibliographic annotations must show in specific ways how a particular source will be useful to the topic at hand.

Step 2. Rough draft, typed. The rough draft should be as close to a final
draft as possible. In other words, students should not merely indicate what
they plan to say but say it. This draft need not include complete
annotations, but should incorporate some system for keeping track of
sources. Subsequent fine-tunings will likely involve work on organization,
clarity, and "voice."

Step two is essentially what many students are accustomed to cranking out the
night before the due date. Since their efforts often receive a rubber-stamp grade
and next to no critical commentary, their approach is not without its logic.[17]
But it will never help students realize their full potential. It also deprives them
of an advantage we as musicologists take for granted: feedback. In submitting
our work for publication, we enjoy multiple rounds of editorial comment from
colleagues, referees, and editors. It has never seemed fair to me that students,
often in the greatest need of such counsel, seldom receive it. Yet one must be
practical. Even given the understanding that feedback is to the writer what
audience response is to the performer, thinking about a student's draft, marking
it up, and, as is often the case, consulting with the student author, is so time-
consuming that I have never been able to manage this kind of assignment in a
class of more than twenty. However, the *pièce de résistance,* as described in
step three, is well worth everyone's efforts:

Step 3. Final draft. The final version will reflect the student's mastery of
sources, rhetorical strategy, and engagement with the material. It should
read well, even elegantly. The difference between steps two and three is
comparable to the difference between a truly convincing performance and
one in which the performer plays "just the notes."

Having developed their ideas through this process, students are likelier to
produce thoughtful, organized essays. Relieved of the temptation to assemble
their papers at the last minute, they come to recognize that clear-headed
preparatory work contributes to succinct expression and an easy flow of ideas
in the final draft. They are also likelier to appreciate, rather than avoid,
thoughtful criticism, and think more seriously about the role of process in their
intellectual development.

What's in it for us? A lot of extra time to be sure, although if step two is
given the proper attention, reading step three is a pleasure. Still, from the
standpoint of improving writing skills, step two yields the greatest benefits. A
pedestrian observation? In his witty commentary on the state of Americans'

written and spoken language, Steven Pinker has referred to extensive revision as the "banal but universally acknowledged key to good writing," noting that "good writers go through anywhere from two to twenty drafts before releasing a paper."[18] By his own admission, this conclusion has disappointingly unsexy ramifications:

> Imagine a Jeremiah exclaiming, "Our language today is threatened by an insidious enemy: the youth are not revising their drafts enough times." Kind of takes the fun out, doesn't it? It's not something that can be blamed on television, rock music, shopping mall culture, overpaid athletes, or any of the other signs of the decay of civilization. But if it's clear writing we want, this is the kind of homely remedy that is called for.[19]

We who teach the Western musical canon face several challenges. Not the least of these is pessimism, even ridicule, from within our profession about our students' abilities, evident in the "howlers," or student gaffes of dubious provenance that intermittently make their way around the Internet. Would not it make more sense to focus on finding ways of enabling students' musical habits to enhance their writing? Awakening in our students the writing urge—the desire to say in the best possible way what one really means—is a time-consuming, even draining act of vigilance. Seeing that desire begin to be realized, however, is as heady as any other performance thrill.

*I wish to thank John Stenzel and Milton Azevedo for helpful comments on earlier drafts of this essay and Brian Kern for research assistance.*

## Notes

1    See Christopher Shea, "What's Happened to Writing Skills?" *The Chronicle of Higher Education* 39, no. 22 (3 February 1993): 33–34; Daniel J. Singal, "High Achievers in Education: An Invisible Crisis," *Current* 339 (1992), especially pp. 6–7, 9; David Rothberg, "How the Web Destroys Student Research Papers," *The Education Digest* 63, no. 6 (1998): 59–61.
2    Alison Schneider, "Taking Aim at Student Incoherence," *The Chronicle of Higher Education* 45, no. 29 (26 March 1999): A16–18.
3    On unnecessary anxieties over "hopefully" and the split infinitive, see Steven Pinker, *The Language Instinct* (London: Penguin, 1994), 381–83 and 371–74. Similar matters are discussed in Edward C. Good, *Mightier than the Sword* (Charlottesville, VA: Blue Jeans Press, 1989).

4     For special problems on writing on music see D. Kern Holoman, *Writing about Music* (Berkeley, Los Angeles, and London: University of California Press, 1988). A welcome recent handbook is Jonathan Bellman, *A Short Guide to Writing about Music* (New York, Reading, et al.: Longman, 1999). On the study of general history in the United States see Polly Morrice, "The Past Wiped Clean," *New York Times*, 7 December 1998, A25. Among the numerous sources on student writing, see Barbara E. Fassler Walvoord, *Helping Students Write Well: A Guide for Teachers in All Disciplines*, second ed. (New York: The Modern Language Association of America, 1986) and Barbara E. Walvoord and Lucille P. McCarthy, *Thinking and Writing in College* (Urbana, IL: National Council of Teachers of English, 1990).

5     Allusive motives are discussed in David Brodbeck, *Brahms: Symphony No. 1* (Cambridge: Cambridge University Press, 1997), 40–50. See also the same author's "Brahms," in *The Nineteenth Century Symphony*, ed. D. Kern Holoman (New York: Schirmer, 1998), 224–29. These motives, however, have been questioned by John Daverio. See *Crossing Paths: Perspectives on Schubert, Schumann, and Brahms* (New York: Oxford University Press, forthcoming).

6     On the politicization of grand opera see Jane Fulcher, *The Nation's Image: French Grand Opera as Politics and Politicized Art* (Cambridge: Cambridge University Press, 1987).

7     Joseph Kerman, *Contemplating Music: Challenges to Musicology* (Cambridge, MA: Harvard University Press, 1985), 16.

8     Ibid.

9     Eduard Hanslick, *Music Criticisms 1846–99,* trans. and ed. by Henry Pleasants, revised ed. (Baltimore: Penguin Books, 1963), 293–95.

10    See Richard Taruskin, *Stravinsky and the Russian Traditions* (Berkeley and Los Angeles: University of California Press, 1998), 2: 1006–7. See also Modris Eksteins, *Rites of Spring* (New York: Doubleday, 1989), 10–16.

11    Jann Pasler, *"Pelléas* and Power: Forces Behind the Reception of Debussy's Opera," *19th-Century Music* 10 (1987): 243–64.

12    Of the extensive literature on critical thinking a provocative discussion is in Chet Meyers, *Teaching Students to Think Critically* (San Francisco and London: Jossey-Bass, 1988).

13    David Lodge, *The Practice of Writing* (London: The Penguin Press, 1996), 172.

14    Instructors may wish to explore the historical context of certain common sources of confusion, such as the use of the apostrophe and the hyphen. On "the aberrant apostrophe's" see David Crystal, *The Cambridge Encyclopedia of the English Language* (Cambridge: Cambridge University Press, 1995), 203; hyphenation is discussed on p. 129.

15    Some of these limitations, which include imprecision in instructions and emphasis on form rather than content, are discussed in Meyers, *Teaching Students to Think Critically,* 69–71.

16    On argumentation, structure, and organization in research see Wayne C. Booth, Gregory G. Colomb, and Joseph M. Williams, *The Craft of Research* (Chicago and London: University of Chicago Press, 1995). Probably everyone recommends favorite sources to students launching a full-scale writing project. Topping my list is the classic and inexpensive *Elements of Style*, third ed. by William Strunk Jr., and E. B. White (New York and London: Macmillan, 1979). Other personal favorites include William Zinsser, *On Writing Well,* fifth ed. (New York: Harper and Row, 1994) and George Orwell's "Politics and the English Language," in *Essays by George Orwell* (New York: Doubleday, 1954), 162–77. A good laugh over difficulties encountered in academic writing can be had in Frederick Crews's *The Pooh Perplex* (New York: Dutton, 1963). A grammar and punctuation manual and editorial style sheet (Chicago, MLA, or APA) should also be part of a student's basic equipment.

17    Shea, "What's Happened to Writing Skills?" 34.

18    Pinker, *The Language Instinct,* 401.

19    Ibid., 401–2.

Chapter Fifteen

# Peer Learning in Music History Courses

*J. Peter Burkholder*

The traditional music history course requires students to read one or more textbooks and other assigned readings, listen to and study a variety of music from the period or repertoire under study, hear lectures, participate in class discussion, write papers, and take exams that may include everything from true/false questions to essays. With the exception of listening to music and studying scores, this is much like traditional classes in any field, from history to physics. Students interact with the material and with the instructor, but they seldom interact with each other except during class discussions and, for some, cramming together for exams.

My experience in my first graduate course in music history at the University of Chicago convinced me that the major missing piece in this format was the interaction of students with each other, working together to gain mastery over the information, perspectives, and skills the course aimed to convey. It was a course in medieval monophony (primarily the history of chant) taught by Edward E. Lowinsky, the renowned Renaissance scholar. On the first day of class, we were given a syllabus that listed dozens of articles, book chapters, books, and editions that were required reading, all of it at a high scholarly level and much of it in German or French. Most of the articles were very dense, requiring slow careful reading and constant reference to background information and to the music under discussion. We were expected to understand and remember the point of view taken and evidence presented in each article or book so that we could write coherent essays contrasting the writers' perspectives on the final exam, which would be the sole basis for our grades. Older graduate students who had been through the course before told us that the only way to survive was to work in teams. Some friends and I took this advice to heart, deciding which readings we all should read, dividing the others among ourselves, sharing notes, and meeting regularly to disuss the readings and to drill and test each other on their contents. I learned far more from going through the material together with my peers than I did from my initial reading of each article or from our class sessions, and I retain a surprising amount of it a quarter century later.

What we discovered for ourselves was peer learning, a process through which students learn course content by working together. At first I used it as a strategy to survive graduate school, but as I began to teach I tried to find ways to induce my students to collaborate. I wanted to go beyond encouraging them to study together outside of class (which I do in some courses by giving a bonus point on the exams if they list the classmates with whom they studied), and beyond Mr. Lowinsky's method of giving them too much work to handle alone (which I admit I do all too often). I soon encountered the *Writing Across the Curriculum* movement, which seeks to use writing as a way to learn the content of courses in every field.[1] Many of the methods involve peer learning in some way, such as using writing as a springboard for discussion or involving students in reviewing and evaluating each other's papers. Drawing on these models, borrowing good ideas from colleagues, and occasionally stumbling across other techniques that work, I (and my teaching assistants) have developed over the years a variety of exercises in and outside the classroom that involve collaboration, conversation, peer review, and other forms of peer learning. These augment and occasionally replace traditional reading and listening assignments, lectures, and examinations. Students' course evaluations and performance on examinations and comments from former students suggest that they learn more, remember more, and tend to enjoy class more when peer learning is included than they do using only the traditional methods.

Successful peer learning depends on observing many of the same ground rules as learning in general. It is easiest and most effective to learn when (1) the goals are clear, (2) you proceed from what you know already to what is new or less familiar (often from a general overview to specific examples, or vice versa), (3) you do not try to do too much too fast, (4) you put what you are learning into your own words through writing and speaking, (5) you apply what you are learning, (6) you repeat and review what you have learned, and (7) you have fun in the process.[2] The peer collaboration exercises in my classes are designed to help students learn the material by applying most or all of these principles. Giving a group a specific task makes the goals clear and divides the work into units small enough to accomplish in the time allowed. Most of these exercises involve writing, often in more than one stage, and several involve making presentations. Typically students work alone and then together, so that the group learning builds on what they have already learned individually. All these exercises involve applying what they know as they learn it. Review is built into the conversation. And working together is usually more fun than working alone. For many students, talking is more fun than listening, and having several group conversations going at once allows more talking from more students than is ever possible in a discussion involving the whole class. While it is possible to structure a lecture based on these principles, peer learning exercises can often apply them more effectively. In any case, it is my experience that variety in the classroom is very helpful, and developing a wide variety of methods capable of conveying the same content provides for the most effective teaching.

Peer review adds some further elements to this. By peer review I mean any process, formal or informal, in which students read or hear other students' work and offer evaluation and feedback. Peer review helps reinforce goals, helps students apply and review what they know, and can be fun. In addition, it adds several other benefits. First, in the process of evaluating someone else's work, each student applies the criteria on which the assignment will be evaluated by the instructor. This familiarizes students with the criteria, helps them understand and internalize the criteria, and thus makes it easier for them to evaluate their own work objectively and see ways to improve it. It also makes it easier for me to explain why they received the grade they did and makes them less defensive about their work. Second, writing for or speaking to their peers helps students pay attention to their purpose and their audience. When students address each other, they have a real audience who may misunderstand or may not have necessary background information, and this helps them learn to present ideas clearly, supply the information the audience needs, and organize the paper or presentation in a way that is easy to follow. This is much closer to real-world experiences than the relatively private act of submitting a paper that only the instructor reads. Third, the process of peer review lets students see the work of other students. This may provide models of excellent work, but will most likely show that each student's work has some strengths and some weaknesses, and that everyone's work can be improved, including one's own. Fourth, knowing that their work will be seen by several people can stimulate students to do their best and makes each assignment matter more. Finally, each student's work is evaluated by more than one person, and having multiple perspectives is often helpful.

In my classes, I have used four general types of peer learning exercises. In order from most to least structured, these involve: (1) formal peer review, (2) formal or informal group presentations, (3) in-class group work based on a written assignment, and (4) group work based on in-class writing. In what follows, I give two examples of each type. These do not exhaust all possibilities, but are meant to suggest the range of options, from formal peer review to informal collaboration and discussion.

**Formal peer review**

*Research paper with peer review of proposal and draft*

In an undergraduate survey of music history to 1750, students are given the following assignment on the first day of class:

> Write a research paper, ten to fifteen pages in length, on a specific topic related to music in European culture before 1750 and appropriate to the objectives of the course. Your paper must be a detailed study of whatever topic is selected, it must have a single main point and a convincing argument, and it must represent your own independent work and thinking, reflecting both thorough research and original interpretation.

> Originality need not imply that your point is startlingly new; you may, for instance, take an idea you find in your reading, such as what makes Rameau's operas different from Lully's, and test it out by comparing specific pieces to which it applies. But it does mean that you go beyond your sources in some way and demonstrate your own thinking.[3]

The assignment includes the following criteria for evaluating the paper:

> *Ideas*: Does the paper have a clear thesis, a main point to which everything else relates? Is the argument persuasive? Is enough evidence presented to support each point, and does each point support the thesis? Are possible counter-arguments considered and refuted? Does the paper treat the topic comprehensively and in depth? Are the ideas original and insightful? *Organization*: Is the organization clear, both in the paper as a whole and within each paragraph? Have unnecessary details and redundancies been eliminated? *Style and mechanics*: Is the paper enjoyable to read? Does it convey the writer's thought efficiently? Are diction, spelling, usage, sentence structure, punctuation, and bibliographic form correct?

The paper is prepared in three stages: a proposal, due the fourth week of the semester; a preliminary version of the paper, due the ninth week; and the final version, due the thirteenth week. Only the final version is assigned a grade. The proposal and the first version are reviewed via peer evaluation sheets and small-group discussions, as well as by the instructors, with the goal of providing guidance and feedback to the writer before the paper is submitted for a grade. For this, each student is assigned to a peer review group of three or four students for the semester.

In the proposal, each student is asked to indicate the idea or subject he or she is interested in exploring: "explain in about 200–400 words how you plan to proceed, including your proposed thesis or main point and a brief sketch of your argument; and present a preliminary bibliography of at least ten items relevant to your topic."

Preparing a proposal like this, after a few weeks of preliminary research and thinking, helps the student follow the guidelines for successful learning listed above: it forces the student to articulate the goals of the project at an early stage; by focusing on the central idea and the main point, it helps the student see how the details discovered in research fit into a big picture; by focusing the student's attention on certain aspects of the paper, it helps to divide the task into manageable units; and by requiring the student to write out the core ideas and argument early on, it helps the student articulate his or her thinking at this stage and also to review and apply what has been learned so far.

The proposal is reviewed by the course instructors who offer detailed feedback in writing and in an individual meeting. But it is also reviewed by the other members of the student's peer review group. Group members distribute their proposals to each other in one class session and discuss them in the next session. In between, they read the proposals and fill out an evaluation sheet for each one. The sheets have the following questions, which are keyed to the requirements of the assignment. (Students will have seen the evaluation sheets before submitting their proposals, so they know what to expect. This is an important aspect of using any formal set of questions or criteria for evaluation, as students do not react well to surprises when evaluation is involved.)

1. What is the topic of the proposed term paper?

2. What question or set of questions does the writer plan to answer in the paper?

3. Does the writer articulate a thesis (the main point the paper will make)? If  so, paraphrase the thesis in your own words. If not, how does the writer plan to proceed in investigating the topic and arriving at a thesis?

4. Does the writer present an argument for the thesis? If so, does the argument seem persuasive? What counter-arguments could you pose?

5. Does the bibliography contain at least ten items relevant to the topic? Are there any items that seem irrelevant or peripheral?

6. Is the bibliography in correct form? If there are any specific problems of style or mechanics, point them out and suggest ways to improve.

At the next class session, students in the peer review group discuss each of their proposals in turn, using their answers to these questions as guidelines, but ranging beyond them as appropriate, to offer any comments that may help each student plan and write the best possible paper. At the end of the session, the evaluation sheets for each proposal are given to the writer of that proposal. Later, when the student meets with the instructor to discuss the proposal, the instructor may ask what feedback the student received from the group but will not necessarily see the evaluation sheets.

Five weeks later, the students hand in the first versions of their papers. These are evaluated through a similar process, with an evaluation sheet whose questions address the criteria announced for the paper:

1. What is the writer's thesis (the main point of the paper)? Is it clearly presented?

2. Is the argument persuasive? Is enough evidence presented to support each point? Does each point support the thesis? Or are there holes or weak spots in the argument?

3. What possible counter-arguments or alternative interpretations are considered in the paper, and are they successfully refuted? What other counter-arguments could you pose?

4. Is the organization clear? How could it be improved?

5. If there are any parts of the paper that seem unrelated to the thesis or provide unnecessary or redundant details, point them out and suggest ways to improve or eliminate them.

6. Is the paper enjoyable to read? Does it convey the writer's thought efficiently? If there are any specific problems of style and mechanics (diction, spelling, usage, sentence structure, punctuation, bibliographic form, and so on), point them out and suggest ways to improve.

The order in which these questions appear is calculated to make the students focus first on the most important issues, the thesis and argument; second on the organization; and last on format, style, and mechanics. Students tend to focus on grammar and style, in part because their previous education encourages them to do so, and in part because it is easier than engaging the ideas of the paper. Thus they need encouragement to focus on the thesis, argument, and organization, both through the evaluation sheet and in their discussions. The instructor (usually one of my teaching assistants) monitors the peer group conversations, as unobtrusively as possible, to make sure they are talking about ideas rather than punctuation and, if a group gets off track, to steer it back to the paper's thesis and argument.

These two stages of peer review yield the benefits listed above: the students apply the criteria to each other and thus internalize them; because there is a real audience for their writing, they are stimulated to pay close attention to issues of purpose and audience; they see each other's work, which provides models to emulate and helps them see how each paper can be improved; they may work harder, knowing their peers will see their work; and they receive feedback from several different readers. These sessions tend to be fun, allowing students to discuss the ideas they have been working with in their papers (always a pleasure for writers) and relieving some of the isolation writers often feel when working alone. And because the written work under review—the proposal and the first version—will not be graded, the focus can be on helping each other, and the atmosphere can be more relaxed. Ultimately, students write better papers and show better command of the content of the course, fulfilling my goals for them as their instructor.

*Research paper and presentation with peer review of both*

In a course devoted to a single composer such as Monteverdi, Beethoven, Ives, or Stravinsky (for music majors at the undergraduate or graduate level), students are asked to write a paper that makes an original contribution to understanding a topic related to the composer's music, career, or context, and to make a presentation of about twenty minutes to the class that is related to the topic of the paper. The topic must be approved in advance, and both paper and presentation must have a single central point, a logical set of secondary points, and sufficient evidence to support the thesis. (A similar assignment can be used in any course, but it works best if the repertoire is relatively focused, rather than a general survey.) The assignment states that presentations and papers will be evaluated using the following criteria:

212 Teaching Music History

1. Usefulness/value of the contribution: how useful is this? What impact does it have on our understanding of the composer and his music?

2. Originality: does this represent the presenter's or writer's own best thinking, including a synthesis of what others have done?

3. Soundness and persuasiveness of the argument: is the argument logical, persuasive, and based on solid evidence? Are there weak spots in the argument? What possible counter-arguments have not been dealt with?

4. Command of the relevant primary and secondary materials: does the presenter or writer know what he or she needs to know?

5. Presentation (organization, order of ideas, clarity of expression, and so on): does the presentation facilitate getting the point and subpoints across?

Here again, the students prepare a first version of the paper, which is evaluated in peer review groups in the same way as the previous exercise. The presentations are scheduled in the final weeks of the semester, after the first version of the paper has been evaluated, so that feedback from this exercise can be incorporated into the presentations. Each presenter is asked to give the instructor and one or more fellow students a run-through of the presentation a few days in advance. This is an opportunity for informal feedback and guidance, using the questions on the evaluation form that will be used at the time of the formal presentation (see below). Because students tend to have less experience with making presentations than with writing papers, much of the feedback at this stage is oriented toward the manner and style of presentation, but of course the content has already been reviewed through the evaluation of the paper and can be sharpened at the run-through. This preliminary presentation is not graded, but the comments and suggestions from me and the presenter's peers are often extensive. Moreover, students often find they are much less nervous at the time they present in class because the instructor and some of their peers have already heard them. The final presentation is almost always better than it would have been without this opportunity for evaluation and feedback.

At the time of the presentation in class, I ask three to five class members (who were not members of the peer review group for the paper or for the informal run-through) to fill out an evaluation sheet on the presentation. Once again, this form is keyed to the criteria announced for the assignment, which reminds both presenter and evaluators of those criteria:

1.  What is the presenter's thesis (the main point of the presentation)? Is it clearly stated?

2.  Usefulness/value of the contribution: how useful is this? What impact does it have on our understanding of the composer and his music? (e.g., What old problems does it help to solve? What new questions does it raise?)

3.  Originality: does this represent the presenter's own best thinking, including a synthesis of what others have done?

4.  Soundness and persuasiveness of the argument: is the argument logical, persuasive, and based on solid evidence? Are there weak spots in the argument? What possible counter-arguments have not been dealt with?

5.  Command of the relevant primary and secondary materials: does the presenter know what he or she needs to know?

6.  Presentation (organization, order of ideas, clarity of expression, correctness of usage, and so on): does the presentation facilitate getting the point and subpoints across? If there are specific problems, point them out and suggest ways to improve.

The presentation is graded. I incorporate the students' comments into my own evaluation (although I write most of my comments before reading theirs) and share these evaluations with the presenter, but the peer evaluators do not assign the grade. Feedback from the presentation is normally available before the final version of the paper is due, so that students can incorporate into their papers any new thinking that arises from the process of making the presentation. In addition, the questions, comments, and discussion after the paper from the class as a whole can show which points came across well and which did not and can give the presenter new ideas about content, organization, and expression.

This exercise has the same benefits as the previous one but adds the experience of sharing one's work with the entire class. This makes even more salient the issues of purpose and audience, of good organization, and of clarity in thesis and argument that good speakers and writers must address.

## Group presentations

### The formal group presentation

In a graduate-level survey of twentieth-century classical music (with primarily performers, but including composers, musicologists, music theorists, and music educators), students are asked to collaborate in groups of four or five to plan, research, and present a class session of seventy-five minutes on a type of music that is often excluded from the modernist "canon," such as romantic and tonal music, music by women composers, music for the totalitarian state (chiefly the Soviet Union and Nazi Germany), film and television music, choral music, wind music, Broadway musical theatre, jazz, and classic rock and pop music. Students are asked to indicate their preferences for topics they would like to present on or hear about, and I assign them to groups accordingly.

Here peer collaboration plays a very significant role. Each group meets with me to describe its initial plans and then presents a run-through to me a few days before the group's class session. Most of the students' work, however, is done out of class time and out of my sight. They must decide what to cover, how to divide up the topic, what each will research, and what each will present. Often, each student takes a separate short block of time, like a series of related presentations, but the more inventive groups divide the time in more interesting ways. Knowing that all students will share the same grade encourages them to work together and to support and coach each other, as in the natural collaboration in a business enterprise or performing group. This provides an informal kind of peer review. In addition, I ask about five students in the class to fill out evaluation sheets on each presentation and use these in making my own evaluation, adding an element of formal peer review from outside the group.

### Informal group presentation on assigned topic

In the small-group discussion sections of a large undergraduate music history survey, students are arranged in groups of two to five and assigned a carefully circumscribed topic on which to make a brief presentation. It is important to pose the question or issue the group is to address in concrete and specific terms, so that what they have to do is as clear as possible. For instance, in a unit on the sixteenth-century madrigal in Italy, each group may be asked to take a particular madrigal and prepare a five-minute report on how the music relates to the text. If the pieces are part of the course repertoire and available in the course anthology, or are relatively short and can be analyzed quickly from a handout, the students may be assigned to a group and piece during class and given ten minutes to prepare their presentation; if the pieces are too long or unfamiliar, the assignment may be given for the next class session. In either case, the presentation is followed by class discussion.

Several of my teaching assistants have devised especially inventive variations on this procedure. Felicia Miyakawa often splits her class in two, each half representing one side in a famous musical debate (such as Plato versus Aristotle, the Lullistes and Ramistes, the *guerre des bouffons*, or the Brahms/Wagner controversy). She has each side caucus to review and clarify the arguments for its position as gleaned from the readings and then stands back as the two sides role-play the debate, sometimes fiercely. Luiz Fernando Lopes has given each group of three or four students a set of images from a particular time and place—often part of a city map, a page from a piece printed in that city and era, and two or three paintings or engravings—and asked them to study these images together and prepare to tell the class what connects them to each other and what story they tell. It is like piecing together a detective story from a few pieces of evidence, combined with background knowledge taken from readings or lectures. In a segment on seventeenth-century opera, Jennifer King divided the class into three groups and gave each the task of listing for themselves the distinctive characteristics of one national operatic tradition—Italian, French, and English respectively—and devising a five-minute improvised miniature opera that embodied as many of those traits as possible. After each mini-opera was presented, the other students had to name the characteristics it exemplified. Thus, for example, the French group began with a brief French overture (slow dotted section and fast imitative section, as well as their best pianist could improvise on the spur of the moment), quick prologue with praise for the King, mythological characters, a dramatic recitative, a jolly air, and a group dance to close. The groups were given fifteen minutes to plan but no time to rehearse. Unrehearsed group improvisation in a relatively unfamiliar style can be hilarious, but the other class members easily recognized the elements being represented, and everyone agreed that it was a fun and memorable class.

Whatever the details, the point of the exercise is to encourage collaboration in applying the general information covered in the texts and lectures to a specific example, whether that be a piece of music, a set of ideas, a historical problem, a genre, or something else. This can be a perfect application of the principles outlined above: the goal is clear (if the instructor has outlined the task clearly enough); the students proceed from the general information they already know from their reading to the specific instances at hand; the task is limited; the students put their findings into their own words (spoken rather than written, although they often write notes for themselves); the exercise requires them to apply and review what they know; and this tends to be more fun than hearing the instructor talk or having an unfocused discussion.

## Group work based on written assignments

*Short paper on assigned topic with in-class discussion*

In any sort of course, students are assigned a short paper on a topic related to the material covered on a particular day. For example, in a course on Charles Ives, students were asked to write a brief paper of about 600 words responding to chapters they had read in two books and relating the ideas to two of his pieces about the American landscape and experience, answering the following question:

> What do Peter Conn's sociocultural approach in *The Divided Mind: Ideology and Imagination in America, 1898–1917* and Stuart Feder's psychoanalytic approach in *Charles Ives, "My Father's Song": A Psychoanalytic Biography* contribute to your understanding of Ives's character and of his music, particularly *Three Places in New England* and *A Symphony: New England Holidays*? Which aspects of their approaches do you particularly like, and which do you question or reject?

A short writing assignment like this affords students the opportunity to digest what they have just read and to apply the themes derived from their reading to the music they are studying, again in accord with the guidelines given above. Putting their thoughts in writing prepares them for discussion in class much better than merely reading, listening, and taking notes. A short paper can be much more effective here than a long one, as it forces them to distill the ideas from the readings and their own thoughts into brief statements that are easier to read or summarize in class.

In class, they share what they have written with each other. They are randomly arranged in small groups of about three people, and each group is asked to choose a spokesperson.[4] In each group, they read each other's papers (or read them aloud, if the papers are brief), make a list of views they hold in common and points where they differ, and discuss and evaluate these shared and differing views. After about ten to fifteen minutes (longer if necessary), I ask the spokesperson for each group to report to the class on its consensus views and points of difference. Frequently there will be agreements and disagreements across groups as well as within them. I then lead a class discussion evaluating the differing views that have emerged, aiming either to find a consensus or to articulate two or more alternative positions, sometimes contradictory and strongly held.

Through all this, peer review is implicit rather than explicit. The students are not asked to evaluate each other's papers as examples of writing, but to work with the ideas that are presented and to weigh them against each other. In the process, the groups, and then the class as a whole, develop a better, more thorough and more nuanced understanding of the readings and of the music than any student is likely to achieve working alone. Thus each student can correct or deepen his or her own initial understanding. The lesson comes across loud and clear that the class as a whole has a wider range of interesting ideas and observations than any one member alone and that sharing these can enrich everyone's understanding. The ideas come from the students, not from the instructor (unless I cannot resist adding some of my own during the discussion). This means that the class collectively demonstrates its command of the material and maintains ownership of the process. My role becomes that of guide, helping students to choose the best and most useful insights, rather than being the source of all wisdom and knowledge. This process of collective learning through writing and discussion can become a model for students' informal joint study sessions outside of class.

*Journal entry with in-class discussion*

In many of my classes, students are asked to keep a journal in which they summarize the readings and describe the pieces on the listening list.[5] The journals are collected and evaluated three or four times in the semester, but they can also be used as the basis for group discussion as in the previous example. For instance, in a course on twentieth-century music, the students read Anton Webern's "The Path to the New Music" and are asked to summarize in their journal the chain of events that Webern argues led inevitably to twelve-tone music, and to identify and comment on the assumptions Webern makes along the way. As in the previous example, putting their responses in writing prepares the students to discuss the material more thoroughly, even when what they write is not collected and graded. The procedure followed in class is the same as above.

## Group work based on in-class writing

*In-class reading, writing, and discussion assignment*

In a large undergraduate survey of about 120–160 students, I have found some alternatives to the traditional lecture. One approach that I have used with both majors and non-majors combines some lecture with an in-class reading and writing assignment followed by discussion in groups and group reports to the entire class.

In one such fifty-minute class session on Vivaldi, I start with the old canard that "Vivaldi didn't write 500 concertos, he wrote the same concerto 500 times," and then address the ways in which this is true or untrue. I introduce the principles of ritornello form through a series of examples from Vivaldi concertos, playing four fast movements and guiding the class through the formal diagram for each movement that I provide on a handout. I use these to make the point that although all Vivaldi fast movements alternate ritornellos played by the large group with episodes played by a smaller group, all begin and end with tutti statements in the tonic, and all modulate to the dominant and perhaps other keys (marking modulations with statements of the ritornello), there is still a great deal of variety from movement to movement. The initial ritornellos divide into units in different ways; subsequent statements may use any of those units; the key scheme varies; the final ritornello takes many forms; and as a result, each movement is unique in form, despite drawing on the same formal strategies. This lecture-demonstration takes about twenty minutes.

Then I pose a question: why did Vivaldi write music this way? Why does this approach make sense, given his circumstances? Instead of answering, I direct students to a set of questions on the second page of the day's handout about Vivaldi and his music.[6]

> How did the way Vivaldi earned a living affect *what* he wrote?
>     Why did he write all those concertos?
>     Why did he write two operas a year for twenty-five years?
>     Why didn't Vivaldi, a priest, write more sacred music than he did?

How did the way Vivaldi earned a living affect *how* he wrote?
　Why do his concertos have the shape they have?
　How was ritornello form useful to him?

How was Vivaldi's reputation made?
　during his lifetime?
　during the 19th and 20th centuries?

Did his death in virtual poverty mean that his genius went unrewarded
　　　　in his lifetime?
　Why did the Bach revival precede the Vivaldi revival?
　Why would it be an Italian publisher that put out the modern
　　complete edition?
　Why does that "complete" edition include only the instrumental
　　music?
　Why don't we hear Vivaldi operas today?

I divide the class into four quadrants and assign each quadrant a set of questions from this list: (1) the questions on how the way Vivaldi earned a living affected *what* he wrote; (2) the questions on how this affected *how* he wrote, particularly concertos and ritornello form; (3) the questions on his reputation and his death in virtual poverty; and (4) the questions on the revival of his music over the last century. Then I ask the students to read (on the third and fourth pages of the handout) a summary of Vivaldi's career, largely taken from Michael Talbot's article in *The New Grove Dictionary*. They then write out answers to the questions assigned to them, based on what they read, what they just heard in my lecture and in the Vivaldi movements, and their own speculation.

It takes about ten to fifteen minutes for them to read the material and sketch out answers to the questions. Then I ask them to discuss their answers with one or more other students. After a few minutes, I interrupt and go around the classroom quadrant by quadrant, asking for responses to the questions. Not all students in a quadrant need to volunteer, but several will, until all the necessary points have been made—usually by the students, sometimes supplemented by me. The first few questions have clear answers based on the written material: for example, Vivaldi wrote concertos and operas because he was paid to do so, whereas he had fewer requests for sacred music. But some questions require a stretch. For example, concertos were a particularly appropriate form for Vivaldi to write for his students at the Pio Ospedale della Pietà because the girls and young women he was training were of varying abilities from virtuosic to pedestrian, and concertos were perfect for showcasing the best while allowing much weaker players a role. Vivaldi's approach to concerto writing and his use of ritornello form made sense for him because he could generate a large amount of music quickly, as he was required to do, while allowing constant variety and invention.

In short, this exercise asks the students to practice the discipline of musicology in a nutshell. They absorb the information for themselves, then immediately apply it to answer specific questions. They relate biographical and historical context to the music itself, trying to establish how the music was shaped by its context, and how the music solves the problem posed by the historical situation. Where evidence is lacking ("Why don't we hear Vivaldi operas today?"), they are encouraged to speculate, based on what they know (the operas don't exist in modern editions? the instrumental music has eclipsed the operas?). They test their interpretations against those of their peers and then go public by volunteering during class discussion. Most find it much more fun than listening to me drone on.

*In-class short writing and discussion*

When there is no take-home writing assignment or in-class reading to do, one can still use in-class writing to generate discussion. Sometimes class discussions fall flat because the students do not know what to say in response to a question from the instructor, or comments will veer from the topic as students respond to each other. If I ask everyone to write for one or two minutes in response to a question, everyone has a chance to think of something to say about it. So most will have something to say when called on, and if the discussion veers off topic it can quickly be brought back by asking a student who has not yet participated to read what he or she wrote. Such in-class writing can also be used to generate group discussion and reports as in previous examples.

Here the peer learning portion of the exercise—the discussion—is already part of most teachers' routines, but it can be helpful to add the brief period of working alone before discussion. This process of starting with one's own direct engagement with the material through the act of writing down one's thoughts, and then moving into discussion with the group, reproduces in miniature the process of the most formal peer review of a writing assignment or presentation. In each case, the student is required to think through the issue for himself or herself first, which provides a much better basis for engaging with the ideas and interpretations of others. Preparing for discussion with a short period of in-class writing (or with short papers and journals, as discussed above) often results in increased participation from the quieter members of a class.

## Conclusions and cautions

These kinds of exercises provide peer review for formal assignments and encourage peer learning in both formal and informal assignments. They help people learn because they work with the natural ways we have of learning. They tend to be fun, although the formal peer assessment can be difficult for some students. They encourage students to apply what they know and to learn by doing. However, some cautions are appropriate.

First, the goals of each exercise need to be very clear. You cannot just gather students into a group and get them talking; you need to give them something very concrete and specific to do. Having them present a report to the class in five minutes may really focus their attention. Giving no clear assignment may just leave them to wallow around in conversation.

Second, it is inevitable that some exercises will work better than others and some groups will work better with each other. The best exercises engage students where they are and stretch them in interesting ways, and which ones do this best is likely to vary from class to class, year to year, and student to student. Over the years, the approaches that are most dependably successful for each individual teacher tend to become clear. The best groups are those in which students bring complementary strengths, each member contributing a different set of skills, information, and understandings from which the others can learn. But since individual students vary in their abilities, groups will too. There will be groups in which the students do not like each other or do not work well together, or in which some of the necessary strengths of focus, discipline, and willingness to engage the material are missing. As an instructor, I sometimes have to intervene when a group is not working well. Assigning students to different groups over the semester is important, as students often bring their experiences with successful group interaction into each new group, and variety gives everyone a chance to participate in groups that work well together. As in any kind of teaching, it is helpful to be attentive to how well things are going for each student and to invite frequent feedback.

Third, this is not a recipe for content-free teaching. The point is to use the strategy that best communicates the content. The Vivaldi exercise described above conveys everything I would want to get across in a fifty-minute session on Vivaldi's concertos, but it makes the students do the discovery and arrive at the conclusions rather than listening to me. This makes it more likely that they will understand and retain the material. In fact, I devised this strategy after planning a lecture that would have led my students through Vivaldi's career and arrived at the same conclusions, only to realize I was providing far too much detail for them to absorb by listening and as a result was obscuring my point. By giving the facts about his career in writing on the handout and having them read it themselves, mining it for the answers to the questions I wanted them to focus on, I established the right balance between the details and the larger themes and made it far easier to remember how the facts relate to the overall picture. But if lecturing is the best way to convey the content in a memorable way, give a lecture.

One strength of this kind of teaching is that it allows you to teach a skill alongside the content. For example, peer review of each other's written work helps teach students about writing, and group exercises that try to summarize a reading or relate information from the readings to the music at hand help students learn how to discern the main points in a reading and apply them. These skills will transfer to other situations.

In the final analysis, the only reason to use any technique is because it works. In my experience, peer learning offers a wide range of methods that help students learn, develop their abilities, and keep them interested in the subject at hand, and consequently their grasp of the content of the course improves. Given how interactive music-making can be, it is appropriate that our music history classrooms be interactive as well, not just between student and instructor, but between students themselves, like performers in an ensemble listening to each other and playing better as a result.

*This essay is adapted from a keynote address on "Writing and Peer Learning in the Music History Classroom" at the international conference on "Peer Learning and Peer Assessment in Music and Cognate Disciplines," sponsored by the University of Ulster Peer Learning in Music project, University of Ulster at Jordantown, Belfast, Northern Ireland, 11 September 1998. The original talk, including copies of several assignments, is reprinted in "Peer Learning in Music," Desmond Hunter and Michael Russ, eds.,* Part Two: Conference Proceedings *(Belfast: University of Ulster, 2000), 11–27.*

## Notes

1    The book that was my introduction to the subject was C. Williams Griffin, ed., *Teaching Writing in All Disciplines* (San Francisco, Washington, and London: Jossey-Bass, 1982). There is a large literature now in this field, surveyed in *Writing Across the Curriculum: An Annotated Bibliography*, compiled by Chris

M. Anson, John E. Schwiebert, and Michael M. Williamson (Westport, CT: Greenwood Press, 1993). Significant collections of essays on the topic include: Art Young and Toby Fulwiler, eds., *Writing Across the Disciplines: Research into Practice* (Upper Montclair, NJ: Boynton/Cook, 1986); Anne Herrington and Charles Moran, eds., *Writing, Teaching, and Learning in the Disciplines* (New York: Modern Language Association of America, 1992); and Charles Bazerman and David Russell, eds., *Landmark Essays on Writing Across the Curriculum* (Davis, CA: Hermagoras Press, 1994).

2    For a more formal statement of these guidelines, see J. Peter Burkholder, *Study and Listening Guide for 'A History of Western Music' and 'Norton Anthology of Western Music'* (New York: W. W. Norton, 1996), vii.

3    The precise details of the assignment vary from year to year. Given here are the assignment and related materials for Fall 1998. The complete assignment for the most recent semester is available on the World Wide Web as a link from the main course page, <www.music.indiana.edu/som/courses/m401>. Linked to the research paper assignment are several other web pages offering guidance on many aspects of researching and writing the paper.

4    Since students often sit near their friends or choose the same seat each time, I often assign them to groups or have them number off, so that they are randomly grouped with people they know less well and with different people each time. For example, in a class of thirty, I may have students count off from one to ten, then put all the "ones" in one group, all the "twos" in another, and so on. However it is done, if one makes a practice of breaking a class into small groups, it is best to introduce variety in the way groups are formed and in group membership, so that the students have a chance to interact with as many different classmates as possible.

5    Sample journal assignments are available on the World Wide Web at <www.music.indiana.edu/som/courses/m656/M656jrnl.html> and <www.music.indiana.edu/som/courses/Monteverdi/journal.html>. Recently, I have been experimenting with portfolios that can be revised over the course of the semester instead of handwritten journals. Online discussions offer another option, although these tend to lack the permanence of a journal or portfolio and can mean students do not have their own written work available to them during class discussion.

6    I typically use the last movement of "Autumn" from *The Four Seasons*, Op. 8, No. 3, the second movement of Concerto Grosso in G Minor, Op. 3, No. 2 (which is included in the *Norton Anthology of Western Music*, the usual anthology for the course), and the first and last movements of Violin Concerto in G Minor, Op. 8, No. 8.

Chapter Sixteen

# Creating Anthologies for the Middle Ages and Renaissance

*Russell E. Murray, Jr.*

## Anthologies: repertories and canons

*"When I was a child... I thought as a child..."* I Corinthians, 13:11

This essay is, in large part, a discussion of anthologies and how we use them. It is also a discussion of how we can create and manipulate anthologies and why we should. Anthologies are a fact of life for anyone who teaches survey courses, and by and large, they have been a great boon. We use them, expand on them, and sometimes complain about them, but we seldom stop to think about what they represent. We can think of anthologies in a number of ways. On one hand, they are like museums, holding the great masterworks that we want our students to know and understand. We walk through them with our students, seeing "pieces at an exhibition" and pointing out this work or that. On the other, they are like zoos: musicological gardens containing various species that we can use to create a taxonomy of musical styles—a *Hortus Musicus* in its truest sense. They are pedagogical aids and commercial ventures, the vision of an individual scholar or the product of an editorial committee. But they also represent something else: repertories and canons.

I remember as an undergraduate getting a gift from my wife-to-be: a copy of the first volume of the *Historical Anthology of Music*. I still enjoy pulling it off my shelf. It has a feel, a look, and even a smell that brings back memories. But there is another quality of this experience that I have been considering recently. When I first held that volume, many years ago, I felt that I was, in fact, holding the entire history of music. A naive thought, and surely even at that time I realized that there was much more to the history of music (beyond, of course, volume two). I had, after all, used the *Norton Scores* and had held in my hand individual scores. Yet at the same time there was a certain completeness to this volume, a certain authority. And in the back of my mind I am sure I thought that if this was not *the* history of music, it was a perfect stand-in; that if I had a mastery of these works, so carefully selected by eminent scholars with foreign names, I would have a mastery of history itself.

As my education continued, I began to see the limits of this view. I discovered the vastness of even so small a field as the sixteenth-century madrigal, or the various stages of the development of the sequence. And as I began teaching, I looked at anthologies with a more sophisticated, perhaps even jaundiced eye. For me, the teacher, the anthology was merely a neutral collection of pieces. It was, for good or for ill, a starting point for the works I wanted my students to know. An anthology was a collection of techniques to explain, as well as favorite pieces to share. I recognized it as a result of personal whim, marketing forces, and the exigencies of copyright difficulties. And as I taught classes again and again, I found myself moving outside of the anthology in order to reflect my own personal tastes and interests.

In short, I had in the words of Paul, "put away childish things," and had made peace with the anthologies, looking ahead with mild curiosity to what the next edition might bring, and constantly looking out for new and interesting works to add. But in all of this sophistication, I had forgotten something very basic; that for my students, especially those exploring the music of the Middle Ages and Renaissance for the first time, these anthologies still represented the whole history of music. And my changes were merely putting my own personal spin on that history. We were, my students and I, looking at these anthologies in different lights and using them for different purposes. This gap between our differing expectations creates both a challenge and an opportunity. For if we can understand these differences, perhaps we can bridge that gap in a creative way and make our anthologies a more useful tool in our teaching.

One way to understand these different views of anthologies is to investigate how they serve as both repertories and canons.[1] Viewing them in these ways suggests different uses—and different expectations—from the body of works that form our anthologies. It is the purpose of this essay to explore these different qualities, especially as they are reflected in the sacred music we teach, and to suggest some strategies for exploiting these qualities. Let me begin by offering some basic definitions of the two terms.

Repertories are, in effect, lists of useful things (in the Middle Ages and Renaissance, a *repertorium* was simply a list). A concert repertory, for example, is a list of useful pieces for performance. We often view reading and listening lists as repertories, and they tend to be flexible and somewhat permeable. Works in a repertory are chosen for their functional value or their aesthetic/popular appeal. Moreover, they are generally seen as neutral. Pieces easily move in and out of repertories without much fuss being made. In this way, our anthologies are repertories, and we employ them as useful tools for teaching techniques and styles.

Canons, on the other hand, have different characteristics. First and foremost, they are organized around value rather than function. They represent not what is useful, but what is seen as good or necessary. As such, they reflect the biases and agendas of those who put them together. Second, they are exclusive and stable. Items earn their place in the canon and are replaced only when their value is perceived as less, often because of changing tastes or interests (and as we know from recent discussions of canons in the academy, change is often met with hostility). Third, they represent authority. Canonicity is conferred by those who have the training to decide the value of certain works. Finally, they are, as Citron points out, self-replicating. Even as a canon changes in the makeup of its individual components, the general outlines and requirements stay pretty much the same. This relates to their stability, and the proof of this can be found in comparing various anthologies or various editions of the same anthology. In these cases, the categories remain stable (a Mozart symphony) even if the particulars differ *(that* Mozart symphony).

To see the extent of this, compare the pre-Baroque contents of the two most widely-used anthologies: *The Norton Anthology of Western Music,* and its most popular competitor, *The Development of Western Music: an Anthology.*[2] The general categories used in these anthologies, not surprisingly, are similar. What is illuminating is the number of works that they have in common. For the non-specialist, it would be easy to conclude, for example, that Adam de la Halle's *Robins m'aime* and Philippe de Vitry's *Garrit Gallus* were canonic works on the par with Beethoven's Fifth Symphony, and that *Alleluia: pascha nostrum* was the most important work of polyphony to come out of the Notre Dame School. Clearly there is a canon-like quality to these anthologies and that quality, I think, sometimes plays a role in inhibiting many of us from expanding or modifying that body of works.[3]

It is easy (and perhaps comforting) to view our anthologies as neutral repertories (which they are: specifically repertories of techniques and styles to be taught). It is important, however, to keep in mind their status as canons. As such they are synecdoches for the history of music and are presumed by their users to be a measure of quality and importance. All of this was brought home to me recently while speaking to a publisher's representative. We were talking about anthologies and about how I was adding to and changing the pieces that I used. In the course of the conversation, he asked if I was not uncomfortable moving away from the *masterworks* (in this case, choosing a different repertory of organum settings). In his mind, then, the anthology was a canon, and it is also that for our students.

I suppose none of this is really very surprising to the readers of this essay. If we do not think specifically in these terms, I am sure, at least, that it is something we intuitively accept. My purpose is to explore what this means from a pedagogical standpoint and how we might use these conflicting views of anthologies to help our students as they struggle to make sense of the history of music, especially the music of the Middle Ages and Renaissance.

## Anthologies as repertories: teaching technique and style

If we view an anthology as a repertory, we can focus on the pragmatic and functional value of the pieces. In teaching medieval and Renaissance music, there are specific musical and historical concepts that we wish to teach, and examples should be chosen for their ability to illustrate those concepts effectively. But how effective is the repertory of the standard anthologies?

One of the broad paradigms of our view of medieval society is that of building on authority. This is reflected in many ways in the sacred music of the period. Students first see this as reality when they begin to study the process of troping, and it is here that we can see how our choice of pieces can help or hinder us. We can start with a practical exercise. In his *Anthology of Medieval Music,* Richard Hoppin provides an excellent example of a troped introit, the Epiphany introit *Ecce advenit.*[4] The structure of the interlinear trope is well explained in the text, and the troped section is clearly set apart in the anthology by the use of italicized text. It is, at first glance, a perfect example for teaching the concept of troping. But imagine seeing this piece without the italicized text. Without specific knowledge of the original introit, it would be difficult to recognize it as an example of a trope. I do not think our students recognize it either. We have added a bit of shorthand to say, "this is this and that is that," but it is merely a code that identifies rather than explains and has no independent reality for our students. Why do we assume, then, that this code will make sense to them? In part, because we have probably taught them the structure of an introit so that they would have a context in which to place this example. Unfortunately, this usually involves the study of a *different* introit. This is the case in the Hoppin anthology, where the introit studied is that from the Easter Mass.

The reason our students have difficulties is obvious: if they do not know the original chant, they cannot recognize the newly composed departure; they can only have it pointed out to them—a passive mode of learning. Yet anthologies more often than not force students to do just that. Consider, for example, various editions of the *Norton Anthology of Western Music,* certainly the most popular and overall the most useful and well thought out of such anthologies (see figure 16.1). In the first and second editions, students were introduced to the plainsong Mass by way of the Mass for *Septuagesima* Sunday: an interesting Mass to study, perhaps, but flawed as a representative example in that it falls within the penitential season of Lent and thus has neither a Gloria nor an Alleluia. Ironically enough, however, when the first edition presented an example of a trope, it was an interlinear trope of a Gloria. This asks a student to assimilate a new concept within a context of which he or she has no firsthand knowledge. And while we *can* use such an example to explain the process of troping by carefully pointing out the original text and music and then placing the trope in opposition to that, the student will come out with—at best—only an intellectual understanding of the process. We would be fooling ourselves if we made any assumption about the student actually knowing the material in any meaningful sense.

The same holds true in the second edition that uses the trope, *Quem quaeritis in praesepe,* an introductory trope to the introit, *Puer natus est.* While the idea of an introductory trope is clearer, it is still new music attached to an unfamiliar piece. In short, the student is hard-pressed to know where one ends and the other begins. This confusion is heightened by the fact that in the recording accompanying the second edition the introit itself is never heard, only the introductory trope. Again, it is presented as an abstract concept divorced not only from its context but, more importantly, from the students' limited listening experience.

Happily, this problem is ameliorated in the new edition of the anthology. The Mass used as an example is that for Christmas Day, and its introit, *Puer natus est,* is still the basis for the example of a trope, this time with at least the first phrase of the chant sung. This allows the students to connect the new idea, the trope, with something they presumably recognize (in my classes, I often stop the recording right at the point where the trope ends and have them sing the first line of the introit). Unfortunately, the process ends there, for there is no example of an interlinear trope, the hardest for the students to assimilate. Our students would be better served if we made this sort of connection between pieces the rule rather than the exception in some of our repertories, allowing the student to build on what he or she knows. In order to do this I have built such a repertory centered in the complete Christmas Mass (including the prayers and readings as well as the chants). After the students use this to learn the order and structure of the Mass, they can then return to it as a context in order to explore the various types of tropes and, ultimately, early polyphony. This repertory is shown in figure 16.2. When they learn about accretions to the liturgy, then, they add to their working repertory the following items: *Kyrie omnipotens genitor* (a Latin-texted Kyrie associated with Kyrie IV), *Gaudeamus hodie* (an interliner trope of the introit, *Puer natus est*), *Quem quaeritis in praesepe* (an introductory trope to the same introit—the same one included in the *Norton Anthology of Western Music*), tropes to the offertory and communion.[5]

Thus, all the tropes they study are connected to pieces that they have already learned, and they are much better prepared to distinguish new from old. I also use this Mass template to introduce non-troped additions to the Mass. In this case I have added to the repertory two sequences (one attributed to Notker, the other a twelfth-century example) and a processional before the Alleluia, *Ecce annuntio vobis*. These works are tied to the liturgy of Christmas Day, and while there is no musical connection among them, they are all seen as additions to a known quantity, the Mass for a particular celebration. This is an aspect of continuity that I will address later.

All that I have said about introducing these monophonic additions to the basic liturgy is equally true when discussing the growth of polyphonic practice in the West. Just as tropes are attached to specific chants, polyphonic settings up to the time of Perotin (and beyond, within the improvised tradition) are inextricably tied to specific items of the liturgy. Again, with this in mind we can see the effect our anthology can have on a student's learning. When teaching the style of eleventh- and twelfth-century polyphony, we need to make students aware of how the division between the solo and choral portions of a responsorial chant were transformed into an alternation of polyphonic and monophonic sections. We further need to highlight how, in the style of the Notre Dame composers, syllabic portions of the original chant lent themselves to extended duplum settings while the long melismas called for more compact discant settings. These are abstract ideas, and to a certain degree counterintuitive; that is, solo sections of the chant are set polyphonically and the syllabic portions receive melismatic treatment. Once more, introducing these techniques with a chant that students know would make the process clearer and more concrete. Yet this is seldom done in anthologies. In the *Norton Anthology* (see figure 16.1 again), the Notre Dame selection used is Leonin's setting of *Alleluia Pascha nostrum*. The first and second editions, as I noted earlier, had used a Mass that had no Alleluia, and first introduced the Alleluia in a polyphonic setting. Thus, the students had no practical experience whatsoever with the responsorial form of a monophonic Alleluia and had to learn the monophonic form at the same time they were learning the intricacies of a polyphonic realization. In the present edition the situation is better. The Christmas Mass presented does have an Alleluia. Now when students encounter polyphonic settings of such chants, they at least have a general schematic of such a chant to work from.

It would be better, I think, if they had the very chants themselves to work from. Conveniently, the Christmas Mass provides rich ground in its gradual, *Viderunt omnes,* and its Alleluia. It is a missed opportunity indeed that these chants are not studied in polyphonic realizations. This is especially true of the gradual, for we can use fine recordings of three generations of polyphonic versions to present a miniature portrait of the development of polyphonic style and technique. Figure 16.2 provides a list of these pieces along with their provenance.[6] As I will show in the next section, there are some larger pedagogical advantages to looking at multiple settings of the same chant.[7]

In short, the repertory we choose not only decides *what* the student learns; to a great extent it determines *how* he or she will learn. Most anthologies force the student to learn in an abstract mode, with no practical experience to help him or her. It only takes a few changes in the repertory to move to a more active mode of learning.

## Anthologies as canons: creating a history

The repertory outlined above provides me with a group of pieces that make it easier to teach specific subject matter. Seen in that light, it is simply a more personalized listening list. If we accept the idea of the anthology as a canon, we can begin to ask some questions about how these anthologies function in the minds of our students. For me, the most important questions are: What is the *history* that the anthology is giving the students? What are the values embedded in that history? Are they the values that I wish to give them? In short, does the anthology build the same history that I want my students to walk away with? These questions work at all levels: inclusiveness, accuracy, etc. As an obvious example, the canon represented by anthologies has been broadened recently to incorporate the contributions of women. In some cases this has involved the addition of pieces here and there, and in some cases it involves substitution (the first is met, at worst, with indifference, the latter more often with resistance). In all cases, however, the change represents an attempt to create a new history in the minds of the students (and the instructors, for that matter), one in which women have a recognizable role.[8]

In the last few years, I have come to think about the values of change and continuity inherent in the sacred music that I teach in my medieval and Renaissance survey. That is, the change entailed in the development of the techniques of troping and polyphony, as well as the continuity reflected in the liturgy of the Catholic church and of chant-based composition. As has probably become clear, the repertory I have outlined above exhibits a coherence that goes beyond a simple listening list. All these items are chosen from the liturgy of the Christmas Mass at various stages of the development of sacred music in the West. And although they are contained on different recordings, they can be presented to students as complete liturgical services, one from around the year 1000 CE (a complete plainsong Mass), one from around 1100 (the Mass with the addition of tropes), and one from about 1200 (the Mass as it might have been celebrated at Notre Dame).[9] Looked at individually, the pieces have a clear context, but in combination they have a quality of completeness that we might be tempted to call canonic. And as I noted above, one of the qualities of a canon is that it encodes certain values.

Anthologies thus create a musical and historical world for the student. My choice of sacred repertory presents a limited world: the music associated with the feast of Christmas. It could be argued that this is a drawback, for only a small repertory is explored, and the richness of the language of medieval chant is perhaps sidestepped. I accept this as a given. In this world, the students will not hear two of the loveliest chants in the corpus of sacred monophony: the gradual and Alleluia of the Easter Mass. And while they will hear the music of Hildegard of Bingen, it will be outside of this canon (which I purposely do to reinforce the separate, non-canonical status of Hildegard and her music). But the breadth or depth that they will miss is compensated for by their chance to witness the continuity of chant over the course of a millennium. Let me explain this by going back to the pieces just discussed and demonstrate how using them as part of a canon can create new meaning for them in the eyes of the student.

If the pieces studied are seen as creating a musical and historical world, the students are allowed to enter that world and to see the pieces they study within that context. When this is the case, they can view two pieces, such as an introit and its trope, as more than abstract examples of styles or techniques separated by time. Instead, they can see them as part of a continuum and recognize the simultaneous qualities of change and continuity. More importantly, as a piece changes, they can see that it takes its place in a changed musical and historical reality. A plainchant gradual, for example, is not *replaced* by another piece. Rather, it *becomes* another piece, and the students can be first-hand witnesses to that transformation.

As an example, we can look again at the Christmas introit and its tropes. The students are first introduced to *Puer natus est* within the context of the complete Christmas Mass. They therefore know it as both a musical item and as a specific part of the liturgy. They then see it in a more detailed context when they explore it as part of the Entrance Rite, and they learn the general antiphonal structure of the piece. By now, the form as well as the basic melody will have become familiar to them, and they should be comfortable with the historical and liturgical context of the piece. At this point, they are ready to explore the process of troping. As they listen to the two troped versions of a chant they are familiar with, they will have a first-hand experience of hearing something new (the trope) intimately tied to something very familiar.

Thus, the trope has been transformed from an abstract concept to a real experience. But more importantly, the students have an opportunity for an authentic listening experience, one that combines newness and memory. The piece has become part of something larger than an item on a listening list; it has become for them part of a canon. Their experience, therefore, is similar to that of the medieval listener upon hearing a new trope of a familiar chant. They have become, in effect, witnesses to the continuity embedded within the expansion of the medieval liturgy. Finally, they see a work that had grown out of centuries of relatively stable practice take its place in a new context, in a liturgy guided by the creative practices of the beginning of the second millennium. We can explain all of this to them, but it is more relevant (and exciting) for them if they can see the process in action.

This same process works with polyphonic settings of chants. As with *Puer natus est,* the students are introduced to the gradual, *Viderunt omnes,* in detail but also within the context of the Mass as a whole. They will have learned those aspects that will relate to polyphonic performance (the solo/choral nature of the responsorial chant) so that by the time they get to the discussion of chant-based polyphony, they will be quite comfortable with these concepts and have a chance to review them within the context of their polyphonic realizations.

As they study examples from three different generations of composers, the students review two things that are old (the musical material of the chant and the alternation of solo/choral textures) even while they are introduced to new concepts: the alternation of monophony and polyphony, duplum and discant style, and the development of large-scale structure. They can see the change in proportion that accompanied the change of style: a four-minute chant transformed into a fifteen-minute work of polyphony. They can also witness how the polyphonic portions begin to overwhelm the monophonic portions, especially the verse. To make this as real as possible, I turn them into medieval cathedral singers by asking them to listen to the setting while reading (and singing quietly) from the original plainchant so that they can see the styles as they relate to the original chant. Again, they have the opportunity to be a witness to the changes that are occurring to a piece they have come to know. Moreover, they can see that change within the context of the unchanging liturgical canon, and they can put themselves in the place of the singer, who surely saw these pieces not as independent works, but as truly glorified performances of the daily liturgy.

Our students' appreciation of continuity need not stop there, however, and it is important to stress that the tradition they explored for the Middle Ages is just as relevant for the Renaissance (and beyond). To illustrate this, I utilize Paul McCreesh's recording of Palestrina's *Missa Hodie Christus natus est*.[10] McCreesh presents the work as part of a complete Christmas service from about the year 1620. It is a veritable anthology of (mostly) late Renaissance music (vocal and instrumental). I exploit this pre-made anthology as a chance to introduce works of exceptionally high quality over the course of the term and ultimately to allow the students to place them within a context they already know. For example, Palestrina's Kyrie becomes a real liturgical item for them; not because the text tells them that it is but because they hear it immediately after the introit that they have come to know so well. And the other pieces on the recording, worthy of inclusion in any anthology, are given a context that makes their function as ascertainable as their sound.

In short, what I am attempting with my selection of pieces is something of a musical time machine. Set the dial for December twenty-fifth of any year, and see how the world has changed. A simple collection of unidentifiable chants becomes, over the course of the semester, a convenient drawer into which new concepts and pieces can be placed. This miniature canon is linked by the context of the Christmas Mass, but other smaller and self-contained clusters of pieces can be used for the same pedagogical ends, in the secular realm as much as in the sacred.[11] Just as with the previous examples, such pieces can be placed within the context of a dynamic canon of works, and they become more than isolated examples. Instead, they embody an important and core value that I wish for the students to internalize and use to inform their understanding that the history of music is part of an unfolding world.

What I have tried to do with these miniature canons, then, is what that first copy of the *Historical Anthology of Music* did for me, to give the students a sense of holding history in their hands. Certainly not *the* history, but *a* history that encapsulates values of change and continuity, of borrowing and transformation; in short, the kind of coherent understanding that is the hallmark of the mastery of a canon. It is an artificial construct, yet it reflects a reality that guided musical life throughout this period—that change and continuity were intimately linked. My hope is that through this process, my students will enter this world and feel a link to a long and continuous tradition. We can hope as well that the editors of our anthologies continue to improve their choice of repertory and that we attempt to craft these repertories into meaningful canons for our students.

## Notes

1    Marcia J. Citron, *Gender and the Musical Canon* (Cambridge: Cambridge University Press, 1993) discusses this issue in her first chapter. See especially pp. 24–28, where she addresses the canon-like quality of anthologies and their relationship to the performance repertory. While Citron would see less of a clean line between repertories and canons than I will draw, her arguments are nonetheless influential on the ideas presented here. See also Joseph Kerman, "A few canonic variations," *Critical Inquiry* 10 (1983): 107–25.

2    Claude Palisca, ed., *The Norton Anthology of Western Music*, third ed. (New York: W. W. Norton, 1996) and K. Maria Stolba, ed., *The Development of Western Music: an Anthology*, second ed. (Madison: Brown & Benchmark, 1994).

3    As Citron points out, early music is more clearly tied to a scholarly canon than, say, nineteenth-century music. This is likely to change as a performance repertory (and, of late, a markedly eclectic one) develops.

4    Richard Hoppin, *Anthology of Medieval Music* (New York: W. W. Norton, 1978), 33.

5    The Christmas Mass is recorded on: Monk's Choir of the Benedictine Abbey of St. Martin, Beuron, dir. Fr. Maurus Pfaff, *Third Christmas Mass*, Deutsche Grammophon 427 014–2 (1960). The other chants are taken from: Capella Antiqua München, dir. Konrad Ruhland, *Sequentiae*, RCA Victor GD 71953 (1980, re-released in 1989); Die Singphoniker, dir. Godehard Joppich, *Gregorian Chant from St. Gall*, CPO Classic Produktion Osnabrück 999 267–2 (n.d.); and Ensemble Gilles Binchois, dir. Dominique Vellard, *Les Premieres Polyphonies Françaises: Organa et tropes des XI$^e$ siècle*, Virgin 7243 5 45135 2 7 (1996). This last recording has the added advantage of utilizing women's voices, helping to overcome the usual bias that chant was sung exclusively by men. The recording of Kyrie IV is found on: Benedictine Abbey Münsterschwarzach, dir. Godehard Joppich, *Eternal Peace*, Deutsche Grammophon 445 945–2 (1982).

6    The polyphony for this repertory is recorded on: Ensemble Organum, dir. Marcel Pérès, *Les Premieres Polyphonies Françaises: Organa et tropes des XI$^e$ siècle, Leonin: école Notre-Dame: Messe du Jour de Noël*, Harmonia Mundi France 1901148 (1985); and The Hilliard Ensemble, dir. Paul Hillier, *Pérotin*, ECM 1385 (1989).

7    Others have certainly recognized this. *The Norton Anthology*, for example, presents a number of substitute clausulae and motets based on the Easter Alleluia, and Sarah Fuller in *The European Musical Heritage, 800–1750* (New York: McGraw Hill, 1987) includes settings of this Alleluia by both Leonin and Perotin. My point is only that we should consider taking this concept a few steps further.

8    For a cogent discussion of this process as it applies to women's music, see Cynthia J. Cyrus and Olivia Carter Mather, "Rereading Absence: Women in Medieval-Renaissance Music," *College Music Symposium* 38 (1998): 101–17.

9    With the development of easy-to-use authoring software, this connection can be made more real to the students by creating electronic media with listening charts that are linked to the CD recordings of the pieces, making an instant and playable anthology of these disparate works.

10    Gabrieli Consort and Players, dir. Paul McCreesh, *Christmas Mass in Rome,* Deutsche Grammophon 437 833–2 (1993). In addition, this recording presents a wide variety of performance practice issues. Palestrina's Mass, for example, is performed with an early Baroque aesthetic, utilizing instrumental doubling and continuo. The chant is performed in an equalist manner, contrasting with the mensuralist and Solesmes styles that the students hear earlier in the semester.

11    The anthology that accompanies Alan Atlas's *Renaissance Music* (New York: W. W. Norton, 1998) does just this with some of the madrigals. Gastoldi's *A lieta vita* can be seen as it is transformed into Morley's *Sing we and chant it,* and the student gets a front-row seat to the process of 'Englishing' madrigals, rather than a second-hand description.

### FIGURE 16.1
### Examples of Plainchant, Tropes and Early Polyphony
in *The Norton Anthology of Western Music*

| First Edition | Second Edition | Third Edition |
| --- | --- | --- |
| **Mass:** | | |
| *Septuagesima* Sunday | *Septuagesima* Sunday | Christmas Day |
| **Tropes:** | | |
| *Gloria spiritus et alme* | *Quem quaeritis/Puer natus est* (Christmas) | *Quem quaeritis/Puer natus est* |
| *Victimae paschali laudes* (Easter) | *Victimae paschali laudes* | *Victimae paschali laudes* |
| **Polyphony:** | | |
| *Alleluia Justus ut Palma* (Commune Sanctorum) | *Alleluia Justus ut Palma* | *Alleluia Justus ut Palma* |
| *Senescente mundano filio* (Versus) | *Senescente mundano filio* | *Congaudeant catholici* (Benedicamus trope) |
| *Alleluia Pascha nostrum* (Easter) | *Alleluia Pascha nostrum* | *Alleluia Pascha nostrum* |
| *Sederunt* (St. Stephen's) | *Sederunt* | *Sederunt* |

## FIGURE 16.2
## A Repertory of Plainchant, Tropes, and Polyphony for Christmas Day

**Plainchant:**
Introit: *Puer natus est*
Kyrie IV
Gloria II
Collect
Epistle
Gradual: *Viderunt omnes*
Alleluia *Dies Sanctificatus*
Gospel
Credo I
Offertory: *Tui sunt caeli*
Secret
Preface
Sanctus III
Doxology
Pater noster
Pax Domini
Agnus Dei III
Communion: *Viderunt omnes*
Postcommunion: *Praesta quaesumus*
Ite, missa est

**Tropes:**
Kyrie Trope: *Omnipotens genitor*
Introit Trope: *Quem quaeritis in praesepe*
Introit Trope: *Gaudeamus hodie*
Antienne: *Ecce annunciato vobis*
Sequence (Notker): *Natus ante saecula*
Sequence (12th century): *Laetabundus exsultet fidelis*
Offertory Trope: *Qui es sine principio*
Communion Trope: *Radix Jesse virga*

**Polyphony:**
Kyrie (improvised organum)
Gradual: *Viderunt omnes* (11th-century organum from Chartres)
Gradual: *Viderunt omnes* (Leonin?)
Gradual: *Viderunt omnes* (Perotin)
Alleluia *Dies sanctificatus* (Leonin?)
Sanctus (organum)
Ite, missa est (organum)

# Bibliography

Ambrose, Jane. "Music Journals." In *The Journal Book*, edited by Toby Fulwiler, 261–68. Portsmouth, NH: Boynton/Cook, 1987.

Anson, Chris M., John E. Schwiebert, and Michael M. Williamson, comps. *Writing Across the Curriculum: An Annotated Bibliography.* Westport, CT: Greenwood Press, 1993.

Arlt, Wulf. "Jehannot de Lescurel and the Function of Musical Language in the *Roman de Fauvel* as Presented in BN fr. 146." In *Fauvel Studies*, edited by Margaret Bent and Andrew Wathey. Oxford: Clarendon Press, 1998.

Atlas, Alan. *Renaissance Music.* New York: W. W. Norton, 1998.

Avril, François. *Manuscript Painting at the Court of France: The Fourteenth Century (1310–1380).* New York: George Braziller, 1978.

Baltzell, W. J. *A Complete History of Music for Schools, Clubs, and Private Reading.* Philadelphia: Theodore Presser Co., 1905.

Bazerman, Charles, and David Russell, eds. *Landmark Essays on Writing Across the Curriculum.* Davis, CA: Hermagoras Press, 1994.

Bellman, Jonathan. *A Short Guide to Writing about Music.* New York, Reading et al.: Longman, 1999.

Bellonci, Maria. "Beatrice and Isabella d'Este." In *The Italian Renaissance*, second edition by J. H. Plumb. New York: Houghton Mifflin Co., 1985.

Bent, Margaret. "Fauvel and Marigny: Which Came First?" In *Fauvel Studies*, edited by Margaret Bent and Andrew Wathey. Oxford, Clarendon Press, 1998.

Bergeron, Katherine. *Decadent Enchantments: The Revival of Gregorian Chant at Solesmes.* Berkeley: University of California Press, 1998.

Bizet, Georges. *Carmen: Cambridge Opera Guide*, edited by Susan McClary. Cambridge and New York: Cambridge University Press, 1992.

Blackey, Robert, ed. *History Anew: Innovations in the Teaching of History Today*. Long Beach, CA: The University Press, 1993.

Bonta, Stephen. "The Uses of the *Sonata da Chiesa.*" *Journal of the American Musicological Society* 22 (1969): 54–84.

Bonwell, Charles C., and James A. Eison. *Active Learning: Creating Excitement in the Classroom*. ASHE-Eric Higher Education Report No. 1. Washington, D.C.: George Washington University, 1991.

Booth, Wayne C., Gregory G. Colomb, and Joseph M. Williams. *The Craft of Research*. Chicago and London: University of Chicago Press, 1995.

Bordwell, David, and Kristen Thompson. *Film Art: An Introduction*, fifth ed. New York: McGraw Hill, 1997.

Boulez, Pierre. *Notes of an Apprenticeship,* translated by Herbert Weinstock. New York: Knopf, 1968.

Bouzereau, Laurent, ed. *Star Wars: The Annotated Screenplay*. New York: Ballantine Books, 1997.

Brinkley, Alan, Betty Dessants, Michael Flamm, et al. *The Chicago Handbook for Teachers: A Practical Guide to the College Classroom*. Chicago: The University of Chicago Press, 1999.

Briscoe, James R., ed. *Historical Anthology of Music by Women*. Bloomington: Indiana University Press, 1987.

Brodbeck, David. *Brahms: Symphony No. 1*. Cambridge: Cambridge University Press, 1997.

——. "Brahms." In *The Nineteenth Century Symphony*, edited by D. Kern Holoman, 224–29. New York: Schirmer Books, 1998.

Brown, Royal S. *Overtones and Undertones*. Berkeley and Los Angeles: University of California Press, 1994.

Bruffee, Kenneth A. "Collaborative Learning and the Conversation of Mankind." In *Cross-Talk in Comp Theory: A Reader*, edited by Victor Villanueva, Jr., 393–414. Urbana, IL: National Council of Teachers of English, 1997.

Buhler, James, Caryl Flinn, and David Neumeyer, eds. *Music and Cinema*. Hanover, NH: Wesleyan University Press, 2000.

Bürger, Peter. *Theory of the Avant-Garde*. Minneapolis: University of Minnesota Press, 1984.

Burkholder, J. Peter. *Study and Listening Guide for 'A History of Western Music' and 'Norton Anthology of Western Music.'* New York: W. W. Norton, 1996.

Burrows, Donald, ed. *The Cambridge Companion to Handel*. Cambridge: Cambridge University Press, 1997.

——. *Handel*. New York: Schirmer Books, 1994.

Burt, George. *The Art of Film Music*. Boston: Northeastern University Press, 1994.

Cain, William E., ed. *Teaching the Conflicts: Gerald Graff, Curricular Reform, and the Culture Wars*. New York: Garland Publishing, 1994.

Calvino, Italo. *If on A Winter's Night A Traveler*, translated by William Weaver. New York: Harcourt, 1982.

Chambers, David, and Jane Martineau, eds. *Splendours of the Gonzaga*. Catalogue of Exhibition in the Victoria & Albert Museum, London, 1981–82. Milan: Cinisello, 1981.

Chion, Michel. *Audio-Vision: Sound on Screen*, edited and translated by Claudia Gorbman. New York: Columbia University Press, 1994.

Citron, Marcia. "Gender, Professionalism and the Musical Canon." *Journal of Musicology* 8 (1990): 102–17.

——. *Gender and the Musical Canon.* Cambridge: Cambridge University Press, 1993.

Cook, Nicholas. *Analysing Musical Multimedia.* Oxford: Oxford University Press, 1998.

Cook, Susan C., and Judy S. Tsou, eds. *Cecilia Reclaimed: Feminist Perspectives on Gender and Music.* Urbana, IL: The University of Illinois Press, 1994.

Copland, Aaron. "Tip to Moviegoers: Take Off Those Ear-Muffs." *New York Times,* 6 Nov. 1949, sec. 6, p. 28. Revised and incorporated in *What To Listen For in Music.* New York: McGraw Hill, 1988.

Crawford, Richard. *Studying American Music.* I.S.A.M. Special Publications 3. Brooklyn: Institute for Studies in American Music, 1985.

——. *The American Musical Landscape.* Berkeley: University of California Press, 1993.

Crews, Frederick. *The Pooh Perplex.* New York: Dutton, 1963.

Crocker, Richard L. *The Early Medieval Sequence.* Berkeley: University of California Press, 1977.

Crystal, David. *The Cambridge Encyclopedia of the English Language.* Cambridge: Cambridge University Press, 1995.

Cyrus, Cynthia J., and Olivia Carter Mather. "Rereading Absence: Women in Medieval-Renaissance Music." *College Music Symposium* 38 (1998): 101–17.

Daverio, John. *Crossing Paths: Perspectives on Schubert, Schumann, and Brahms.* New York: Oxford University Press, forthcoming.

David, Hans T., and Arthur Mendel, eds. *The New Bach Reader: A Life of Johann Sebastian Bach in Letters and Documents.* Revised and expanded by Christoph Wolff. New York: W. W. Norton, 1998.

Davison, Archibald T., and Willi Apel, eds. *Historical Anthology of Music.* Cambridge, MA: Harvard University Press, 1946 and 1949.

Dressel, Paul L., and Dora Marcus. *On Teaching and Learning in College.* San Francisco: Jossey-Bass, 1982.

DuPree, Mary. "Beyond Music in Western Civilization: Issues in Undergraduate Music History Literacy." *College Music Symposium* 30 (1990): 100–5.

Eisler, Hanns. *Composing for the Films.* London: D. Dobson, 1947. Reprint with introductory essay by Graham McCann. London: The Athlone Press, 1994.

Eisler, Riane. *The Chalice and the Blade.* San Francisco: Harper Collins Publishers, 1987.

Ekstein, Modris. *Rites of Spring.* New York: Doubleday, 1989.

Elbow, Peter, and Jennifer Clarke. "Desert Island Discourse: The Benefits of Ignoring Audience." In *The Journal Book*, edited by Toby Fulwiler, 19–32. Portsmouth, NH: Boynton/Cook, 1987.

Emig, Janet. "Writing as a Mode of Learning." In *Cross-Talk in Comp Theory: a Reader*, edited by Victor Villanueva, Jr., 7–16. Urbana, IL: National Council of Teachers of English, 1997.

Ferris, Jean. *America's Musical Landscape*, third ed. Boston: McGraw Hill, 1998.

Fétis, François-Joseph. "Découverte de manuscrits intérressans pour l'Histoire de la Musique." *Revue musicale* 2 (March 1827): 106–13.

Fillion, Bryant. "Language Across the Curriculum." In *To Compose: Teaching Writing in High School and College*, second edition by Thomas Newkirk, 235–50. Portsmouth, NH: Heinemann, 1990.

Fink, Robert. "Elvis Everywhere: Musicology and Popular Music Studies at the Twilight of the Canon." *American Music* 16, no. 2 (Summer 1998): 135–79.

Fisk, Josiah, ed. *Composers on Music: Eight Centuries of Writings*, second ed. (Jeff Nichols, consulting ed.). Boston: Northeastern University Press, 1997.

Friedman, Thomas. *The Lexus and the Olive Tree: Understanding Globalization.* New York: Doubleday, 2000.

Fulcher, Jane. *The Nation's Image: French Grand Opera as Politics and Politicized Art.* Cambridge: Cambridge University Press, 1987.

Fuller, Sarah, ed. *The European Musical Heritage: 800–1750.* New York: McGraw Hill, 1987.

Fulwiler, Toby, ed. *The Journal Book.* Portsmouth, NH: Boynton/Cook, 1987.

Gann, Kyle. *American Music in the Twentieth Century.* New York: Schirmer Books, 1997.

Gilman, Charlotte Perkins. *The Charlotte Perkins Gilman Reader: The yellow wallpaper and other fiction*, edited by Ann J. Lane. New York: Pantheon Books, 1980.

Good, Edward C. *Mightier than the Sword.* Charlottesville, VA: Blue Jeans Press, 1989.

Gorbman, Claudia. *Unheard Melodies.* Bloomington: Indiana University Press, 1987.

Graff, Gerald. *Beyond the Culture Wars: Teaching the Conflicts Can Revitalize American Education.* New York: W. W. Norton, 1992.

Griffel, L. Michael. "Teaching Music." In *Scholars Who Teach: the Art of College Teaching*, edited by Steven M. Cahn, 193–216. Chicago: Nelson-Hall, 1978.

Griffin, C. Williams, ed. *Teaching Writing in All Disciplines.* San Francisco, Washington, and London: Jossey-Bass, 1982.

Griffiths, Paul. *Modern Music: the Avant-Garde since 1945.* London: J. M. Dent, 1981.

——. *Modern Music and After*. Oxford: Oxford University Press, 1995.

Grout, Donald J. *A History of Western Music*. New York: W. W. Norton, 1960; rev. ed. 1973; third ed., 1980; fourth ed., 1988; fifth ed., 1996.

Hallmark, Anne V. "Teaching Music History in Different Environments." In *Musicology in the 1980s: Methods, Goals, Opportunities*, edited by D. Kern Holoman and Claude V. Palisca, 131–44. New York: Da Capo Press, 1982.

Hanslick, Eduard. *Music Criticisms 1846–99*, edited and translated by Henry Pleasants. Baltimore: The Penguin Press, 1963.

Hawkins, John. *A General History of the Science and Practice of Music*. Reprint of the 1853 ed. (with introduction by Charles Cudworth). New York: Dover Publications, 1968.

Hepokoski, James A. "'Music History' as a Set of Problems: 'Musicology' for Undergraduate Music Majors." *College Music Symposium* 28 (1988): 12–15.

Heriot, Angus. *The Castrati in Opera*. London: Secker and Warburg, 1956.

Herrington, Anne, and Charles Moran, eds. *Writing, Teaching, and Learning in the Disciplines*. New York: Modern Language Association of America, 1992.

Higgins, Paula. "The 'Other Minervas': Creative Women at the Court of Margaret of Scotland." In *Rediscovering the Muses: women's musical traditions*, edited by Kimberly Marshall. Boston: Northeastern Press, 1993.

Hitchcock, H. Wiley. *Music in the United States: A Historical Introduction*, fourth ed. Upper Saddle River, NJ: Prentice Hall, 2000.

Holoman, D. Kern. *Writing about Music*. Berkeley, Los Angeles, and London: University of California Press, 1988.

hooks, bell. *Teaching to Transgress*. New York: Routledge, 1994.

Hoppin, Richard, ed. *Anthology of Medieval Music*. New York: W. W. Norton, 1978.

Hughes, Andrew. *Medieval Music: The Sixth Liberal Art*, revised ed. Toronto: University of Toronto Press, 1980.

Huyssen, Andreas. *After the Great Divide: Modernism, Mass Culture, Postmodernism*. Bloomington: Indiana University Press, 1986.

Isaac, Heinrich. *Five Italian Songs for Three Voices or Instruments*, edited by Bernard Thomas. Thesaurus musicus 28. London: London Pro Musica, 1981.

Jameson, Frederic. *The Seeds of Time*. New York: Columbia University Press, 1994.

Kaho, Elizabeth E. *Analysis of the Study of Music Literature in Selected American Colleges*. New York: Teachers College, Columbia University, 1950.

Kalinak, Kathryn. *Settling the Score: Music and the Classical Hollywood Film*. Madison: University of Wisconsin Press, 1992.

Karlin, Fred. *Listening to Movies: The Film Lover's Guide to Film Music*. New York: Schirmer Books, 1994.

Karlin, Fred, and Rayburn Wright. *On the Track: A Guide to Contemporary Film Scoring*. New York: Schirmer Books, 1990.

Kassabian, Anahid. *Hearing Film: Tracking Identifications in Contemporary Hollywood Film Music*. New York: Routledge, 2001.

Kaufmann, Walter. *The Future of the Humanities: Teaching Art, Religion, Philosophy, Literature, and History*. New Brunswick: Transaction Publishers, 1977. Revised with new material, 1995.

Kelly, Thomas. *First Nights: Five Performance Premiers*. New Haven: Yale University Press, 2000.

Kent, O. T. "Student Journals and the Goals of Philosophy." In *The Journal Book*, edited by Toby Fulwiler, 269–77. Portsmouth, NH: Boynton/Cook, 1987.

Kerman, Joseph. *Contemplating Music: Challenges to Musicology.* Cambridge, MA: Harvard University Press, 1985.

——. "A few canonic variations." *Critical Inquiry* 10 (1983): 107–25.

Kivy, Peter. *The Fine Art of Repetition: Essays in the Philosophy of Music.* Cambridge and New York: Cambridge University Press, 1993.

Koskoff, Ellen. "Gender and Power in Music." In *The Musical Woman* 3, edited by Judith Lang Zaimont, 669–788. Westport, CT: Greenwood Press, 1990.

Långfors, Arthur. *Le Roman de Fauvel par Gervais du Bus publié d'apres tous les manuscrits connus.* Paris, 1914–19.

Larsen, Catherine M., and Margaret Merrion. "Documenting the Aesthetic Experience: The Music Journal." In *The Journal Book*, edited by Toby Fulwiler, 254–60. Portsmouth, NH: Boynton/Cook, 1987.

Lawson, Kay. "Women Conductors: Credibility in a Male Dominated Profession." In *The Musical Woman* 3, edited by Judith Lang Zaimont, 197–219. Westport, CT: Greenwood Press, 1990.

Locke, Ralph. "Constructing the Oriental 'Other': Saint-Saëns's *Samson et Dalila.*" *Cambridge Opera Journal* 3 (1991): 261–302.

Lockwood, Lewis. "Josquin at Ferrara: New Documents and Letters." In *Josquin des Prez: Proceedings of the International Josquin Festival Conference*, edited by Edward Lowinsky and Bonnie J. Blackburn. London: Oxford University Press, 1976.

Lodge, David. *The Practice of Writing.* London: The Penguin Press, 1996.

Lyotard, Jean-François. *The Postmodern Condition: A Report on Knowledge*, translated by Geoff Bennington and Brian Massumi. Minneapolis: University of Minnesota Press, 1984.

MacDonald, Laurence E. *The Invisible Art of Film Music: A Comprehensive History.* New York: Ardsley House, 1998.

Macey, Patrick. *Bonfire Songs: Savonarola's Musical Legacy.* Oxford: Clarendon Press, 1998.

——., ed. *Savonarolan Laude, Motets and Anthems. Recent Researches in the Music of the Renaissance* 116. Madison: A-R Editions, 1999.

Machaut, Guillaume de. *Le Jugement du roy de Behaigne and Remede de Fortune*, edited by James I. Wimsatt and William W. Kibler. Music edited by Rebecca A. Baltzer. Athens: University of Georgia Press, 1988.

Macy, Laura. "Speaking of Sex: Metaphor and Performance in the Italian Madrigal." *Journal of Musicology* 14 (1996): 1–34.

Mann, Brian. "A Response to Kivy: Music and 'Music Appreciation' in the Undergraduate Liberal Arts Curriculum." *College Music Symposium* 39 (1999): 87–106.

Marks, Martin. "Film Music: The Material, Literature, and Present State of Research." *Notes of the Music Library Association* 36 (1979): 282–325.

Marriott, Alice. "*Beowulf* in South Dakota." *New Yorker,* 2 August 1952, 46, 48–51.

Matessino, Michael. Program notes to *Star Wars: A New Hope.* Original Motion Picture Soundtrack, Lucasfilm Ltd., 09026–68746–2 (1997).

Matthews, Lora, and Paul Merkley. "Iudochus de Picardia and Jossequin Lebloitte dit Desprez: The Names of the Singer(s)." *Journal of Musicology* 16 (1998): 200–26.

Mazullo, Mark. "Music Appreciation Revisited." *College Music Society Newsletter* (electronic version). September, 2000.

McClary, Susan. Foreward to *Opera, or the Undoing of Women.* Minneapolis: University of Minneapolis Press, 1988.

Merkley, Paul A., and Lora M. Merkley. *Music and Patronage at the Sforza Court.* Turnhout: Brepols, 1999.

Meyer, Leonard. *Music, the Arts, and Ideas.* Chicago: The University of Chicago Press, 1967.

Meyers, Chet. *Teaching Students to Think Critically.* San Francisco and London: Jossey-Bass, 1988.

Milewski, Barbara. "Chopin's Mazurkas and the Myth of the Folk." *19th-Century Music* 23 (1999–2000): 113–35.

Miller, Mark. *Music and the Silent Film: Contexts and Case Studies, 1895–1924.* Oxford: Oxford University Press, 1997.

Morgenstern, Sam, ed and trans. *Composers on Music: An Anthology of Composers' Writings from Palestrina to Copland.* New York: Pantheon Books, 1956.

Morrice, Polly. "The Past Wiped Clean." *New York Times,* 7 December 1998, A25.

Moser, Hans Joachim. *Musik in Zeit und Raum.* Berlin: Verlag Merseburger, 1960.

*Musicology and Undergraduate Teaching.* The College Music Society Report No. 6. Boulder, CO: College Music Society, 1989.

Naumann, Emil. *History of Music,* translated by F. A. Gore Ouseley. London: Cassell and Co., Ltd., n.d. [1880–85?].

Nettl, Bruno. *Heartland Excursions: Ethnomusicological Reflections on Schools of Music.* Urbana and Chicago: The University of Illinois Press, 1995.

Neuls-Bates, Carol. "Women's Orchestras in the United States, 1935–45." In *Women Making Music: The Western Art Tradition 1150–1950,* edited by Jane Bowers and Judith Tick, 349–69. Urbana, IL: The University of Illinois Press, 1986.

*The New Cartography.* New York: Friendship Press, 1983.

Nochlin, Linda. "Why Have There Been No Great Women Artists?" In *Art and Sexual Politics: women's liberation, women artists, and art history*, edited by Thomas B. Hess and Elizabeth C. Baker, 1–43. New York: Collier, 1973.

Orwell, George. "Politics and the English Language." In *Essays by George Orwell.* New York: Doubleday, 1954.

Page, Christopher. *The Owl and the Nightingale: Musical Life and Ideas in France 1100–1300.* Berkeley: University of California Press, 1989.

Palisca, Claude, ed. *The Norton Anthology of Western Music*, third ed. New York: W. W. Norton, 1996.

*Papers from the Dearborn Conference on Music in General Studies.* College Music Society, 1984.

Parakilas, James. "Teaching Introductory Music Courses with a 'More Comprehensive Perspective.'" *College Music Symposium* 30 (1990): 112–16.

Parker, Roger, ed. *The Oxford Illustrated History of Opera.* Oxford: Oxford University Press, 1994.

Pasler, Jann. "*Pelléas* and Power: Forces Behind the Reception of Debussy's Opera." *19th-Century Music* 10 (1987): 243–64.

Patterson, Daniel W. *The Shaker Spiritual.* Princeton: Princeton University Press, 1979.

Pelikan, Jaroslav. *The Idea of the University: A Reexamination.* New Haven: Yale University Press, 1992.

Pendle, Karen. *Women and Music: A History.* Bloomington: Indiana University Press, 1991.

Pinker, Steven. *The Language Instinct.* London: The Penguin Press, 1994.

Pleasants, Henry. *The Agony of Modern Music.* New York: Simon and Schuster, 1955.

Postman, Neil. *Amusing Ourselves to Death.* New York: The Penguin Press, 1985.

Potter Keith. *Four Musical Minimalists: La Monte Young, Terry Riley, Steve Reich, Philip Glass.* Cambridge: Cambridge University Press, 2000.

Prendergast, Roy. *Film Music: A Neglected Art*, second revised ed. New York: W. W. Norton, 1992.

Prizer, William F. "Music at the Court of the Sforza: The Birth and Death of a Musical Center." *Musica disciplina* 43 (1989): 141–94.

——. "Una 'Virtu Molto Conveniente A Madonne': Isabella D'Este as a Musician." *Journal of Musicology* 17 (1999): 10–49.

Reckow, Fritz. *Der Musiktraktat des Anonymous IV.* Beihefte zum Archiv für Musikwissenschaft IV. Wiesbaden: Franz Steiner Verlag, 1967.

Reich, Steve. *Writings about Music.* New York: New York University Press, 1974.

Reynolds, Simon, and Joy Press, eds. *The Sex Revolts: Gender Rebellion and Rock'n'Roll.* Cambridge, MA: Harvard University Press, 1995.

Rideout, Roger. "The German Model in Music Curricula." *College Music Symposium* 30 (1990): 106–11.

Riemer, Bennet. "Music as Cognitive: A New Horizon for Music Education." *Kodály Envoy* 20, no. 3 (1994): 16–17.

Ritter, August Gottfried. *Zur Geschichte der Orgelspiels* [Leipzig, 1884]. Reprint, Hildesheim: Georg Olms Verlag, 1969.

Rosenberg, Samuel N., and Hans Tischler, eds. *The Monophonic Songs in the Roman de Fauvel.* Lincoln: University of Nebraska Press, 1991.

Rothberg, David. "How the Web Destroys Student Research Papers." *The Education Digest* 63, no. 6 (1998): 59–61.

Rowland, David. "The Nocturne: Development of a New Style." In *The Cambridge Companion to Chopin*, edited by Jim Samson, 32–49. Cambridge: Cambridge University Press, 1992.

Sacks, Peter. *Generation X goes to College: an eye opening account of teaching in postmodern America*. Chicago: Open Court, 1996.

Saint-Saëns, Camille. *Musical Memories*, translated by Edwin Gile Rich. Boston: Small, Maynard & Company, 1919.

Schneider, Alison. "Taking Aim at Student Incoherence." *The Chronicle of Higher Education* 45, no. 29 (26 March 1999): A16–18.

Schrade, Leo. "Diabolus in Musica." *Melos* 29 (December 1959): 361–73.

Sergent, Justine, et al. "Distributed Neural Network Underlying Musical Sight-Reading and Keyboard Performance." *Science* 257 (1992): 106–9.

Shea, Christopher. "What's Happened to Writing Skills?" *The Chronicle of Higher Education* 39, no. 22 (3 February 1993): 33–34.

Sheperd, John. "Difference and Power in Music." In *Musicology and Difference*, edited by Ruth Solie, 46–65. Berkeley: University of California Press, 1994.

Singal, Daniel. J. "High Achievers in Education: An Invisible Crisis." *Current* 339 (1992): 4–13.

Small, Christopher. *Musicking: The Meanings of Performing and Listening*. Hanover: Wesleyan University Press, 1998.

Smith, Jeff. *Sounds of Commerce: Marketing Popular Film Music*. New York: Columbia University Press, 1998.

Smith, Page. *Killing the Spirit: Higher Education in America*. New York: Viking, 1990.

Smith, Ruth. *Handel's Oratorios and Eighteenth-Century Thought.* Cambridge: Cambridge University Press, 1995.

Sokal, Alan. "Transgressing the Boundaries: Towards a Transformative Hermeneutics of Quantum Gravity." *Social Text* 46–47 (Spring–Summer 1996): 217–52.

Sokal, Alan, and Jean Bricmont. *Fashionable Nonsense.* New York: St. Martin's Press, 1998.

Stolba, Kay Marie, ed. *The Development of Western Music: an Anthology,* second ed. Madison: Brown & Benchmark, 1994.

Strohm, Reinhard. *Dramma per Musica: Italian Opera Seria of the Eighteenth Century,* New Haven: Yale University Press, 1997.

Strunk, Oliver. *Source Readings in Music History.* New York: W. W. Norton, 1965.

Strunk, William Jr., and E. B. White. *The Elements of Style,* third ed. New York and London: Macmillan, 1979.

Stunkel, Kenneth R. "The Lecture: a Powerful Tool for Intellectual Liberation." *The Chronicle of Higher Education* (26 June 1998): A52.

Taruskin, Richard. *Stravinsky and the Russian Traditions.* 2 vols. Berkeley and Los Angeles: University of California Press, 1998.

Teachout, Terry. "Masterpieces of the Century: A Critical Guide." *Commentary* (April–June 1999): 46–50.

Thomson, Virgil. *American Music Since 1910.* New York: Holt, Rinehart and Winston, 1971.

Timm, Larry M. *The Soul of Cinema: An Appreciation of Film Music.* New York: Simon and Schuster, 1998.

van der Werf, Hendrik. "Anonymous IV as Chronicler." *Musicology Australia* 15 (1992): 3–25.

van Orden, Kate. "Sexual Discourse in the Parisian Chanson: A Libidinous Aviary." *Journal of the American Musicological Society* 48 (1995): 1–41.

——. "An Erotic Metaphysics of Hearing in Early Modern France." *The Musical Quarterly* 82 (1998): 678–91.

Waite, William. *The Rhythm of Twelfth-Century Polyphony.* New Haven, CT: Yale University Press, 1945.

Wallace, Wanda T. "Memory for Music: Effect of Melody on Recall of Text." *Journal of Experimental Psychology: Learning Memory, and Cognition* 20, no. 6 (1994): 1471–85.

Walvoord, Barbara E. Fassler. *Helping Students Write Well: A Guide for Teachers in All Disciplines*, second ed. New York: The Modern Language Association of America, 1986.

Walvoord, Barbara E., and Lucille P. McCarthy. *Thinking and Writing in College.* Urbana, IL: National Council of Teachers of English, 1990.

Wasowska, Elzbieta, ed. *Mazurki kompozytórow polskich na fortepian: antologia ze zbiorów Biblioteki Narodewej.* 2 vols. Warsaw: Biblioteka Narodowa, 1995.

Weiss, Piero, and Richard Taruskin, eds. *Music in the Western World: A History in Documents.* New York: Schirmer Books, 1984.

Wescott, Steven D. *A Comprehensive Bibliography of Music for Film and Television.* Detroit: Detroit Studies in Music Bibliography, No. 54, 1985.

Wheelock, Gretchen A. *Haydn's Ingenious Jesting with Art: Contexts of Musical Wit and Humor.* New York: Schirmer Books, 1992.

Williams, Christopher. "Of Canons and Context: Toward a Historiography of Twentieth-Century Music." *repercussions* 2, no. 1 (1993): 31–74.

Wolff, Christoph. *Johann Sebastian Bach: The Learned Musician.* New York: W. W. Norton, 2000.

Woodbridge, Linda. "The Centrifugal Classroom." In *Gender and Academe*, edited by Sarah Munson Deats and Lagretta Tallent Lenker, 133–51. Lanham, MD: Rowman & Littlefield, 1994.

*World Map in Equal Area Presentation: Peters Projection.* Oxford: Oxford Cartographers Ltd., [n.d.] and Cincinnati: Friendship Press, [n.d.].

Wright, Craig. "Leoninus, Poet and Musician." *Journal of the American Musicological Society* 39 (1986): 1–35.

——. *Music and Ceremony at Notre Dame of Paris, 500–1500.* New York: Cambridge University Press, 1989.

Wright, H. Stephen. *Film Music Collections in the United States: A Guide.* Hollywood, CA: Society for the Preservation of Film Music (now called The Film Music Society), 1996.

Yardley, Ann Bagnall. "'Full weel she soong the service dyvyne': The Cloistered Musician in the Middle Ages." In *Women Making Music: The Western Art Tradition, 1150–1950*, edited by Jane Bowers and Judith Tick, 15–38. Urbana, IL: The University of Illinois Press, 1986.

Young, Art, and Toby Fulwiler, eds. *Writing Across the Disciplines: Research into Practice.* Upper Montclair, NJ: Boynton/Cook, 1986.

Yudkin, Jeremy. *The Music Treatise of Anonymous IV: A New Translation.* Musicological Studies and Documents 41. Stuttgart: American Institute of Musicology, Hänssler-Verlag, 1985.

Zinsser, William. *On Writing Well*, fifth ed. New York: Harper and Row, 1994.

## Sound Recordings

Benedictine Abbey Münsterschwarzach, Godehard Joppich, dir. *Eternal Peace.* Deutsche Grammophon 445 945–2, 1982.

The Binchois Consort. *Guillaume Dufay: Music for St. James the Greater.* Hyperion Records CDA66997, 1998.

Bukkene Bruse. *Åre*. Grappa GRCD 4100, 1995.

Capella Antiqua München, Konrad Ruhland, dir. *Sequentiae*. RCA Victor GD 71953, 1980. Re-released in 1989.

Dimitry Pokrovsky Singers. *Les Noces*. Elektra Nonesuch CD 79335–2, 1994.

Ensemble Gilles Binchois. *Musique et Poesie a Saint-Gall: Sequences et tropes du IX^e*. Harmonia Mundi France HMC 905239, 1997.

Ensemble Gilles Binchois, Dominique Vellard, dir. *Les Premieres Polyphonies Françaises: Organa et tropes des XI^e siècle*. Virgin 7243 5 45135 2 7, 1996.

Ensemble Organum, Marcel Pérès, dir. *Les Premieres Polyphonies Françaises: Organa et tropes des XI^e siècle, Leonin: école Notre-Dame: Messe du Jour de Noël*. Harmonia Mundi France 1901148, 1985.

Ensemble Project Ars Nova. *Remede de Fortune*. New Albion Records, Inc. NA068CD, 1994.

L'Ensemble de l'a République turque, Kudsi Erguner, dir. *Les janissaires: musique martiale de l'Empire Ottoman*. Auvidis Ethnic B6738, 1990.

Gabrieli Consort and Players, Paul McCreesh, dir. *Christmas Mass in Rome*. Deutsche Grammophon 437 833–2, 1993.

Gothic Voices. *The Mirror of Narcissus: Songs by Guillaume de Machaut*. Hyperion Records CDA66087, 1987.

The Hilliard Ensemble, Paul Hillier, dir. *Pérotin*. ECM 1385, 1989.

The Medieval Ensemble of London. *Heinrich Isaac: Chansons, Frottole & Lieder*. L'Oiseau-lyre, Decca Recording Co. LP 410 107–1, 1984.

Melkus, Eduard, and Kurt Kedel. *Polnische-hanakische Volksmusik in werken von Georg Philipp Telemann*. Deutsche Grammophon LP:Archiv SAPM 198 467, 1967.

The Military Band of the Old Turkish Army. *Turkish Military Band Music of Ottoman Empire*. King Records [Tokyo] KICC 5101, 1987.

Monk's Choir of the Benedictine Abbey of St. Martin, Beuron, Fr. Maurus Pfaff, dir. *Third Christmas Mass*. Deutsche Grammophon 427 014–2, 1960.

Rogers, Nigel, and Charles Medlam, cond. *Claudio Monteverdi: L'Orfeo*. CDC 7 47142 EMI, 1984.

St. Petersburg Orchestra and Chorus. *Alexander Nevsky*. RCA Victor Red Seal 09026–61926–2, 1995.

Die Singphoniker, Godehard Joppich, dir. *Gregorian Chant from St. Gall*, CPO [Classic Produktion Osnabrück] 999 267–2 [n.d.].

Steen-Nokleberg, Einar, and Knut Buen. *Edvard Grieg: Slåtter (Norwegian Dances), op. 72 together with original fiddle tunes*. Simax PSClO4O, 1988.

Studio der Fruhen Musik, Thomas Binkley, dir. *Roman de Fauvel*. Reflexe LP C 063–30 103, 1972.

[Various artists]. *Classic Country Music: a Smithsonian Collection/selected and annotated by Bill Malone*. RDO42, Smithsonian Institution, 1990.

[Various artists]. *Hungarian Folk Music: Gramophone Recordings with Béla Bartók's Transcriptions*, a Hungaroton LP set, LPX 18058–18060, 1981.

[Various artists]. *Pologne: Chansons et danses populaires*, ed. Anna Czekanowska. VDE-Gallo CD 757, 1994.

*White Spirituals from the Sacred Harp*, New World Records NW 205, 1977.

Yurchenco, Henrietta. *Folk Songs of Puerto Rico*. Asch Records AHM 4412, 1971.

*Web pages*

http://falcon.cc.ukans.edu/~bclark

http://www.filmmusicsociety.org/

http://www.movietunes.com/

http://www.music.indiana.edu/som/courses/m401

http://www.music.indiana.edu/som/courses/m656/M656jrnl.html

http://www.music.indiana.edu/som/courses/Monteverdi/journal.html

http://www.physics.nyu.edu/faculty/sokal/

*Video Recordings*

Fontain, Dick. *Sound??* UPC#7 4547580563, 1967. Re-released on video by Rhapsody Films, 1988.

Harnoncourt, Nikolaus. *Claudio Monteverdi: L'Orfeo.* New York, London, 1998.

Jhally, Sut. *Dreamworlds: desire, sex, power in rock video.* [n.p.], 1990.

Waletsky, Joshua. *The Hollywood Sound.* Sony Classical Film and Video, 1995.

# Index

ABBA 29
Abing 26
Adam, Adolphe (Charles) 36
Adams, John
    *Nixon in China* 49
Adés, Thomas 48
Adorno, Theodor 128
Agazzari, Agostino 186
alchemy 84
Allegri, Gregorio
    *Miserere* 55
Ambros, August Wilhelm 186
American Choral Directors
    Association 176
American Musicological Society x,
    146
Anderson, Laurie 54
Anonymous IV 182, 184–85
Arcadelt, Jacques 9
Aristotle 74, 215
Armstrong, Louis 26, 51, 55
art history xi, 71, 72–73
arts management 21

Babbitt, Milton 48
Bach, J. C. 182
Bach, J. S. 16, 17, 26, 28, 219
    Cantata BWV 140 (*Wachet
        auf*)17
    *Durch Adam's Fall* 17
Back Street Boys 35
Baker, Josephine 30
ballads (balladry) 29, 30, 145, 149
Baltzell, W. J. 183
Barry, John 133
Bartók, Bela 28, 38, 50
Bartoli, Cecilia 29
Bates College 157, 158
Beach Boys, The 52

Beatles, The 29, 48, 52, 54, 103,
    112, 157
Beethoven, Ludwig van 16, 35, 44,
    166, 199, 211
    Fifth Symphony 227
    Ninth Symphony 26, 89, 96,
        103
Bellini, Vincenzo 32, 33
Bembo, Pietro 84
Benedictines 3
*Beowulf* 34
Berio, Luciano 45, 57
    *Sinfonia* 48, 52, 57
Berlioz, Hector
    *Symphonie fantastique* 5, 96,
        162
Bernstein, Elmer 123, 128, 133
Bernstein, Leonard 39, 54
    Clarinet Sonata 176
    *West Side Story* 152
Berry, Chuck 30, 55
Bill Haley and the Comets 53
Billings, William 31
Biondi, Fabio 29
Bizet, Georges
    *Carmen* 115
Blake, William 77
Boccaccio
    *Decameron* 3
Bordwell, David 126, 128
Boulez, Pierre 26, 44, 46, 47, 50,
    53, 54
Bowdoin College 157, 158
Bowling Green State University
    (BGSU) 11, 113, 118, 193
Brahms, Johannes 31, 32, 44, 215
    First Symphony 195
Brecht, Bertolt 50
Brel, Jacques 26

Britten, Benjamin 37
    *War Requiem* 176
Broadway 17, 26, 35, 147, 214
Broughton, Bruce 131
Brown, James 54, 57
Brown, Royal S. 128
Buhler, James 128
Burrows, Donald 21
Burt, George 126, 129
Busnoys, Antoine xii
Byrne, David 133

Cage, John 45, 47, 48, 49, 54, 145
    *4'33"* 48, 52
    *Williams Mix* 57
Calvino, Italo 49
canon (canonical) xi, 16, 25–26,
        30–31, 44, 49, 70, 78, 85,
        96, 111, 112, 122–24,
        146–47, 149, 152, 166, 202,
        214, 225–34
cantus firmus 8, 16
Carlos, Wendy
    *Switched on Bach* 54
Carnival songs 8
    *Visin, visin, visin* 8
Carter, Elliott 44, 48
Carter, Tim 188
castrato 17, 57, 188–89
Cerasi, Carole 29
chant 3, 4, 5, 15, 28, 181, 182, 184,
        188, 205, 228–34
    Alleluia 4, 227–34
    *Dies irae* 5
    *Dilecto Deo Galle* 5
    *Ecce advenit* 228
    *Ecce annuntio vobis* 230
    Epistle 4, 5, 188
    Gospel 4, 5
    Gradual 4, 5, 182–84, 231–33
    Introit 228

    *Kyrie Omnipotens genitor* 229
    Mass and Office 2, 4, 5,
        186–88, 228–34
    *Puer natus est* 229, 232, 233
    *Quem quaeritis in praesepe* 229
    Sequence 4, 5, 226, 230
    *Viderunt omnes* 231, 233
Charlamagne 3
Chàvez, Carlos 149
Chernoff, John Miller 38
Chion, Michael 124, 126, 128
Chopin, Frédéric 25, 32–35
    mazurkas 33
    Nocturne in E-flat, op. 9, no. 2
        34
Christie, William 29
Citron, Marcia 112, 227
Clarke, Jennifer 173
Cline, Patsy 26
Coleman, Ornette 52
Coltrane, John 30, 52
Compère, Loyset 8
Conn, Peter 216
Copland, Aaron 47, 122, 126, 148
    *Appalachian Spring* 38
Corelli, Arcangelo 4, 30, 181
Corigliano, John 122, 133
Council of Trent 186, 187
country music 150
Couperin, François 30
Coward, Noel 30
Crawford, Joan 124
Crawford, Richard 149, 150
Crosby, Bing 30
Crumb, George 145
Cubism 47
Curtis, Tony 114
Curtiz, Michael 124, 129, 130
Czekanowska, Anna 34

Dahlhaus, Carl 26

Daniels, David 29
Debussy, Claude 26, 28, 37
  *Pelléas et Mélisande* 197
Del Tredici, David 48
Delibes, Lèo 36
D'Este, Duke Ercole I 8
D'Este, Isabella 8
*diabolus in musica* 187
Dietrich, Marlene 30
Dufay, Guillaume 7, 186
  *Apostolo glorioso* 7
Dylan, Bob 52

Eastman School of Music 25, 46,
  49, 52
Einstein, Alfred 186
Eisenstein, Sergei 132
Eisler, Riane 118
Elbow, Peter 173
Elfman, Danny 122, 133
Ellington, Duke 35, 51, 122
Emig, Janet 170
Enlightenment, The 5
Ensemble Gilles Binchois 5
Etheridge, Melissa 26
Evans, Bill 29
Expressionism 47

Faulkner, Quentin 170
Feder, Stuart 216
Ferneyhough, Brian 44
Fétis, François 186
Ficino, Marsilio 84
Field, John 32, 33
  Nocturne No. 5 in B-flat 34
  Nocturne No. 8 in A 34
Fillion, Bryant 173
Films
  *2001: A Space Odyssey* (1968)
    131

*The Adventures of Robin Hood*
  (1938) 130
*Age of Innocence* (1993) 133
*Altered States* (1980) 133; 130
*Angel at My Table* (1990) 113
*Apollo 13* (1995) 129
*Ben-Hur* (1959) 127
*The Best Years of Our Lives*
  (1946) 129
*Beyond Rangoon* (1995) 133
*Blade Runner* (1982) 133, 129
*Breaking Away* (1979) 127
*Casablanca* (1939) 129, 130
*Charade* (1963) 133
*Citizen Kane* (1941) 129
*Cleopatra* (1963) 125
*The Color Purple* (1985) 133
*Dances with Wolves* (1990) 133
*East of Eden* (1955) 129
*Easy Rider* (1969) 125
*Edward Scissorhands* (1990)
  133
*The Empire Strikes Back* (1980)
  133
*Glory* (1989) 133
*Goldfinger* (1964) 133
*The Graduate* (1967) 125, 130
*High Noon* (1952) 133
*Jaws* (1976) 133
*Journey to the Center of the
  Earth* (1959) 125
*Julius Caesar* (1953) 125, 131
*King Kong* (1933) 123
*The Last Emperor* (1987) 133
*Laura* (1944) 123
*Lawrence of Arabia* (1962) 127
*Mildred Pierce* (1945) 124
*The Mission* (1986) 133
*The Natural* (1984) 133
*North by Northwest* (1959) 127,
  134

*Now Voyager* (1942) 128
*Patton* (1969) 123, 128
*Planet of the Apes* (1969) 133
*The Prince and the Pauper*
    (1937) 125
*Psycho* (1960) 123
*Romeo and Juliet* (1996) 125
*The Sea Hawk* (1940) 130
*Star Wars* (1977) 130, 132–33
*To Kill a Mockingbird* (1962)
    123, 128, 133
*Vertigo* (1957) 132, 133
*Witness* (1985) 128
fixed forms
    ballade 7
    rondeau 7
    viralai 7
    *Douce Dame* 6
Florentine Camerata 74–84
Flotow, Friedrich
    *Martha* 127–28
Fludd, Robert 84
Fluxus 54
Flynn, Errol 130
Forster, E. M.
    *Howard's End* 58
Foss, Lukas
    *Phorion* 48
Foster, Steven 151
Frame, Janet 112
Franconian notation 181
French Revolution 5
Frescobaldi, Archangelo
    *Fiori musicali* (1635) 4
Friedhofer, Hugo 129
Friedman, Thomas 56
frottola 8
fuging tune
    "Northfield" 36
Fuller, Sarah 17

Gabrieli, Giovanni 4
Gamelan 27, 37, 114
Gardiner, John Eliot 29
Genesis 52
Gershwin, George
    *Second Rhapsody* 127
Gesualdo, Carlo 9
Ghanaian (Ewe) drumming 38, 115
Gilman, Charlotte Perkins 113
Glennie, Evelyn 74
Goldsmith, Jerry 123, 133
Gonzaga family 8
Gorbman, Claudia 126, 128
Gottschalk, Louis Moreau
    *Souvenir de Porto Rico* 36
*Graduallied* 4
Graff, Gerald 30, 33
Graham, Martha 152
Grant, Cary 134
Grieg, Edvard 31
    *Slåtter*, op. 72 37
Griffiths, Paul 57
Grout, Donald J. 4, 16, 188
*guerre des bouffons* 215

Halle, Adam de la
    *Robins m'aime* 227
Hammerstein, Oscar II 152
Handel, George Frideric 16, 17, 20,
    21, 106
    *Guilio Cesare* 17–19
    *Jephtha* 18
    *Messiah* 20, 96
    *Admeto* 17
    *Theodoro* 19
    *Water Music* 20
Hanslick, Eduard 196
hardanger fiddle 37
Hargis, Ellen 29
Harmony of the Spheres 83–85

Harvard University xi, 95–96, 100, 102, 104, 106
Hauer, Josef 182
Hawkins, John 182
Haydn, Franz Joseph 162, 174
    "The Joke" Quartet 163
Herreweghe, Philippe 29
Herrick, Christopher 29
Herrmann, Bernard 122, 123, 125, 127, 129, 133
    *Fandango* 127
Hildegard of Bingen 5, 55, 188, 232
Hitchcock, Alfred 127
Hogarth, William 162
hooks, bell 117
Hopper, Dennis 125
Hoppin, Richard 228
Horner, James 129
Howard, James Newton 124
Howard, Ron 129
Hughes, Andrew 187
Hughes, Langston 148
Hume, Robert D. 21
Hupfeld, Herman
    "As Time Goes By" 130

inclusive language 117
Ingalls, Jeremiah 36
Irwin, May 30
Isaac, Heinrich 8
isorhythmic motet, 7; *see also*
    Dufay; Vitry
Italian courts 7–9
Ives, Charles 48, 145, 211, 216
    *Decoration Day* 38
    *A Symphony: New England
        Holidays* 216
    *Three Places in New England*
        216

jazz 26, 28, 29, 30, 47, 51, 53–54, 56, 80, 111, 114, 123, 136, 145, 158, 159, 214
*jíbaros* 36
John, Elton 55
Jones, Quincy 122, 133
Jones, Rev. A. M. 38
Josquin des Prez 7
    *Ave Maria...virgo serena* 8
    *Missa Hercules dux Ferrariae* 8
    *Miserere mei* 8

Kaho, Elizabeth E. xi
Karlin, Fred 126
Kassabian, Anahid 128
Kazan, Elia 129
Kelly, Thomas 95
Kerle, Jacobus de 187
Kerman, Joseph xii, 196
Khunrath, Heinrich
    *Amphitheatrum sapientiae
        aeternae* 84
King, Jennifer 215
Kirk, Rahsaan Roland 54
Kneif, Tibor 26
Kolberg, Oskar 33
Korngold, Erich Wolfgang 122, 125, 130
Koskoff, Ellen 112
Kubrick, Stanley 131
Kulthum, Umm 26

Landini, Francesco 185
    "cadence" 185–86
    *Non avrà ma' pietà* 186
lauda 8
    *Gesù, Gesù, Gesù* 8
Lawson, Kay 114
Lean, David 127
Lemmon, Jack 114
Lennon, John 54

Leonardo da Vinci 7
Leonin(us) 182–85
    *Alleluia Pascha Nostrum* 230
Levi-Strauss, Claude 50
Lieberson, Lorraine Hunt 29
Ligeti, György
    Horn Trio 29
Liszt, Franz 31, 35
    *Totentanz* 5
Lodge, David 199
Lopes, Luis Fernando 215
Lowinsky, Edward E. 205, 206
Lucas, George 132
Ludovico il Moro 7
Luhrmann, Baz 125
Lully, Jean-Baptiste 208, 215
Lutheran Mass 4
Luzzaschi, Luzzasco 9
Lyotard, Jean-François 43, 45

Ma, Yo Yo 193
MacDowell, Edward 31
Machaut, Guillaume de 3, 5, 7, 185
    *Roman de Fauvel* 3, 5, 6
    *Remède de Fortune* 5, 7
Madonna 115
madrigal 9, 28, 87, 215, 226
*Magnus Liber* 182, 184
Mahler, Gustav 54
    Fourth Symphony 57
Mailer, Norman 53
Mancini, Henry 122
Mankiewicz, Joseph 131
Mann, Brian 71
Mantegna, Andrea
    *Parnassus* 8–9
Manze, Andrew 29
Margaret of Scotland 113
Martini, Giovanni 9
Marx Brothers, The 152
McClary, Susan 115

McCreesh, Paul 234
McLuhan, Marshall 53
Medici, Lorenzo de 8
Messiaen, Olivier 50
    *Quatuor pour le fin du temps*
        176
Meyer, Leonard 48, 49
Meyerbeer, Giacomo
    *Les Huguenots* 195
Milhous, Judith 21
Mille, Agnes de 152
Miller, Glenn 30
Minimalism 48, 49, 54
Miyakawa, Felicia 215
Modernism 44, 46, 47, 48, 51–54
Monteverdi, Claudio 9, 183, 211,
        221
    *L'Orfeo* 74, 86–89, 96, 102,
        103
    *Vespers* 26
monody 9
Monroe, Marilyn 114
Morricone, Ennio 133
motet 20
    Arts antiqua 17
    isorhythmic 19
Mozart, Wolfgang Amadeus 4, 5,
        17, 18, 25, 28, 32, 35, 44,
        117, 181–82, 227
    Fifth Violin Concerto in A,
        K 219 36
    Piano Sonata in A, K. 331
        36
Mulligan, Robert 128
*Myth of Er* 83

Napster 55
National Association for the
        Teaching of English 173
National Association of Schools of
        Music 146

Nationalism 34, 35
Native American 34
    powwows 149, 151
Nazareth College 78–80
Nebraska Writing Project 173
Neoclassicism 48, 49
Nettl, Bruno xi
Neuhaus, Heinrich 199
Neuls-Bates, Carol 114
New Objectivity 47
Newman, Alfred 123
Newman, Randy 133
Newman, Thomas 124
Nichols, Mike 125, 130
Nochlin, Linda 112
North, Alex 125, 131
Notker 230
Notre Dame, Paris 4, 183, 185
    School (composers) 227, 229,
        232

O'Dette, Paul 29
*Oklahoma!* 150–51
Oliver, King 50
Ono, Yoko 54
opera x, 3, 26, 115, 126, 150, 152,
        161
    Baroque 9, 17–18, 20, 21,
        73–74, 208, 215
    castrati 188
    Vivaldi 218–20
    grand opera 195
    women and 188–89
    *see also*; Bizet; Debussy;
        Flotow; Handel; Meyerbeer;
        Monteverdi; Pfitzner;
        Torke; Verdi; Wagner
Oppenheimer, J. Robert 21
organum 4, 17, 182, 184, 227
Oswald, John
    Plunderphonics 54, 57

Page, Christopher 4
Palestrina, Giovanni Pierluigi da
    *Missa Papae Marcelli* 186
    *Missa Hodie Christus natus est*
        234
Parker, Charlie 51
Pärt, Arvo
    *Credo* 48
Pasler, Jann 197
Pelikan, Jaroslav 13, 14
Pendle, Karin 113, 115
Perotin(us) 182–85, 230
Pfitzner, Hans
    *Palestrina* 186
philosophy xi, 43, 71, 73–74, 116
Picasso, Pablo 50
Pinker, Steven 202
Plato 74, 215
Pleasants, Henry 51
Pokrovsky Ensemble 38
popular music 29, 30, 32, 52, 69,
        70, 71, 80, 111, 112,
        115–16, 121–22, 125, 165,
        214
Porter, Andrew 196
Portman, Rachel 122
Postmodernism 43, 44, 46, 48, 50,
        52, 54, 55, 57, 169
Prendergast, Roy 126
Presley, Elvis 30, 52
Press, Joy 115
Printemps, Yvonne 30
Prokofiev, Sergey 132, 174
    *Classical Symphony* 174
psalmody 146
psychology xi, 71, 74, 216
Public Enemy 57
Pythagorian proportions 83

Queen
    *Bohemian Rhapsody* 57

Rachmaninoff, Sergey 5
Raksin, David 123
Rameau, Jean-Philippe 208, 215
Rammstein 29
Rapper, Irving 128
Ravel, Maurice 31, 50
Reeve, David Wallace
    *Second Regiment Connecticut
        National Guard March* 38
Reformation, Lutheran 4; *see also*;
    Lutheran Mass; *Graduallied*
Reich, Steve 48, 54, 55
    *The Cave* 39
    *Clapping Music* 38
    *Different Trains* 39
    *Tehillim* 39
*Rent* 152
Reynolds, Simon 115
Richardson, Samuel 162
Richter, Sviatoslav 199
Riemann, Hugo 186
Riley, Terry
    *In C* 54
Ripperton, Minnie 55
Ritter, August Gottfried 186
Rochberg, George 8, 54
rock'n'roll 52, 53, 56, 112, 114,
        115, 126, 202, 214
Rogers, Richard 152
Rore, Cipriano de 9
Roseman, Leonard 129
Rossini, Gioachino 181
Rousset, Christophe 29
Rozsa, Miklos 122, 131

Saint, Eva Marie 134
St. Mark's, Venice 4
St. Peter's, Rome 4
Saint-Saëns, Camille
    *Samson et Delila* 37

Sakamoto, Ryuichi 133
Sanders, Ernest 185
Satie, Erik 47, 48, 49, 50, 57
Savall, Jordi 29
Savonarola, Girolama 8
Scarlatti, Alessandro
    *Griselda* 17
Schaeffer, Pierre
    *Symphonie pour un homme seul*
        56
Schaffner, Franklin 128
Schifrin, Lalo 122
Schnittke, Alfred 54
Schoenberg, Arnold 44, 181, 182
Schopenhauer, Arthur 50
Schubert, Franz 28, 166, 193, 200
Schumann, Clara 117, 195
    *Liebst du um Schönheit* 116
Schumann, Robert 117, 195
Sforza, Cardinal Ascano 7
Sforza, Duke Galeazzo Maria 7
Shakespeare, William 131
    *The Merchant of Venice* 83
Shelley, Mary
    *Frankenstein* 5
Sheperd, John 112
Shrude, Marilyn 113
Simon and Garfunkel
    "Mrs. Robinson" 130
Small, Christopher 151
Smith, Bessie 30
Smith, Jeff 128
Smith, Page 170
Socialist Realism 47
Society for American Music
    (SAM) 145
Sokal, Alan 43
Sontag, Susan 53
Spears, Britney 35
Stalling, Carl 57

Steiner, Max 123, 124, 125, 129, 130, 131
Still, William Grant
    *Afro-American Symphony* 148
Stockhausen, Karlheinz 50, 52
Strauss, Richard
    *Also Sprach Zarathustra* 131
    *Death and Transfiguration* 196
Stravinsky, Igor 28, 47, 48, 103, 211
    *Le sacre du printemps* (The Rite of Spring) 26, 96, 196–97
    *Les Noces* 38
Styne, Jule 26
Su, Cong 133
*Sumer is icumen in* 31

Talbot, Michael 219
Talking Heads 54
Tan Dun 54
Tchaikovsky, Pyotr Il'yich
    *Giselle* 37
    *Swan Lake* 37
Telemann, Georg Philipp 35
Thompson, Kristin 126
Thomson, Virgil 149, 196
Timm, Larry M. 126
Tiomkin, Dmitri 133
Tischler, Hans 185
Torke, Michael
    *Strawberry Fields* 29
Tower, Joan 28
Turkish music (Janissary) 35, 37

University of California Los Angeles (UCLA) 51, 53, 55, 56
University of Chicago 205

Van der Rohe, Mies 50

Van der Werf, Hendrik 185
Vangelis 133
Vassar College 121
Verdi, Guiseppe 17
    *Rigoletto* 19–20
Véron, Louis 195
Vienna Philharmonic 114
Vitry, Philippe de 7
    *Garrit Gallus* 227
    *Tribum/Quoniam/Merito* 7
Vivaldi, Antonio 16, 218–22

Wagner, Richard 46, 181, 199, 215
    The *Ring* Cycle 57
Waite, William 183, 184
Waller, "Fats" 30
Walton, William 122
Warhol, Andy 50
Warner Brothers 124
Wasowska, Elzbieta 32
Waxman, Franz 123
Webern, Anton 44, 217
Weerbeke, Gaspare van 8
Weill, Kurt 47
Weir, Peter 128
Wells, Orson 129
Wheelock, Gretchen 163
Williams, Christopher 44
Williams, Hank 30
Williams, John 122, 130, 132, 133
Wolf, Hugo 200
Wolff, Christoph 21
Woodbridge, Linda 169, 171
Wright, Craig 185
Wright, H. Steven 134
Wyler, William 127, 129

Yates, Peter 127
Young, Lester 50

Zimmer, Hans 122, 133

Zimmermann, Bernd Alois
    *Requiem for a Dead Soul* 48

Zorn, John 45, 48, 52